TOM GILMARTIN

The Man Who Brought Down a Taoiseach
and Exposed the Greed and Corruption
at the Heart of Irish Politics

FRANK CONNOLLY ∾

Gill & Macmillan

Gill & Macmillan
Hume Avenue, Park West, Dublin 12
www.gillmacmillanbooks.ie

© Frank Connolly 2014
978 07171 6047 1

Index compiled by Róisín Nic Cóil
Typography design by Make Communication
Print origination by O'K Graphic Design, Dublin
Printed and bound by CPI Group (UK) Ltd, Croydon, CR0 4YY

This book is typeset in 12/14.5 pt Minion.

The paper used in this book comes from the wood pulp of
managed forests. For every tree felled, at least one tree is
planted, thereby renewing natural resources.

A CIP catalogue record for this book is available from the
British Library.

5 4 3 2 1

For my parents, Frank and Madeleine, who instilled in me the wisdom and humanity of an equal and just society.

CONTENTS

PREFACE

Tom Gilmartin believed, as many of the Irish diaspora still do, that it was his responsibility to assist in stemming the tide of emigration that forced so many young people of his and later generations to England, the United States, Australia and many other far-flung places to seek decent work and a better life.

The graft and corruption described in the 2012 report of the Mahon Tribunal, which destroyed his efforts to develop his ambitious business projects and create substantial employment in Ireland during the late 1980s and early 1990s and almost caused his financial ruin, sowed the seeds of the recent economic collapse that has so deeply indebted future generations of Irish people. For this reason, the story of his journey from humble origins in the west of Ireland to success in the world of mechanical engineering and property development in England and his return to do business in Dublin deserves to be told.

I first spoke to Tom Gilmartin in the summer of 1998, a year after the Tribunal of Inquiry into Certain Planning Matters and Payments was established by the Fianna Fáil and Progressive Democrat coalition Government and a few months after its legal team had tracked him to Luton in order to hear his extraordinary allegations concerning his encounters with the political and planning systems in Dublin.

Gilmartin's claims were more dramatic, and more sensitive, than anything I had come across in years of investigating official wrongdoing by politicians and public servants. It centred on how he was forced from control of the company he formed to develop an ambitious retail and business park at Quarryvale, near Lucan in west Dublin, now the site of the commercially successful Liffey Valley Shopping Centre.

Work on this book began in 2004 but could not be completed, primarily for legal reasons, until Tom Gilmartin and the other characters central to the Quarryvale module of the tribunal had given their evidence and the inquiry had published its conclusions, which it did in the spring of 2012. Those conclusions largely vindicated the version of events provided to the tribunal by Gilmartin, who had been accused of inventing his various claims regarding the behaviour of various politicians and public servants he encountered.

This story is based on direct interviews with Gilmartin over several years, his private statements to the tribunal, his public evidence and that of many other witnesses, and other documents and information from a range of sources. It also leans heavily on the complex four-volume 3,000-page report of the tribunal and its damning conclusions, and I believe it helps to make the tribunal's detailed investigation into Gilmartin's claims more readily accessible to a wider audience. The report exposes deeply disturbing questions concerning the political culture that prevailed in Ireland during those years and the manner in which systemic corruption contaminated other organs of the state, including the civil service, the Garda Síochána, the legal system and the media.

Tom Gilmartin was initially reticent about his life and that of his family being the subject of a book. Indeed one chapter concerning some extraordinary events in Luton during the 1970s and 80s that dealt with the mistreatment endured by many in the Irish community in Luton during the conflict in the North of Ireland was removed at his request. He emerged with nothing but credit as a reluctant mentor and adviser to those in the Irish community who sought his assistance during those dark years.

Eleven years after he proposed the establishment of the inquiry to the Oireachtas, Bertie Ahern was forced to resign as Taoiseach because of its investigation into his personal finances and the large and unexplained amounts of money he accumulated when he was Minister for Finance in the early 1990s. Ahern's resignation, in April 2008, resulted directly from information provided to the tribunal by Gilmartin. However, the tribunal did not directly link financial transactions that Ahern could not adequately explain to the claims it heard from Gilmartin. For this reason the following narrative makes a clear separation between the conclusions of the tribunal in this regard and the role played by the former Taoiseach in the Quarryvale affair and his involvement with Gilmartin and the prominent Cork businessman Owen O'Callaghan, who ultimately took control of the retail development.

In September 2008, only weeks after the tribunal completed hearing public evidence, the Government led by Fianna Fáil plunged future generations of Irish people into austerity when it agreed to guarantee the billions in debt of the country's insolvent banks, including Allied Irish Banks and Anglo-Irish Bank, and of Irish Nationwide Building Society, all of which feature in this story.

In early 2011 Fianna Fáil was devastated in a general election three months after the Government it led was forced into the arms of an EU-ECB-IMF loan facility.

The circumstances that brought the country to its knees have been well explored and documented by others, but it is my hope that this book will assist those seeking answers to the question of where the political and financial rot began that has wreaked such havoc on the lives of so many Irish people. The final report of the Mahon Tribunal, published in March 2012, revealed in shocking detail the level of political and corporate corruption and deceit that prevailed in Ireland over many decades.

In exposing the treatment he endured at the hands of some of the most powerful and influential in Irish society, Tom Gilmartin helped to expose the greed that motivated many in the corridors of power during those times. In conversations during what were to be his final days, he expressed his hope that he would be around to see this work published. He believed that the tribunal report had been put on the proverbial shelf by the establishment and that his story had yet to be properly told. Unfortunately, he did not live to see the publication of this book, despite his strong wish to do so. Tom Gilmartin died unexpectedly in Cork University Hospital on Friday 22 November 2013.

ACKNOWLEDGEMENTS

Since this work began over ten years ago I have had the assistance and encouragement of many people, far too many to allow for individual mention. Some indeed would prefer to remain anonymous, as identifying them as sources or contributors to this story may not be in their best interests.

This book could not have been written without the co-operation of its central character, the late Tom Gilmartin, who kindly provided me with access to his files, his friends and his family over the past decade and more. His son Thomas has also been an invaluable adviser, providing observations and corrections on the manuscript up to its completion. His sisters, Chris and Una, kindly lent some personal photographs and contributed to my greater understanding of the family's history.

Others who helped to improve earlier drafts include Richard Roche, David Burke, Greg O'Neill and Suzanne Connolly, while David Connolly, Justine McCarthy, Stuart Carolan and Theo Dorgan made valuable comments on later versions. Others who read the manuscript in its final stages and offered words of encouragement include Eamon Dunphy, Niall O'Dowd, Sebastian Hamilton, Scott Millar and Fintan O'Toole. Over the years, many others have offered advice and practical assistance, including the former tribunal chairman Feargus Flood, Karen Hackett, Deirdre Price, Sonia Slevin, Pat Pidgeon, Colm Keena, Miriam Lord, Christy Moore and the extremely helpful staff at the National Library of Ireland in Dublin and at Sligo Central Library. Padraic Ferry and Kieran Kelly provided wise legal counsel. Mary Webb also worked extensively and expertly on several drafts.

Derek Speirs added his creative touch with photographs, as did Eamon Farrell of Photocall Ireland, and Trevor McBride. My sincere gratitude also goes to Fergal Tobin, now retired, and Conor Nagle of Gill & Macmillan for recognising its value and bringing this work to publication. Their colleagues Deirdre Rennison Kunz, Jen Patton and Teresa Daly helped with the editorial process, photo acquisition and layout, and cover design and promotion, respectively.

My beautiful and talented children, Oisín, Saoirse, Caomhán, Síomha and Liadh, grew up with this story and all that comes with a father embroiled in the often controversial, and always intense, world of investigative journalism. This book is for them, with the hope that the errors and abuses of the powerful it reveals can inspire them, and their children, to insist that they will not be tolerated in their society of the future.

Finally, this work, carved out over many years, could not have been completed without the constant encouragement, unerring insight and tender love of Mary Tracey.

For the rest of what you read in these pages I bear sole responsibility.

PROLOGUE

It started on the 'Late Late Show'

It was a normal Friday night in the home of the Gilmartin family in Luton, Bedfordshire. As usual, Vera Gilmartin and her husband, Tom, were watching that evening's 'Late Late Show', the long-running and sometimes controversial chat show on RTE Television. The programme was available to its large audience in England through a live satellite service provided by Tara Television of London.

The programme broadcast on Friday 15 January 1999 was hardly memorable until its host, Gay Byrne, introduced the Irish member of the European Commission and former Fianna Fáil minister, Pádraig Flynn, as a guest. A former schoolteacher from county Mayo, Flynn was one of the country's more colourful politicians and could always be counted on to enliven a television debate, usually through some controversial, and sometimes outrageous, observation. It was he who notoriously referred to Mary Robinson's 'new-found commitment to the family' during the 1990 presidential election campaign, querying whether she had ever played the role of a proper mother or housewife during her long career as barrister, human rights and feminist activist, senator and advocate for the marginalised. It was a remark that backfired spectacularly on Flynn, and Mary Robinson went on to achieve a historic victory over the Fianna Fáil nominee in the election.

Flynn's appearance on the 'Late Late Show' came four months after an allegation had surfaced that in 1989 he had accepted a donation of £50,000 from a property developer, Tom Gilmartin, which was intended for Fianna Fáil but which, it was claimed, the party never received. When the story was first published, in September 1998, Flynn denied that he had received the money from Gilmartin. The claim was now under scrutiny by the Tribunal of Inquiry into Certain Planning Matters and Payments, which was set up to investigate corrupt practices in the planning system in Dublin.

After some initial chat about Flynn's EU career, during which Flynn was his usual ebullient self, Gay Byrne asked, 'What are you going to do about the Flood Tribunal and the £50,000 [and] Gilmartin?' The family watching in Luton had paid little heed to the conversation up to that point, but Flynn's answer and his subsequent comments on the Gilmartins created outrage in the household that would eventually lead to the exposure of unheard-of depths of corruption back in Dublin and, ultimately, the fall of a Taoiseach.

Flynn's immediate response was to adopt his usual jocular tone and say, 'Well, I want to tell you about that. I've said my piece about that. In fact I've said too much, because you can get yourself into the High Court for undermining the tribunal, so I ain't saying no more about this . . . except to say just one thing, and this is all I'll say: I never asked nor took money from anybody to do favours in my life.'

Prompted by Byrne, 'But you know Gilmartin?' Flynn replied, 'Oh, yeah, yeah. I haven't seen him now for some years. I met him. He's a Sligo man who went to England and made a lot of money. Came back. Wanted to do a lot of business in Ireland. Didn't work out for him. Didn't work out for him. He's not well. His wife isn't well. And he's . . . he's out of sorts.'

Winding up that section of the interview, Byrne pressed Flynn with a last question. 'But you're saying you never took money from anybody at any time, for whatever reason?' Looking directly at his questioner, Flynn replied with a variation on his earlier denial, saying, 'I never took money from anybody to do a political favour as far as planning is concerned.'

After that the conversation moved on to other matters, with Flynn complaining about the fact that his daughter, the Fianna Fáil TD Beverly Cooper Flynn, had been the victim of allegations of irregular practices when she worked for National Irish Bank. He also remarked how difficult it was for him to survive on an annual salary of £140,000 when he had to look after three homes, raising eyebrows all over the country when he moaned about the cost of maintaining his three separate houses in Brussels, Dublin and his native Castlebar, county Mayo. Running three homes, with three housekeepers, was a 'very expensive business,' he said, and he suggested to the audience: 'Try it some time.'

Flynn might have thought this latter bit of frivolity would be what would be talked about next day, and that his comments on the Gilmartin issue would be forgotten. He couldn't have been more mistaken.

In the Gilmartin household Pádraig Flynn's comments went down like the proverbial lead balloon. Vera Gilmartin, an intensely private woman, became upset as she heard herself and her medical condition discussed on live television. Christmas 1998 had been a hard time for them, as Vera's multiple sclerosis had gradually worsened over the preceding months and she was largely immobile. Now her family and friends in her native county Donegal and the length and breadth of Ireland were watching this politician making ill-considered remarks about herself and her husband.

Tom's sister Una phoned RTE from her home in Sligo to complain, and researchers on the show contacted Flynn. As the two-hour show neared an end, Gay Byrne told viewers that 'Pee' Flynn, as he was known to the public, had corrected his earlier comments about Tom Gilmartin. 'In the interview it was suggested by Pee Flynn that Tom Gilmartin was sick. As far as Pee is concerned, Tom Gilmartin is not sick and has never been seriously sick, and we would just like to say sorry and apologise for that,' Byrne said.

But it was too little, too late.

As the show ended, the telephone in Luton began to ring, with friends and family from Ireland calling to express their concern at Flynn's performance. Tom Gilmartin was furious. 'When I saw that clown on TV I was incensed,' Gilmartin told me in the days immediately after the programme. 'The only thing that was missing was the red nose. I never wanted to be the centre of attention, and I never wanted my wife to be involved in any of this. And then that comedian went on TV. The irony is that Flynn was not the worst of them, and I'm not saying that because he is from the west of Ireland.'

On the morning after the programme Gilmartin's home was under a media siege. Television crews and newspaper journalists set up camp outside the house, pleading for Gilmartin to give more details about his claims of corruption in Dublin. Some months earlier Gilmartin had revealed to a number of journalists some details about the donation of a £50,000 cheque. He said that Flynn had asked him to leave the payee section of the cheque blank, and that it had never been passed on to Fianna Fáil, as intended.

Notes seeking interviews were dropped in the letter-box, and one reporter delivered a bouquet of flowers, presumably for Vera, in the hope of getting a chat with the man now at the centre of a mounting political storm in Ireland.

Gilmartin decided to throw a couple of highly charged grenades in the direction of those now seeking to depict him as 'unwell', as Flynn had suggested. Without too much thought, he responded to some of the media queries and confirmed that he had been contacted by Flynn when the news of the £50,000 donation, and the fact that it had not been handed over to Fianna Fáil, had emerged a few months earlier, in September 1998. Flynn, he said, was concerned about Gilmartin's contact with the Flood Tribunal and wanted to know what he had told the inquiry about the donation. This revelation now placed the hapless Flynn in a position where he stood accused of siphoning off party funds as well as attempting to interfere with the tribunal of inquiry.

Flynn's 'Late Late Show' performance ensured that Gilmartin's claims became known to huge numbers of people who had previously never heard of the reclusive developer or his allegations of corruption among Dublin's political elite.

Just as Gilmartin was besieged in Luton, so the press pack chased down Flynn back in Ireland. But the man who was usually prominent in his local church in Castlebar for Sunday mass was nowhere to be seen. He headed for the privacy of the five-star Ashford Castle Hotel, some miles from his home, where he met his party colleague and former EU commissioner Ray MacSharry for urgent consultations. Flynn had decided to keep his head down, and the usually voluble politician refused to respond to any further media queries, which, of course, only led to further speculation.

In the few comments he made immediately after the 'Late Late Show', Gilmartin assured reporters that his health was 'the very best.' He also told reporters that he had never intended to generate controversy and had been reluctant to get involved with the tribunal of inquiry set up in 1997. The fact that he had been contacted by the tribunal had already been confirmed some months earlier in the Irish media.

'I didn't want to get involved. I kept my mouth shut for ten years,' he told the *Irish Independent*. But Flynn's remarks had changed his mind. 'I will be giving evidence now. Flynn has seen to that. On the "Late Late Show" he made me out to be a mental patient. I am not a bitter man, and I was never money-oriented . . . But as far as I am concerned I am the victim of the most scurrilous carry-on perpetrated right from the top—including the current top.'

Asked what he meant by this last remark, he said, 'I think I will leave that for the tribunal. But I can tell you this: they all have a lot to worry about, right from the top. Everything I say will be proved; it will all be proved . . . What I have to tell the tribunal will explode at the heart of the current Government . . .'

It was a comment that significantly raised the political stakes; but few could have thought at the time that it would end up embroiling the Taoiseach, Bertie Ahern, in such a dramatic political controversy, or that it would lead to Ahern's resignation from office less than a decade later.

PART 1

An emigrant's return

Chapter 1 ⤲

THE LONG ROAD FROM LISLARY

Tom Gilmartin's reluctance to engage with a tribunal—any tribunal—can be seen in a comment he made on hearing of the decision by the Revenue Commissioners in December 1998 to waive any tax demand on the disgraced former Taoiseach Charles Haughey after details of his illegal Ansbacher accounts had emerged in an earlier judicial inquiry. In his typically blunt fashion, Gilmartin said that 'tribunals are about as useful as tits on a bull.' The expression, picked up from his early days living on the land in county Sligo, was published, to much amusement, and provoked more questions about the nature and background of this character who had emerged sensationally onto the already crowded set of the tribunal drama.

So who was Tom Gilmartin? And how had this west of Ireland lad become such a significant player in business and property development?

Born in 1935 in Lislary, near Grange, county Sligo, to James and Kathleen Gilmartin (née McDermott), Tom was the first son after three girls, Maudie, Eileen and Patsy; later came Una, James, Julann and Christina. Another child died at birth, while Julann died at six months. James Gilmartin supplemented his income from the thirty-acre farm with his various skills: he made shoes, harnesses for horses, and was a carpenter as well as a champion ploughman. Using expertise he had acquired with explosives during the War of Independence, he also did blasting work for the county council.

Tom Gilmartin was encouraged by his father to work with him on the land. He left school at thirteen, having decided that he was learning nothing there. 'It was a small national school with one teacher, who chain-smoked and was quite heavy-handed with the stick, to say the least. The only thing I ever saw on the blackboard was *Tá mé go maith* [I am well] and *Sin é an madra* [That is the dog]; we never learnt much else. I wanted to learn, but there was nothing. You had to bring a sod of turf every day for the fire. The place was freezing, and there was ice on the floor in winter time, and the teacher would have his arse to the fire all day.'

He got his first job cleaning drains with the county council after altering the age on his birth certificate from thirteen to sixteen. He also helped his father with work on a land reclamation scheme recently introduced by the Government. For a few years the work of clearing scrub and briars, draining and reclaiming land, took up his days. However, he was ambitious for more, and at night he attended the local technical school, despite his father's opinion that there was little worth in the education there.

Through perseverance, and despite missing years of formal education, he won a scholarship to the agricultural college at Ballyhaise, county Cavan. As the course neared its end he applied for a post with the Department of Agriculture and came first in the civil service examination for the position; however, he was disqualified on the grounds that he had not completed his course, which ended the same week as the exam. His place was awarded to another young man, who had achieved poorer results but who had a well-placed relative in the public service. Several of those who gained places had ended the course at exactly the same time as the young Gilmartin, so it seemed to be a case of 'who you know and not what you know' that sealed his future.

Hordes of young people left Ireland for England in the 1950s. It was a reflection of the deep depression throughout the country, and it was only a matter of time before Gilmartin decided to join his many friends from Grange, Cliffoney and other parts of north Sligo who had headed for job-rich Luton, thirty miles from London, where a number of people from his home area had already settled.

'I was back at home saving hay with my father when I stuck the fork in the ground and I said, "I'll be in England tomorrow." He wouldn't believe me. He didn't want to believe me, so he called me in the morning to go down at the hay, and I told him, "No, I'm going to England." And he went mad and he said, "You go to England and you need never come home again." It might have been different if I was going to America or somewhere, but he never wanted me to go to England.'

It was understandable. James Gilmartin's past history with the British colonisers was not a happy one. Born in 1898 in Lislary, he joined the

Irish Volunteers some time after the Easter Rising in 1916 and became something of a crack shot and an explosives expert. The exploits of Gilmartin and his group of volunteers during the War of Independence were the stuff of local legend. He was captured during what was also known as the 'Tan' war, so called after the brutal and infamous Black and Tans, the undisciplined force of irregulars, mostly former British soldiers and convicts recruited to swell the ranks of the Royal Irish Constabulary. He escaped from Cliffoney barracks with the help of an RIC officer.

The search for his group of IRA volunteers, and his subsequent arrest, followed a daring attack on the RIC barracks at Breaghwy, near his home, when another Lislary man, Dominic Hart, scaled the chimney of the high-walled house and descended into a room where the two most senior British officers were sitting down to tea. Local folklore has it that Hart, two revolvers in hand, told the officers to order their men to lay down their weapons and leave the barracks. The officers were not to know that Hart's weapons were empty; in fact the whole purpose of the raid was to stock up on guns and ammunition, of which there were precious little among the local IRA unit. The column of British troops and RIC men left the barracks, which was promptly seized in one of the more dramatic and less well-known actions by the IRA in county Sligo.

Having joined the anti-Treaty forces after the War of Independence, James Gilmartin was lucky to escape death during the vicious and bitter civil war that tore communities and families apart. He once helped a group of volunteers evade arrest at Lissadell, the ancestral house of the Gore-Booth family and home of Constance Markievicz, by hiding them in the sea with reeds in their mouths to help them breathe. He then returned home to Lislary. Soon afterwards, pro-Treaty forces, led by General Seán Mac Eoin, dragged him out of the house and put him up against the gable wall. His mother, Mary, threw herself in front of her son to prevent him being put to death on the spot. He was taken prisoner and transported to the Curragh prison camp, in county Kildare, for the remainder of the conflict.

Some of his comrades were not so fortunate. In September 1922 the Free State armoured car *Ballinalee* (named after Mac Eoin's home town), equipped with a machine gun, was captured by republicans at Rockwood, county Sligo, and was used to mount attacks on government troops. When the pro-Treaty forces launched an operation to retake the armoured car a gun battle took place near Drumcliff. The republicans took to the hills after dismantling the car and the machine gun and were pursued by government troops on the Horseshoe Mountain deep into the slopes of Benbulben. In one of the most infamous episodes of that bitter conflict, six republicans, including Brigadier-General Séamus Devins TD and his adjutant, Commandant Brian MacNeill, son of a government minister, Eoin MacNeill, were captured. After their surrender, troops under the command of Tony Lawlor, a government officer of some notoriety, shot the six: Séamus Devins, Brian MacNeill, Joseph Banks, Patrick Carroll, Thomas Langan and Harry Benson.

Two of the bodies were not found for a fortnight. The bodies of the other victims were removed by an uncle of the future Fianna Fáil ministers Brian Lenihan (senior) and Mary O'Rourke to his mother's family home at the foot of Benbulben. The uncle, Brian Scanlon, was subsequently forced into exile in Australia because of the assistance he gave the anti-Treaty soldiers. The Free State government claimed that the men were preparing an ambush when they were shot, but republicans in the county said that the six had been shot and savagely bayoneted by soldiers after they had surrendered and had been disarmed.

The killings on Benbulben left a legacy of bitterness in county Sligo that persisted long after the final shots of the Civil War were fired. For James Gilmartin, like many on the defeated anti-Treaty side, the newborn state had been christened with the blood of too many of its young, and the reward for his contribution was a life of hard work on the soil. The victors took the spoils, including the best public-service jobs and positions; the losers returned to the land or faced the emigrant boat.

'My father never talked to me very much about it,' Gilmartin said. 'If you asked him questions he didn't answer. The six that were shot on the mountain were great friends of his. Martin Brennan was a great friend of ours too. They took him out of the house and shot him up against the wall at Mount Edward. They riddled him with bullets. A lovely fellow who had nothing much to do with anything. My father always believed he was shot for his piece of land.'

James Gilmartin took little interest in politics in later life but fervently supported de Valera and Fianna Fáil, the party joined by many of those who fought on the losing side in the Civil War. The party won power in 1932, thus ending nearly a decade of rule by Cumann na nGaedheal, which was identified with the victorious pro-Treaty forces. De Valera built a mass movement with a promise to develop an independent, self-sufficient economy, support and extend the use of Irish, and finally achieve the long-held objective of a united Ireland, which appealed to many like James Gilmartin.

———

Tom Gilmartin readily understood his father's opposition to his decision to emigrate, but was determined on this course. 'My father never wanted me to go to England. It was the old thing about England; but everybody around us, every able-bodied man, was gone. My mother was heartbroken. She had raised us well, and although there was not much money around we were always turned out in the best of clothes. She was a great cook and we always ate well. She was sorry to see any of us leave. My sister had gone before me, but she died of meningitis at twenty-three. My mother was a highly intelligent woman, and she regretted never having gone to America herself with her sisters. I am very proud of my parents, and my mother in particular. But there was no chance here at that time.'

Although reluctant to see him go, his mother would help him to advance in any way she could, while his father resisted in vain his eldest son's departure to the land of the old enemy.

Tom Gilmartin took the boat on 27 July 1957. Arriving at Euston Station in London, the fresh-faced young man from county Sligo headed for St Pancras Station and the train to Luton. His first encounter was with a friendly English man from whom he asked directions. 'I wasn't quite sure where I was going. So there was this fellow standing on a corner. "Oh, you've just arrived," he says to me. I said I was going to Luton. "Ah, you don't have to go to Luton. I have a lovely place, and you can stay with me." I thought, What a lovely fellow to meet after arriving in a strange place! The next thing this woman passed by and she looked at me. She asked if I was lost and then said she assumed I had just come off the train. She kind of moved away from the bloke, and she said to me, "Do you realise what he is?" I said no, and she said he was a homosexual. And I said, "What's that?" She took a big fit of laughing and said, "You bloody Irish, you're so innocent." She pointed out St Pancras Station, which was right beside me.'

After arriving in Luton and a night of searching for digs, with many refusals by landladies who didn't take Irish tenants, Gilmartin found a bed. A few days later he joined up with the crowd from Grange and found more permanent lodgings with an Irish landlord.

It was boom time for the British economy, with new industrial towns spreading across the Home Counties. His first job was as a conductor on the buses of the United Counties bus company. His next stop was at the Vauxhall car factory in Luton. He was put to sweeping the floors, a job that suited him perfectly, as it meant he could work seven days a week and boost his wages with overtime. After a while he was approached by a manager to help with maintenance on the conveyor system in the manufacturer's new chromium plant, where the cars were painted. It was not long before his talent for fixing and maintaining complex engineering equipment was noticed and he was encouraged to go on a basic training course on the mechanical handling system, paid by the company. 'I started working with mechanical handling systems, and they fascinated me. I then joined Simpsons of Round Green, who were building special-purpose machinery as well as overhead runways and conveyors.'

At Simpsons he spent several months working on Britain's first prototype space rocket. 'I was the only Irishman among them. They had the rocket ready, and they used to test the engines underground. When they turned on the big engines the whole town used to vibrate.' The project was eventually closed down by the British government under Harold Wilson. Many of the scientists went to work on the NASA space programme in the United States. 'America ended up building what the English had pioneered. It was referred to as the brain drain, because all of the scientists and specialists went to America and Germany and other places.

'I was determined to learn about everything, so I had a chequered employment history, as I never stayed too long with any one company, because I wanted to learn something else. I did structural engineering as well. I had a plan to set up my own company over about two to three years, and I did that. I built it up with any type of engineering or steel jobs I could get. I started on my own, literally on my own.'

As well as expanding his knowledge of specialist engineering work, he took night classes in the local technical school, where he obtained a certificate in welding. He had discovered that he had the eye for precision engineering, as well as mathematical skill and excellent recall.

He also threw himself into improving the social life of the Irish in Luton. His entrepreneurial flair came to the fore in organising events within the thriving Irish community. 'I knew a lot of Irish people, and I started the Gaelic football in Luton. I set up the Erin's Hope club and got football pitches. Over seventy thousand Irish arrived in Luton during those few years, and there were some very good footballers from every county. There were a few clubs: St Dymphna's, the Owen Roe Hurling Club and Erin's Hope, where I was chairman.'

Chairman in those days was a fancy name for chief fund-raiser and bottle-washer. Tom organised dances and chartered the first aeroplanes from Luton to Dublin for football matches. 'I suppose I was the equivalent of the first Ryanair, as it happens. We organised chartered plane trips to Dublin Airport for all-Ireland finals and other events. There was a man who came back from the war with one arm. He was a travel agent and he used to beg me to join him in setting up an airline service. I was actually offered the use of Luton Airport, which at the time was used for training pilots and testing aircraft built in the nearby factories.'

It was while he was selling tickets for a flight to a football match in Dublin that Tom Gilmartin met his future wife, Vera Kerr, who had recently arrived from county Donegal. 'I met Vera while I was collecting money for the trip at a dance in the George Hotel ballroom,' he said. A native of Urris, Clonmany, in the Inishowen peninsula, Vera had recently arrived in Luton with her sister, Sarah. She was from a small farming family, and she and her sisters and brothers all spent years working in England.

When Vera met Tom, who was five years older, she was working as a waiter in the Red Lion Hotel in Luton. 'She was gorgeous, petite, and always looked much younger than her age. She was a very sensible and down-to-earth girl,' Gilmartin said.

It was 1959, and Gilmartin was fast gaining a reputation as a man who would try any engineering job, no matter how complex or dangerous. Setting up in Cross Street, Luton, on the site of a former hat factory, he took on a variety of structural engineering and other jobs. Despite his relatively basic engineering training he was hired by some of the giant corporations in the south-east of England to come up with innovative solutions to practical problems, particularly with the developing conveyor-belt technologies. He became an expert in mechanical handling systems and special-purpose machinery, helping to design and develop the first computer-controlled conveyor systems and assembling the cast-steel equipment that put the car bodies in place.

At the Ford factory in Dagenham he helped to remove equipment weighing thousands of tonnes by constructing a special lift table. Over several weeks he manoeuvred the equipment onto his self-made conveyor system and used huge poles to gradually move it from the factory. It saved the company hundreds of thousands of pounds, as other experts had determined that the only way to move the equipment was by removing part of the factory roof. When he was asked how much he wanted for completing the job, Gilmartin asked for £200. The manager paid him and then told the self-trained engineer that he would have paid £50,000 to have the job done.

By the early 1960s Gilmartin was building special-purpose steel handling equipment required by the car and other heavy industries. He went on to specialise in the construction and installation of conveyor systems for prominent customers, including the biggest car manufacturer in the area, Vauxhall, owned by General Motors, as well as the chemical giant ICI and the prestigious Rolls-Royce.

In 1965 he registered his company, Gilmartin Engineering, with Vera, whom he married the same year, as the other director. He built a customised factory at Eaton Green Road, close to Luton Airport, and developed computerised car production systems as well as heavy lifting and handling equipment for the steel industry, to cope with the demands posed by the large and complex engineering contracts the company was taking on. The work force grew from fifty to several hundred at peak times.

Gilmartin installed the first automated conveyor at Vauxhall, which allowed for the efficient assembly and passage of car parts from the massive pressing machines to the installation of panels, wings and engines and then the final stages of chromium-plating, dyes and finishes. He came up with an overhead system worked by a panel of switches that had the added benefit of a more efficient use of space in the factory. He also developed new airport baggage-handling carousels and conveyors.

'The real money was in the shut-down at Vauxhall over the summer. We worked flat out ripping out the old conveyor system and installing new ones. We had to have it all running on the day they came back from holiday. It meant working around the clock, twenty-four hours a day. There was no time for socialising. There were some hellish ups and downs.

I was determined to make it work. It might sound romantic and exciting, but it was hard work and an absolute nightmare at times. I often went to work on a Friday and didn't come home until the Tuesday night.'

The hard work, the constant pursuit of new skills and his innate entrepreneurial drive paid off. The immigrant from county Sligo had become a success.

But despite his achievements and the increasingly lofty circles in which he was moving, Tom Gilmartin remained very much a Sligo man. On one occasion an Irish-American senior executive of the giant American car manufacturer General Motors visited the Vauxhall plant to view the quality of Gilmartin's engineering work. Sir Reginald Pearson, a director of Vauxhall, commented on Gilmartin's Irish accent, asking why he hadn't learnt to speak 'proper' English after all his years in Britain. It was not a remark that sat well with the Sligo man, who said he was proud of his roots and his accent. The conversation was overheard by the American visitor, who praised him for facing down the snobbery of the British director.

As Luton continued to attract Irish immigrants, Gilmartin and other expatriate business people worked hard to ensure that the social, sporting and spiritual needs as well as the employment needs of the new population were met. Father Liam Murtagh, who ministered in the city during much of the 1960s, told me how Gilmartin, along with the Connolly brothers from county Mayo, the Shanleys from county Leitrim, the McNicholases and other Irish business families helped the Irish community. 'These businessmen had their own companies and they came together to build the Harp Club, where the huge Irish community congregated for sports and social events. They also contributed to building Catholic churches and schools in the area.'

Father Tom Colreavy, who came to Luton in the late 1960s, also remembered Gilmartin as 'a hard-working devil who tried his best at everything...He was an ambitious fellow as well, and that is why I believe he was very successful in his business life. Others were very capable, but you had to admire Tom because he bit the bullet and went for it. He was very hard-working, and his family were well liked in Luton.'

In 1970, after the birth of their first two children, Liam and Anne, the Gilmartins moved from their home at 111 Merrick Avenue to a detached house at 22 Whitehill Avenue in one of Luton's leafier suburbs, where Thomas and James were born.

Gilmartin spread his engineering work to the United States, where he assisted with major commercial projects, including the construction of monorail systems at the new Disneyworld developments in Florida and California. His work brought him into contact with the US air force and army engineering corps, for which he did design work through a new company he established, the Minnesota Engineering Group, in Minneapolis in the 1970s. He was also involved in the design of the complex engineering work used in the construction of the Silverdome, the American football venue in Vancouver, Canada, which opened in 1975.

Thousands of Irish people were still hitting the emigration trail to England and the United States. In the winter of discontent in 1978 a wave of industrial disputes pitted hundreds of thousands of workers in Britain against the Labour government, which continued when an ascending Conservative Party, led by Margaret Thatcher, came to power one year later. The disputes affected Gilmartin's business and, while his employees were not on strike, the work force was effactually prevented from working, though he continued to pay their wages for months.

Eventually he was forced to wind up Gilmartin Engineering in 1981, resulting in more than four hundred workers losing their jobs. 'You were only as good as the next contract. We were working night and day just to keep our heads above water. We had to quote prices below cost. The economy was in free fall. Thatcher took on the trade unions and destroyed the steel industry. All our bread and butter was gone. The car industry was a shambles. I couldn't compete with the big players, who were bidding at a loss for contracts. I put the company into liquidation.'

For the determined Gilmartin it was time to explore other avenues. He got £1 million for a factory he had been building in Northampton that was almost finished. Using these funds, he began a business in which he identified suitable sites for office and retail property schemes, which he then helped to design.

———

Gilmartin made the transition to property developer with some ease. In his first foray into this area he acquired, and then sold on, a proposed scheme in Milton Keynes, a town north of Luton where a new city was under construction. The sale raised another £1 million for Gilmartin, which helped restore his finances after the difficult years trying to keep his engineering business afloat. He worked with the auctioneer Richard Forman of Wilson and Partners (later Connell Wilson) in designing other schemes for office and retail developments and selling them on before construction.

Among the schemes he was asked to examine was a planned development at Tiger Bay, close to the home of Welsh rugby at Cardiff Arms Park. He controversially proposed the demolition of the 'Park' and the construction of another one at a different site, though he was not involved in the project that was completed in 1999, when the Millennium Rugby Stadium was constructed on a much expanded and redeveloped Cardiff Arms Park.

Through various projects Gilmartin restored his finances, and after a few years of astute property investments he accumulated several million pounds, which ensured that his family would enjoy a comfortable life-style in England. In the course of his work in property development he was getting a name for himself as a shrewd investor who recognised the commercial potential of sites throughout the country, and as a consequence he came to the attention of senior executives in the major finance companies and pension funds, including Capital and Counties, the London Edinburgh Trust, and Norwich Union. His ability to identify potentially profitable property schemes and to envisage their long-term development was widely recognised, and his services were in significant demand as the British economy recovered. His contacts at the highest level within these finance houses provided him with access to capital for investment and also introductions to the main retailers that would anchor various schemes, including such prominent retail names as Marks and Spencer, Selfridge's and Boot's.

Gilmartin was now regarded as a successful and respected businessman, not only in his community but among banking and financial institutions in England. He had an interest in the development of Milton Keynes, where he had been offered a 99-year lease on a three-acre site earmarked for the extension of the new shopping centre in the town following his successful construction, and sale, of an office block in the new city. Another project was suggested by the grandees of Winchester, who asked him to come up with a scheme for redeveloping its city centre.

At the same time that Gilmartin was expanding his business as a
developer in Britain, Ireland's economy remained in a depressed state,
resulting in another wave of emigration. Thousands of young Irish men
and women arrived on the streets of London, Liverpool and Luton, and
Gilmartin has nothing but praise for the ordinary English people who
helped them while they were looking for work and shelter during this
time. The welfare state provided a basic income, and the social services
ensured that the new immigrants were treated fairly. A number of Irish
nuns from the Sisters of St Clare, including Sister Antoinette from Dublin
(an aunt of the former Irish international soccer player Ronnie Whelan)
and her friend Sister Eileen from Cork set up a day centre in Park Street
for the huge numbers of immigrants still flowing into Luton. Gilmartin,
along with other Irish business people and individual donors, helped
them get the project off the ground.

His encounter with one such young Irish immigrant about this time
was to inspire Gilmartin with the idea of investing in Dublin. 'I was in
town shopping. I came out of the supermarket with bags of groceries
and was waiting for a taxi to arrive. I noticed this young fellow looking
in the window of McDonald's next door. I could see he was straining
to read the menu. He put his hand in his pocket and took out whatever
money was there, and he started counting it. He'd look at the money
and then at the price list. He stood there for a good while. A young Irish
fellow passed and said hello to him and I realised he was Irish. I started
chatting to him and asked him if he was long in Luton. He said he had
come a month or two earlier. He couldn't get work. He had no luck at all.
He was a decent enough young lad from Tipperary. I said, "Why the hell
don't you go home? Anything is better than the streets of Luton." I asked
him if he had any money. He was very embarrassed and said he was a bit
short at the moment. He said he didn't have the fare to go home. Then
he said, "If I go home there's no hope at all," and that was the thing that
hit me.

'Here was a fellow walking the streets of Luton looking for a job,
without a penny to buy himself a burger, but he considered going home
the greater of two evils. That struck me more than anything. I told him
I could understand, because I came over in the 1950s, when there was no
hope either. But I felt it was a damning indictment of Ireland. I said, "If

you want to go home, I'll pay the passage." He didn't want to take it. I handed him some money to get himself a feed. With a bit of persuasion he took the money. I said I knew a few people in Milton Keynes and that there was work starting on a site there. I told him to mention my name. I gave him two hundred pounds and said, "That should take care of you." He didn't want to take it, and he wanted my address so he could pay me back. I said, "I'm all right. God is good to me, and I hope he'll be good to you." It was then and there I decided to see if I could do anything to help rescue the Irish economy and keep these kids at home.

'Since Ireland was at rock bottom, it hit me that it would be a good time to start. I put the feelers out to see would there be any interest.'

Invited to a function in London attended by executives from a number of banks and investment houses, Gilmartin raised the prospect of doing business in the then flagging Irish economy. The notion was greeted with some incredulity by potential investors, who considered Dublin a backwater, with little to offer by way of a healthy return. As the event came to a close he was introduced to Raymond Mould, chief executive of Arlington Securities, and also met executives from the London Edinburgh Trust and Capital and Counties, who were more open to his ideas. After discussions with the investors in London he was told that funds were available for any potentially successful scheme he could identify in Dublin.

Gilmartin had already been invited by the Northern Ireland Office in Belfast to discuss plans for the redevelopment of Belfast along the River Lagan and of Derry along the Foyle, and had made a successful investment with local business people in the Clandeboye Shopping Centre in Bangor, county Down, which was a commercial success despite the continuing and bitter conflict in Northern Ireland. 'I was told that money would be no object if I put the right deal together.'

Armed with that promise, Gilmartin came to Dublin.

Chapter 2

'AN IDEAL SPOT FOR DEVELOPMENT'

T he economic and political landscape in Ireland in the mid-
1980s was bleak. Unemployment was at a record level, and tens
of thousands emigrated every year, including many young,
skilled and educated graduates. The country was weighed down by
poor growth, high inflation and mounting public debt. In the North
of Ireland the Troubles continued to rage, with nearly seven hundred
people killed between 1980 and 1987.

What would later emerge—in part as a result of Tom Gilmartin's
evidence to the tribunal—was that there was also a culture of political and
business corruption in the 1980s, and nowhere more so than in Dublin,
which reached all the way to the leader of Fianna Fáil, Charles Haughey.
Throughout the 1980s Haughey encouraged taxpayers to tighten their
belts and after 1987 inflicted deep cuts on public services while living in a
mansion in county Dublin, owning an island off the Kerry coast, buying
expensive tailor-made shirts in Paris, and entertaining his friends in the
luxury to which he had become accustomed.

Such a life-style would be impossible even on a Taoiseach's salary. It
was later revealed that Haughey maintained it by receiving large secret
payments from businessmen during most of his career. With the help of
Des Traynor, a former accountancy partner in his firm Haughey Boland,
he stashed huge amounts of money offshore in the Cayman Islands,
as did other well-connected individuals, all this at a time when public
hospital wards were being closed through lack of funds. Haughey's
influence, and that of his party, penetrated all levels of society, and none
more so than the lucrative world of construction and development.

If lands were purchased at agricultural prices around the capital
they multiplied in value if they were eventually rezoned for housing or
commercial developments. Advance information about rezoning was

available from plans that were accessible to the politically influential. Corrupt politicians, planners and senior council officials could provide much of the information to those who were willing to pay the price.

A crucial moment was the creation in 1966 of Taca, an organisation specifically designed to allow wealthy businessmen access to Fianna Fáil politicians for a donation to the party of £100—a considerable amount in the 1960s. Taca became public knowledge in 1967, and as a result of the disquiet that resulted it was wound up in 1969, but the connections between powerful political figures and wealthy businessmen continued, although in a more informal and surreptitious fashion. But the important feature of Taca, noted even at the time, was how many of those involved came from the property and construction sectors. What Taca first showed was the deep connection between Fianna Fáil and the building industry, a connection that both would use in the future to their mutual advantage but often to the great detriment of the state the politicians were meant to serve.

The political and commercial culture in Dublin was not what Tom Gilmartin anticipated when he arrived there from Luton in late 1986. He had studied maps of the city several years earlier and had already identified possible sites for retail developments in the rapidly expanding western suburbs and the city centre. Since the mid-1970s he had also identified the need for an integrated development plan for the city and had a vision of what could be achieved, which he had discussed with the influential executives of financial institutions and pension funds he knew in London. The vision was quite extraordinary, though Gilmartin's potential backers felt that it was a realistic objective.

Dublin at the time was run by two authorities. Dublin City Council (called Dublin Corporation at the time) was responsible for an area that extended outwards from the city centre to the suburbs of Sutton and Santry in the north, Finglas and Ballyfermot in the west, and Donnybrook in the south, while Dublin County Council (now split into Fingal, South Dublin and Dún Laoghaire-Rathdown County Councils) was responsible for the area beyond that out to the county boundary. These authorities were responsible for issuing planning permission and for rezoning lands, so any developer wishing to assemble a project needed to deal with them. At times the developer would have to work with both authorities, as lands required might cross the boundary between city and county.

The ambitious plans Gilmartin created for Dublin involved a massive reconstruction of an area linking the shopping quarter of Grafton Street with a new footbridge across the River Liffey to Henry Street, close to O'Connell Bridge in the heart of the city centre. He was in discussions through his London solicitors, Cameron Markby (later Cameron Markby Hewitt) and with several leading banks and finance houses in Britain and Ireland about these plans. Among those involved at various stages were the American banking giant Citicorp and, in Dublin, Investment Bank of Ireland and Standard Life.

The plans included acquiring a number of the leading retail names in Dublin, including Brown Thomas and Switzer's in Grafton Street and the fashionable but at the time unprofitable Arnott's and Clery's in Henry Street and O'Connell Street, respectively. Gilmartin held discussions with the chief executive of Independent Newspapers, Joe Hayes, on the possible acquisition of its premises in Middle Abbey Street, which involved the proposal that Gilmartin and his investors would acquire land owned by the state transport company, CIE, near the mouth of the Liffey, where the media group could set up more modern production and printing facilities.

The figures involved were staggering, with Arlington Securities and other investors considering a scheme that would require up to £200 million in finance and the prospect of twenty thousand new jobs for Dublin. The plan also included a monorail link from Connolly Station to Heuston Station and new roadways to divert traffic from the badly choked artery along the quays. Gilmartin had an even greater long-term vision that would involve the construction of an entire new city in the midlands near Athlone to relieve the pressure on the ever-expanding capital, to which more than a third of the population had drifted over recent decades, depopulating vast swathes of the countryside and making towns and villages commercially unviable. He proposed a six-lane motorway from Cork to Derry, which he also discussed with the authorities in the North, which would open up dozens of towns along the route for residential, commercial and industrial development.

Gilmartin had recognised that Bachelor's Walk, the strategic street along the Liffey adjoining the city's most important and busiest thoroughfare, O'Connell Street, was ripe for development. He had also noted the Government's plan for a ring road around the city, the proposed M50 motorway, and reckoned that there was an ideal site for retail and other commercial development where the planned motorway would meet the N4, the main road to Galway and the west. 'I noticed the M50 and I had an idea that somewhere on the N4 around Palmerstown would be an ideal spot. I realised that was it: bingo! And then I saw Bachelor's Walk, derelict, with half the buildings knocked down, and I thought that would also be an ideal prospect for development. I went back to England. A number of people had made me offers of funds, and Arlington Securities was one of them.'

Gilmartin's success in exciting the interest of powerful investors in London and Dublin did not go unnoticed, and as the scale of his vision and plans became known among the financial and political elite it became apparent that there would be attempts to get a slice of the action or, failing that, to cause obstruction to his plans. When he sought to purchase a site in an affluent south Dublin suburb in 1986 a shocked Gilmartin was told by an agent that a leading financier would appreciate a tidy £75,000 under-the-table payment in exchange for closing the deal. Gilmartin made it clear that it was not the way he did business. In the event he did not proceed with the purchase, as he realised that it would be made unviable by the county council's plan for a motorway through the site.

Arlington Securities, a public company that had successfully developed major retail projects in England, backed by a number of prestigious pension funds and other investment houses, was the first to declare a real interest in Dublin as an investment prospect. Ted Dadley, whom Gilmartin knew from a property venture in Wales and who had previously worked for the supermarket chain Tesco, had recently joined Arlington. Raymond Mould agreed to travel to Dublin to look at the Bachelor's Walk site. Gilmartin had made sketches of the scheme, and by early 1987 a plan for a large shopping centre at Bachelor's Walk was well under way. He was offered £250,000 by Arlington Securities, as well as the reimbursement of expenses and a percentage of the profits generated in the project.

The site was made up of derelict buildings, which pockmarked the quays, stretching back to Middle Abbey Street, most of which had lain idle for years. Almost all were unoccupied, though there were preservation orders on some of the Georgian houses, a few of which had retained their rich interiors. Like the north end of O'Connell Street, the area was in sore need of regeneration, and part of it had been included under the urban renewal incentive scheme of 1986, which offered tax incentives to anyone willing to invest.

'When they saw the location and the numbers of people who were passing by, they were amazed that such a prime site could lie derelict for so long. So they allocated £200 million and told me to start assembling the site. As it happened, I had already agreed to buy numbers 9 to 14 Bachelor's Walk for £600,000, from Hill Samuel Bank.' He went on to purchase numbers 5 and 6 for a further £170,000 and then numbers 1 to 4 for £150,000.

By the end of 1987 Gilmartin had met several Government ministers, including Ray MacSharry (Finance), Bertie Ahern (Labour) and Pádraig Flynn (Environment), with whom he had discussed the prospect of tax designation, which would extend the incentives under the urban renewal scheme to cover the entire Bachelor's Walk site. Until then the scheme covered only a part of the site, most of which he had already assembled. Gilmartin's view was that the designation should be extended to cover the entire area or be removed altogether, as the development was unviable if there was only a partial designation. He was seeking consistency.

In February 1988 Pádraig Flynn proposed, and the Government accepted, that the entire area back to Middle Abbey Street would be included under the scheme. A similar designation was given to the Custom House Docks area further down the Liffey, where there was already a plan to develop an International Financial Services Centre. But Gilmartin was fearful that if Arlington's proposal for a massive retail scheme was revealed to the public, the remaining sites that they had yet to purchase would suddenly increase in price. He urged the company to buy up the rest of the sites; but Arlington executives, having already poured £10 million into the area, wanted to be certain that Government support in the form of tax designation would be guaranteed.

When they got the guarantee in writing from Pádraig Flynn they decided to proceed, but Gilmartin's fears were soon realised. Asking prices began to spiral upwards as other business interests learnt of Arlington's apparently deep pockets. 'We had a contract to buy the Abbey Shopping Centre at Liffey Street for £400,000. It went up to £1.5 million because these Mickey Mouse men were appearing.' This was Gilmartin's name for middlemen who promised owners they could secure a higher price for their properties in return for a commission.

Other Government ministers had become directly engaged with the plan for Bachelor's Walk, including the Minister of State for Trade and Marketing, Séamus Brennan. Government officials proposed that the developers include a bus station in the complex and asked Arlington Securities at a series of meetings, including one attended by Brennan and Flynn, to consider the idea, which would be paid for with EEC structural funds. Gilmartin and Arlington welcomed the idea and included it on land belonging to CIE adjoining the planned shopping centre.

When they were told that the EEC would finance only a station within the complex, Gilmartin was outraged and argued that siting the bus station above the shopping centre, as officials were proposing, would make the plan unworkable. 'At the first meeting it was full steam ahead with the bus station as far as the Government was concerned, even though it had never been part of our original plan for the area. They told us that CIE owned a big chunk at the back of the quays and that they wanted to put a bus station there. The Government said it would be paid for out of European structural funds. So we designed the whole bus station. We did all the costing and the estimates for acquiring the sites. Then the promised money disappeared. Arlington said, "Well, we are not going to pay."'

Media reports later spoke in denigrating terms of Arlington's 'bus station in the sky' proposals, despite the fact that the idea for the station, and the ludicrous suggestion of siting it at the top of the shopping complex, had emanated from CIE and Government officials.

There was also concern among conservationists about the manner in which historic Bachelor's Walk was to be redeveloped. A reflection of the growing unease about Arlington's proposal to transform the lower end of O'Connell Street and the quays appeared in an article in the *Irish Times* on 4 February 1988. The paper's environment correspondent, Frank McDonald, wrote of a 'serious threat that hangs over Bachelor's Walk,' where, he said, 'an English property company called Arlington Securities is now assembling a large site for comprehensive redevelopment.' He described how An Taisce, the environmental watchdog, had warned the city's chief planning officer, Gay McCarron, that the demolition of buildings would 'have a disastrous effect on the scale of Bachelor's Walk and the quays generally.'

Meanwhile Gilmartin was keeping his eye on the site at Quarryvale, at the junction of the M50 motorway and the N4 near Lucan that had been first introduced to him by an auctioneer a year or two earlier. He had already learnt that three sites in west Dublin, at Blanchardstown, Tallaght and Neilstown, near Clondalkin, had been earmarked as new town centres in the Dublin Development Plan by the city council several years earlier. From the early 1970s the Government-sponsored Myles Wright Plan identified the need for three town centres in west county Dublin, where hundreds of thousands of people, many from inner-city communities, had moved into local authority housing schemes. The developer Phil Monahan, through his company Monarch Properties, had secured control of land for a new town centre at Tallaght, a rapidly growing urban community with negligible shopping, leisure and other facilities, while John Corcoran of the Green Property Company was pushing ahead with a large-scale retail, leisure and business complex at Blanchardstown. Dublin City Council had also zoned the site at Balgaddy and Neilstown for a third town centre, between Tallaght and Blanchardstown and close to the proposed new M50 ring road around the city.

In early 1988 Gilmartin was shown the Neilstown site by Michael McLoone, chief valuer for Dublin City Council, who provided valuation and similar services to both local authorities, in an effort to encourage the developer to fulfil the county council's plans for the area and in particular to service the growing needs of the nearby north Clondalkin-Balgaddy community. It did not take Gilmartin long to realise that the site was unsuitable for such commercial development. He had already realised that the Quarryvale site had more strategic potential and was determined to pursue it. At first he identified a 180-acre parcel of land that would be ideal for a development, while there was a potential extra 300 acres available for acquisition.

A friend, Paul Sheeran, was manager of the Bank of Ireland in Blanchardstown, and in May 1988 Gilmartin asked him how he could establish the ownership of the lands at Quarryvale. Sheeran knew little about the ownership of the lands, but he asked a customer who worked in Palmerstown and who happened to be in the bank at that very moment, Brendan Fassnidge, a garage-owner. Fassnidge said he was aware that Dublin City Council had land for housing in the area and that Des Bruton, a cousin of a prominent Fine Gael politician and former Minister for Finance, John Bruton, had a large holding there. 'He wasn't sure about the rest of the land, but he said he knew a fellow who would know every bit of that land. He said, "I'll give him a ring and find out if he'll meet you." He went out to the car to make a phone call and came back in to ask me was I available that evening.'

Fassnidge asked Gilmartin if he could meet the man at seven o'clock in the Dead Man's Inn, a pub in Palmerstown. 'I was in the Dead Man's Inn for about ten minutes when this big man came tearing in the door, all "hail, fellow, well met." He wasn't the slightest bit interested in what I wanted to know. He only wanted to talk about Bachelor's Walk, which he said was on his patch. He told me he knew I was involved in a big scheme in Bachelor's Walk, and he said the Government had allocated him to take care of me and get the deal into Dublin. He said that he wanted to meet the people behind the proposed development. I said that I was meeting the people in London on Thursday and I would ask them if they would like to meet him. I told him I was interested in a piece of land in the Palmerstown area. He said that this land was zoned industrial, and he told me he would have a map for me the next time I came over from England. That was my first encounter with Liam Lawlor.'

Chapter 3 ∽

| THE CORRIDORS OF POWER

The following week Gilmartin sat down with the Arlington executives in their London boardroom at Brewer's Green. 'The meeting had just started and we were discussing Bachelor's Walk, with maps and plans in front of us. The next thing the phone rang and Raymond Mould picked it up. I could hear him ask, "Who is he?" He looked around and said that there was a fellow who claimed to be a Government representative from Dublin. He wanted to join the meeting and said that I had invited him. He said, "His name is Lawlor." I nearly went through the floor. I said I never invited him; I said I met him but I never invited him to the meeting. Mould said, "We'll hear what he has to say." The next thing the fucker walked in, as brazen as brass. He pulled up a chair and sat at the table. He told them he had been appointed by the Government to look after Bachelor's Walk, that they would have to have him on board if the scheme was to get off the ground. He went on to say that, at the very least, he could knock two years off the time to develop the scheme if he was on board. I objected. I said I had never invited the gentleman and that I didn't even know him. I had met him on one occasion. He contradicted me and said I had invited him. So here I was in a situation where there's two Paddies in the room going to start an argument, so I decided to bite my tongue. The meeting broke up, and Mould and Price spoke together with Dadley.

'Dadley came in and suggested we go for a cup of tea to a nearby hotel while Mould and Price talked to Lawlor. I said to him, "That guy is a hustler. He lied when he said I had invited him." I told Dadley to tell Mould to have nothing to do with him. I said I wanted Mould to know that he had lied. I couldn't figure it out.

'We were there half an hour when Lawlor came haring into the hotel. He sat down and said that he was on board, that they had appointed him. He said that he had asked the Arlington executives for £100,000 up front and a 20 per cent stake in the Bachelor's Walk project. They had refused to give him a 20 per cent stake. Then he said that Mould had agreed that I would give him half of my stake and £100,000 up front. I said he would get nothing of my stake and no hundred thousand. He said they had agreed to pay him a consultancy fee of £3,500 a month. "You have to work with me or you are going no further," he declared.'

The Arlington executives told Gilmartin that Lawlor, a Fianna Fáil TD and county councillor in west Dublin, had insisted that he could help them traverse the difficult political landscape in Dublin: 'He said he could help us through the corridors of power.'

Lawlor had convinced them that he could win the necessary 'political support' for the Bachelor's Walk project, and they agreed to the monthly consultancy fee, which Gilmartin was to pay and then be reimbursed by the company. Gilmartin had no choice but to reluctantly accept the decision of the Arlington executives to pay the monthly fee to Lawlor. The first cheque for £3,500 was given to Lawlor, with the payee section left blank at his insistence, and was subsequently lodged to the account of Advanced Proteins Limited, a company controlled by Lawlor, in the Bank of Ireland in Lucan near Lawlor's home, while on other occasions the cheques were made out to his brother-in-law Noel Gilson, who was an innocent party and unaware of Lawlor's activities. (See appendix 1, paragraph 1.)

A week or so later, in late May or early June, Gilmartin returned to Dublin, to be met at the airport by his new self-appointed friend and minder. After that Lawlor would often meet Gilmartin at the airport and, according to Gilmartin, would 'chauffeur me around, despite the fact that I never asked him to do so, and he would generally turn up without me having arranged for him to do so. On many occasions I really had no idea how he managed to find out the details of my flights into Dublin.

'I arrived back in Dublin and Lawlor collected me. He brought me into the offices of Dublin County Council in O'Connell Street. He brought me to George Redmond's office. He introduced me to Redmond.'

George Redmond, assistant city and county manager, was the most powerful man in planning in the greater Dublin area. The city of almost a million people was spreading outwards to the county boundary, and Redmond had a handle on all the plans that showed which areas should be rezoned and where the roads, water and sewerage services would be available. It was information that was invaluable for prospective builders and developers. Redmond and Lawlor had assiduously courted many business people in a relationship that was to be mutually beneficial. In Gilmartin they identified another developer who might prove to be a cash cow, and it did not take them long to let him know the cost of their co-operation.

Gilmartin explained that he was interested in buying some land along the Dublin–Galway road and was looking for the map that could identify the owner of each plot of land at Quarryvale. Almost immediately after their introduction Redmond produced a 24 by 24-inch colour-coded sheet providing the details he required.

Before he did so, Lawlor and Redmond engaged in bit of theatre to make it plain to Gilmartin that the information would come at a price. 'Redmond got up from the desk and picked up the phone at another desk. I knew he was talking to nobody. While he was "occupied" Lawlor asked me for £100,000 for himself, and said that Redmond would have to be paid £100,000 as well. I didn't say yes, aye or no. I said, "I told you before I will not give you a penny." Redmond came back and handed me a drawing, a layout with every landowner in Quarryvale identified. It was colour-coded for each owner. Again, Lawlor told me I'd have to pay Redmond £100,000. I said I'd think about it.

'I didn't know what to do. I had the map. On the way out to the car Lawlor said again that George would have to be looked after. "If you're going to go anywhere you have to pay George, you have to take care of George," Lawlor said, adding, "and you have to have me on board."

'I never trusted Redmond from the first time I met him. I thought he was a sneak. By the second or third meeting he had confirmed my impression that he was a gangster.' As he left the meeting in the council offices in O'Connell Street, Gilmartin realised that he had learnt, at first hand, the cost of doing business in Dublin.

He had not let either Lawlor or Redmond in on his detailed plans for Quarryvale, though the two men were obviously keen to find out what this new arrival from Luton had to offer. The price of their co-operation was £200,000, and it had been made abundantly clear to him that if he did not pay up, his ambition to purchase and develop the lands would not be realised. The map came in useful in subsequent discussions with landowners and bankers, but Gilmartin's refusal to accede to the financial demands made by Lawlor for himself and Redmond were to haunt him over the coming months and years. Soon after the encounter he informed his friend Paul Sheeran of the demand, while many others in senior positions of power were to learn of them before too long. (See appendix 1, paragraph 2.)

Gilmartin went on to negotiate with Des Bruton for his lands at Quarryvale. Bruton wanted a stud farm in exchange. Gilmartin bought Convie Stud, near Luttrellstown, for him for £400,000 after some tense negotiations with the owners, who at first sought a higher sum for the somewhat run-down estate.

Lawlor, as was his tendency with any business deal he came across, continued to press for a 20 per cent share in the Quarryvale development. Gilmartin refused to concede. 'I said, "That site could cost £3 to £5 million. If it is developed and comes to be worth £200 million, you are telling me you have to be paid £40 million. What investor is going to come in on this site if they know it's already tied up between you and me? It's not on. You are not getting any 20 per cent." I told him that he had conned Arlington into giving him money and that he was not getting any from me. Lawlor said something to the effect that that is the way things are done. "You'll go nowhere. You'll go no fucking place if you want to get this off the ground," he said.' (See appendix 1, paragraph 3.)

After a further year of fruitless discussions, and with £12 million invested in the Bachelor's Walk project, Arlington got fed up with the delays and in particular the blind alley of a bus station they had been asked to research and pursue. The company eventually pulled out of Dublin, amid bitter recriminations over the obstructions it had faced, and it was subsequently taken over by British Aerospace.

———

While still employed by Arlington Securities, working out of an office in St Stephen's Green that was paid for by the company, Gilmartin had begun to concentrate on his other site, the proposed retail development at Quarryvale. He had formed a company, Barkhill, to develop the project and by the autumn of 1988 had assembled the main blocks of land necessary to ensure the project's success, using finance he raised himself. Acquiring the land out of his own funds was a protracted and complicated affair, with Gilmartin taking on various professional advisers, including auctioneers, solicitors and accountants, while seeking to maintain some secrecy about his long-term intentions in order to avoid a repeat of the Bachelor's Walk experience. He also assembled a team of architects and engineers and a public relations firm to prepare the elaborate plans that went with a multi-million retail development on a green-field site on the outskirts of the city's fast-expanding western suburbs.

Gilmartin had been offered the Neilstown site by senior officials but refused it, on the grounds that it was unsuitable for such a development. In his view it was not economically viable and nowhere near as attractive as the lands at Quarryvale, which had frontage onto the Galway road. The development plan's choice of the Neilstown lands for a town centre was ill-advised, in Gilmartin's view, despite its proximity to the local population centre of Clondalkin. He argued from the time he first viewed it that the site would not work. It still had official zoning, however, as the preferred site, but Gilmartin believed that the working-class people of the area would benefit more from a development on a more accessible site, which would ensure its commercial success, generate local employment and finance a range of essential social, sports and other facilities for the community.

While the city council officials were sympathetic to Gilmartin's arguments about the commercial non-viability of the designated site, and indeed were encouraging him in his efforts to develop Quarryvale, the control of the Neilstown lands, which had the all-important zoning, emerged as a significant obstacle to his plans. The first hint of difficulty came from Liam Lawlor, who continued to shadow every move Gilmartin made in Dublin. Lawlor quickly identified the potential ransom value of the Neilstown lands and was not slow to pass on this information to others if he thought it could be to his advantage. He had maintained constant contact with Gilmartin and in September 1988 even drafted a letter on his behalf to the Minister for the Environment, Pádraig Flynn, though Gilmartin was already in contact with the minister and had no need to write such a letter. 'Mr Lawlor's consultancy services effectively consisted of drafting this one letter,' said Gilmartin. 'I was already speaking to Flynn, so I never actually sent the letter.' He was not aware that Lawlor was also busy lining up others who might have an interest in the potentially lucrative west Dublin development.

In November 1988 Gilmartin had arranged a meeting with his architects, Taggarts of Belfast, in the Trust House Forte Hotel at Dublin

Airport. He had worked with the firm some years earlier on the successful Clandeboye Shopping Centre that he developed in Bangor, outside Belfast. As they sat around the table Gilmartin had another unexpected visit from the busy politician. Lawlor had heard about the meeting from Gilmartin's son after he had made a phone call to Gilmartin's home in Luton. Lawlor was now on a mission to persuade Gilmartin to bring the Cork developer Owen O'Callaghan into the project. 'Lawlor told me I would have to deal with the developer Owen O'Callaghan. He told me O'Callaghan had another site at Neilstown, near Quarryvale, which he had an option to buy from Albert Gubay. He said O'Callaghan was a property developer who had done the Merchants Quay Shopping Centre in Cork.'

Challenged by Gilmartin that no-one in their right mind would build on the Neilstown site, Lawlor replied: 'It doesn't matter. You'll go nowhere, because Mr O'Callaghan, all he has to do is threaten to build it and you'll be [stuck] there for ever.' Ultimately Gilmartin had no choice but to deal with O'Callaghan.

Long before the publicity-shy millionaire came to national attention as one of the country's most successful developers, Owen O'Callaghan was well established as a determined and shrewd operator in property and political, mainly Fianna Fáil, circles. He had been appointed to the board of An Bord Gáis, the state-sponsored energy company, by Charles Haughey and was recognised as a powerful back-room influence in the party. By the time Gilmartin met O'Callaghan for the first time, O'Callaghan had spent twenty years building houses and retail projects and was involved in both the Merchants Quay retail development in his native city and another, smaller retail project at Arthur's Quay in Limerick. He had already been tipped off by Lawlor and other contacts in Dublin about Gilmartin and his ambitious plans and quickly recognised the potential of the lands acquired at Quarryvale. He had met Lawlor in early November 1988, along with Finbarr Hanrahan, a Fianna Fáil councillor for Lucan, who had assisted O'Callaghan some five months earlier in supporting a 'section 4 motion' in the council (subsequently withdrawn) in respect of lands at Cooldrinagh, near Lucan, where O'Callaghan was proposing to develop a shopping centre. This was a controversial method of obtaining changes to the Dublin Development Plan under section 4 of the Planning and Development Act. Before he met Gilmartin, O'Callaghan was briefed by Hanrahan on the relative advantages of the Quarryvale site over the designated Neilstown lands, and how the new arrival from Luton had secured a foothold on the better option and had already made progress on its rezoning.

After a meeting on 2 November 1988 O'Callaghan recorded in a memo dated 4 November that Hanrahan 'told me about the Gilmartin site some three months ago.' He was referring to lands with direct entry to the Galway road on which Gilmartin had taken an option. The land was zoned for residential use by councillors using a section 4 motion, but the county management had refused to carry out this instruction. This decision was challenged in the High Court, which upheld the motion. 'The case is now with the Supreme Court and a decision will be made on Tuesday next, 8th November. Hanrahan is confident the decision will be in favour of Gilmartin and the councillors. All Gilmartin has then to do is get a change of use to retail. This site [Quarryvale] is obviously a better location than Clondalkin [Neilstown].'

It was evident that O'Callaghan was informed in some detail about Gilmartin's plans during the summer and autumn of 1988 through his contact with Hanrahan and Lawlor, and he was also aware that only by gaining control of the Neilstown lands could he leverage his way into the Quarryvale project. By early November he had secured the option on the Neilstown lands from the Welsh retail and property developer Albert Gubay, which could now be used for what is known in the ruthless property game as their 'ransom' value. In short, O'Callaghan could now use his option on Neilstown as a lever with which he could negotiate with Gilmartin. In his memo of the meeting with Lawlor and Hanrahan, O'Callaghan also recorded that the Neilstown site was 'going nowhere' but that the Quarryvale option had the support of Government ministers, who, Lawlor claimed, had 'asked him to look after Gilmartin.' O'Callaghan also noted that Lawlor 'was confident that Gilmartin will get permission' but that 'we are in the driving seat for the time being.' His political and banking contacts also confirmed to O'Callaghan that Gilmartin was about to become a significant player with control over what was recognised as potentially the most important retail site in Ireland.

Gilmartin described his first encounter with O'Callaghan on 7 December 1988. 'Lawlor gave me O'Callaghan's phone number and he said, "You have to deal with this man or you are going nowhere." I went away and I was thinking about it. I spoke to council officials who confirmed that if O'Callaghan went ahead with his site at Neilstown it would cause problems for me. Quarryvale could not go ahead unless Neilstown wasn't built on. I realised I had goofed. I should have got control of that site first. I had been offered the site by Michael McLoone, in early 1988, but I didn't think it could ever be built on. At the time the corporation owned it. Some weeks later Albert Gubay offered the corporation £3 million for the site and provided a deposit of £300,000. He had a clause inserted in the contract which stated that if anything was built close by he did not have to build on the Neilstown land. O'Callaghan learnt about the option secured by Gubay and moved in on the site.'

O'Callaghan recognised that control of the Neilstown-Balgaddy land could provide him with vital leverage in any negotiations with Gilmartin over Quarryvale. The fact that it had the town-centre designation was crucial, in that it would require a council vote to have it transferred to the more strategic site at the junction of the M50 and N4.

In all these calculations there appeared to be little or no consideration of the people of Neilstown or north Clondalkin, who were already enduring high levels of unemployment and poverty and were still awaiting some decent shopping and leisure facilities for their community. Gilmartin recognised that in any proposal for the Quarryvale lands, which he envisaged could be used for much more than a retail scheme, it would have to service the wider needs of these local communities for their shopping, cultural and sports amenities as well as providing much-needed employment.

Gubay had put the property into the name of a company called Merrygrove, which O'Callaghan bought for £500,000 plus the £300,000 deposit Gubay had paid to the city council. Recognising that he would have to come to some accommodation with O'Callaghan, Gilmartin decided to phone him at home. O'Callaghan agreed to meet him the following day in the Royal Dublin Hotel in O'Connell Street and had a room booked upstairs. He presented a drawing of the 33-acre Neilstown site to Gilmartin and a sketch of a shopping centre prepared by his architect, Ambrose Kelly, and then said that he had outline planning permission for the development. 'He wanted me to hand over the Quarryvale site to him, or to go fifty-fifty on the deal. He said he'd spent a lot of money on the Neilstown site and if he was to pull out of the deal there would have to be something in it for him.'

O'Callaghan went on to press Gilmartin on the supposed benefits of such a partnership. 'You would think butter wouldn't melt in his mouth. I had some business cards with me, and when I put my hand in my pocket to take them out a religious artefact fell on the floor. I stopped to pick it up and he said, "So you're a religious man." I said I could do better. He went on talking about religion and how religious he was, and he couldn't understand people who didn't say the Rosary, and things like that.'

O'Callaghan wanted £7 million for the Neilstown lands. Gilmartin wouldn't give it to him. 'By that time I had control of the site at the junction of the Galway road at the M50. He and his financial advisers knew they couldn't do anything with Quarryvale without me. They also knew it was one of the best sites in Europe.'

But Gilmartin also knew that he needed to get control of Neilstown so that it would not be used to obstruct his quest for zoning and planning permission on the Quarryvale lands. He was forced to deal, and the price was high. He came to an agreement with O'Callaghan, signed in January 1989, to pay £3½ million for the Neilstown lands, to be delivered in stages. 'First I had to give him the £800,000 he paid Gubay, and on the anniversary of that [January 1990] I would pay him £1.35 million, and the final £1.35 million when zoning for Quarryvale was approved, or in January 1991, whichever came sooner. That was that. I had bought the site off him.'

The contract, subsequently the subject of some dispute between the parties, was made in the offices of Gilmartin's solicitor, Seamus Maguire, in Blanchardstown. Gilmartin was aware that developing the Neilstown site was impractical. Council houses obstructed the entrance to the land, and a flyover would have been necessary. However, he had no choice but to do the deal with O'Callaghan, who, he believed, had no real intention of developing the lands.

During their first meeting O'Callaghan also let Gilmartin know of his extensive political contacts and the fact that only days earlier he had met the Minister for Industry and Commerce, Albert Reynolds, and senior executives of Allied Irish Banks at a function in Cork, where discussions on the Quarryvale site had taken place. The local newspaper, the *Evening Echo*, had published a photograph of O'Callaghan with Reynolds during the minister's visit to the developer's shopping centre in the city.

There were more wheels within wheels in Irish commercial and political life than Gilmartin had been prepared for.

Chapter 4

'THE PLACE WAS TOTALLY CORRUPT'

With the encouragement of Dublin City Council officials, who were desperate to advance development to the west of the city, Gilmartin proceeded with the acquisition of lands around Quarryvale. All the assembled property was vested in Barkhill Ltd, of which he and his wife were sole directors. By the end of 1988 he had purchased the crucial sites at Quarryvale, including 68.62 acres from Dublin City Council and a further 12.04 acres from Dublin County Council, both deals negotiated with the city's chief valuer, Michael McLoone. He had completed his option agreement on the Neilstown lands with O'Callaghan, which was signed, in its fourth draft, on 31 January 1989. This meant, he felt, that he could move on with some confidence now that the main obstacles to progress were removed. If only life was so simple . . .

Within a matter of days Gilmartin gained some idea of the difficulties he was to face in getting his dream project off the ground. Again Liam Lawlor was at the centre of events. On 1 February 1989 Lawlor met Gilmartin at about 5 p.m. in Buswells Hotel in Molesworth Street, across the road from Dáil Éireann in Kildare Street. Lawlor had told him that 'the Boss' wanted to meet him. The Boss was, of course, Charles Haughey, then Taoiseach and leader of Fianna Fáil, which made him Ireland's most powerful politician. Gilmartin followed Lawlor across the road into the Dáil building and ascended by lift to an upper floor. Ray Burke, a Government minister, was in the lift on the way up but they hardly exchanged a word. Gilmartin recalled being led by Lawlor along a gangway, past partitioned offices on each side and towards a lobby area. He was then ushered through dark oak double doors.

Lawlor stayed outside when Gilmartin entered a large meeting-room where a group of Government ministers were gathered around a large rectangular table. Pádraig Flynn sat at the top left-hand corner of the table and beside him Albert Reynolds. Beside Reynolds was Gerry Collins, Minister for Justice, while along the right-hand side were Bertie Ahern, Minister for Labour, Brian Lenihan (senior), Tánaiste and Minister for Foreign Affairs, and Séamus Brennan, Minister of State for Trade and Marketing. Standing behind Brennan was a man whom he did not recognise and to whom he was not introduced. Ahern, Brennan and Lenihan, all of whom he had previously met, greeted him. Burke then entered through a door in the middle of the room, followed by Charles Haughey.

'I know you: you're Gilmartin from Lislary,' Haughey said as he walked around the table towards his visitor. He told Gilmartin that he knew of Lislary because he had a holiday home by the sea in the townland. After chatting about the two projects at Bachelor's Walk and Quarryvale, the Taoiseach gave Gilmartin an assurance that no obstacles would be put in his way at a time when jobs were desperately needed.

During the brief conversation Gilmartin mentioned that he knew Seán Haughey, the Taoiseach's brother, who, like George Redmond, was an assistant city and county manager for Dublin. The Taoiseach took this to be a reference to his son Seán, a politician who, he told Gilmartin, was or was about to become Lord Mayor of Dublin, and encouraged him to call in to him at the Mansion House. Before he ended the conversation Haughey asked whether 'Liam was taking good care of you.' At some point during the conversation Mary O'Rourke, Minister for Education, entered the room and was introduced by Pádraig Flynn to Gilmartin, to whom she nodded.

After the brief and informal encounter with these members of the Government he was ushered from the room by the unidentified man who had been standing behind Brennan. As he entered the lobby area outside, Gilmartin says he saw Lawlor and another man in conversation to his left. He was then approached by yet another man, short in stature with 'salt and pepper' (i.e. black and white) hair and a casual jacket. This man, whom he did not know, told him he would do well out of his business projects. He gave Gilmartin a piece of paper with a number written on it. It was the number of a bank account with Bank of Ireland in the Isle of Man. The man asked him to deposit £5 million in the account.

Describing the incident in detail, Gilmartin told me:

Well, he approached me, I looked around, and . . . he says: 'Do you realise that you're going to get every assistance to get these two projects off the ground?' and I said, 'Well, it's a major investment that I'm bringing into Ireland, so I would expect that they would be happy to see it under the current economy,' and he says to me, 'You're also—we're all aware that you are going to make hundreds of millions out of these two projects,' and I said, 'Well, not me. Whoever invests in it will. It won't be me that will make hundreds of millions.' And he said to me, 'Well, we think that you should give us some of that money up front.' So I say, 'Yeah?' And he said, 'Yes, we would like you to deposit five million pounds before you start.' And I say, 'What do you mean?' and he says, 'Well, we want you to deposit five million pounds, and we want it deposited into an Isle of Man account,' and I said, sarcastically, 'That's not much,' or words to that effect.

With that—he had his hands in his jacket pocket and he took out this piece of paper . . . a striped piece of paper about an inch and a half wide . . . and he says, 'I want you to deposit the money into that account.'

Gilmartin took the piece of paper, put it in his pocket, turned to the man and said, 'You make the fucking Mafia look like monks.' The man grabbed him by the hand in an apparent attempt to take back the piece of paper, which Gilmartin had put in his pocket, and as he did so the unidentified man said, 'You could fucking wind up in the Liffey for saying things like that.'

'I told him to "fuck off" and walked on.'

There were no witnesses to the conversation. Lawlor, who had been present in the hallway when he left the meeting with the Government ministers, was nowhere to be seen.

As Gilmartin walked towards the lift, Seán Walsh, then a Fianna Fáil TD for Dublin West, beckoned to him to come into his office. He warned Gilmartin that he was being set up by Lawlor and named other councillors, including Finbarr Hanrahan, as well as George Redmond, as individuals he 'needed to watch out for.'

'Remember, you are being shafted, you are being set up . . . You must watch your back' were the words used by Walsh.

Not surprisingly, his first experience at the highest levels of political power in Dublin left Gilmartin with the distinct impression that corruption was rampant at every level. It is not clear whom the man who approached him represented, or who controlled the Isle of Man account, but it was the most dramatic moment thus far in Gilmartin's confrontation with the elusive and powerful interests that influenced commercial and political life in the city.

'I was invited by Mr Lawlor to meet the Taoiseach. I went to meet the Taoiseach. I went into the Dáil. I met the majority of ministers, who were sitting around the table, and on my way out, just at the door, a gentleman asked me—told me, because of the amount of money I was going to make out of all the help they were going to give me . . . that I should give them five million pounds . . . So all in all I could only come to one conclusion, that the place was totally corrupt.'

The Isle of Man was a favoured place for Irish banks and building societies wishing to provide offshore facilities for their customers, with its promise of confidentiality and protection from the unwelcome attention of the revenue authorities. The identities of account-holders were frequently hidden behind shelf companies created by local legal firms or company service providers.

Later Gilmartin assessed the potential significance of Haughey's remark about whether 'Liam was looking after' him. Given that Lawlor had already hit him for substantial sums of money, it was not surprising perhaps that his visit to the Taoiseach would be used as another opportunity to get a slice of the multi-million investment Gilmartin was bringing to town, either for the party or for prominent individuals in it.

But there may have been another issue at play for Haughey at the meeting. This concerned his reference to the Gilmartins of Lislary. Several years earlier Haughey had acquired a property close to the Gilmartin family land and had then sought to extend his holding onto a portion of their land through his company Larchfield Securities Ltd. When it emerged that there was an attempt to alter the ownership with the Land Registry, Chris Gilmartin, Tom's sister, objected. After an exchange of legal correspondence and a complaint by her to the Land Registry, Haughey's company withdrew its claim to the 1½ acres.

Haughey had obtained the land from John Andrew Currid, a relation of the Gilmartins who left Lislary to find work in the 1930s. Currid had inherited an amusement-arcade business in Dublin and Bray from a Jewish family that had left Ireland when the Second World War broke out in Europe and did not return. The now wealthy Currid had returned to Lislary, rebuilt and renovated his seaside family home at Lislary, and had given small plots of land to various neighbours and relations, including James Gilmartin. On the latter's death his daughter Chris was given some of the rough grazing land at what was known as the 'Bent', a turn in the road close to her family home and overlooking the sea. Haughey's accountancy firm, Haughey Boland, had acted for Currid, and on his death Charles Haughey took over the house and the land around it for use as a holiday home.

In the late 1970s Haughey sought to spread his holding onto the Gilmartin lands but perhaps did not anticipate the opposition he would meet. In June 1984 a firm of Sligo solicitors, Horan, Monahan and Company, wrote to Haughey's solicitor, J. S. O'Connor, on behalf of Christina McGoldrick (Chris Gilmartin's married name) asking whether Larchfield Securities intended to pursue an interest in the lands at Ballinfull, county Sligo, but she received no reply. Two years later, in May 1986, Haughey, then leader of the opposition, was confronted by Chris Gilmartin during a visit by him to the town. She approached him as he was meeting and greeting members of the public and asked when he was going to relinquish his claim on her land. Haughey invited her to meet him to discuss the matter later that evening in the Ballymount Entertainment Centre in the Silver Slipper Hotel in Strandhill, where he was to address a Fianna Fáil function. As she waited to meet him after the event she was informed that Haughey had already left for Dublin.

Finally, Chris Gilmartin contacted the Land Registry directly and was informed that an agent for Larchfield had sought to register ownership of the land by telephone but that no written application had been made. The Land Registry then gave ten days to Larchfield to respond in writing with a submission. When it failed to do so, the land was registered in Chris Gilmartin's name.

Haughey was not used to being challenged and even less so to losing such a battle. It was undoubtedly an embarrassment for him and perhaps one that he had not forgotten when he encountered Tom Gilmartin at the Leinster House meeting less than three years after his confrontation with the developer's sister in Sligo. Given his character, it was an experience Haughey was unlikely to forget, or forgive, but whether it would have motivated the extraordinary efforts to interfere with, and jeopardise, Tom Gilmartin's ambitious plans for Dublin is another matter.

Although Gilmartin was aware of the dispute over a piece of land involving Haughey and his sister in county Sligo, it never crossed his mind that it might influence the Taoiseach or those around him in respect of his investment and job-creation initiatives. 'I would never have considered that a piece of scrub land at the edge of the sea in Lislary would have any bearing on my discussions with Haughey or anyone else in Dublin. It never crossed my mind at the time, but when you consider his comments about Liam "taking care" of me and what followed, you could never rule it out,' Gilmartin remarked years later.

————

Back in February 1989 he just could not believe that he would be confronted with such an outrageous financial demand as the one he faced after his meeting with the Taoiseach and several other members of the Government.

In the days and weeks that followed, a shocked Gilmartin told, among others, Paul Sheeran, Michael McLoone and the investment banker Johnny Fortune of his extraordinary encounter in Leinster House. Fortune, director of corporate finance in Investment Bank of Ireland, recalled that an 'ashen-faced' Gilmartin told him within days of his meeting with the Taoiseach that a demand for a 'seven-figure sum' had been made of him in relation to his business interests in Quarryvale just after he had emerged from a meeting with the Taoiseach and his Government. (See appendix 1, paragraph 4.)

He had a taste of more of the greed and graft that epitomised Irish political life when he met Councillor Finbarr Hanrahan. Gilmartin had been advised by Lawlor that he should get a few councillors 'on board' and had contacted Hanrahan to meet him in Buswells Hotel. When he arrived at the hotel he saw Owen O'Callaghan, his solicitor, John Deane, his architect, Ambrose Kelly, and Lawlor in the bar along with 'another gentleman'. When the other gentleman moved away from the group, O'Callaghan indicated to Gilmartin by nodding that he should approach the man who had just left their company. It was evident that this man was Councillor Hanrahan, although Gilmartin had not informed anyone of their intended meeting.

Gilmartin showed the councillor a brochure outlining the Quarryvale scheme and spoke about its potential to bring a significant number of jobs to west Dublin. He remembers the politician saying, 'Well, this is going to damage quite of a few of my friends in Lucan, and there's little people who were taking care of me over a number of years, and if I'm going to support your scheme I expect to get something for it. I want £100,000 for my support, because those people have taken care of me for a number of years and they're all going to be damaged by this scheme.'

'So then [Hanrahan] said: "I've met people like you," or words to that effect, "who when they get what they wanted didn't pay up, so I want £50,000 up front." I exchanged a few words and walked out.' As Gilmartin left the bar in disgust he was asked by O'Callaghan, 'Did he tap you?' to which he replied, 'What do you think?'

By this time Gilmartin would have been down almost £6 million if he had acceded to all the demands for money from various quarters. He had told a number of people, including O'Callaghan, Sheeran and some of the politicians, of the constant demands made on him for money. The demand by Hanrahan and the approach after his meeting with Haughey and his ministers prompted Gilmartin to make his complaints more widely known to the authorities, with unexpected results. (See appendix 1, paragraph 5.)

———

On the day after the encounter with Gilmartin in Leinster House the Taoiseach summoned senior officials of Dublin City Council and Dublin County Council to meet him and other ministers on 2 February 1989 for a discussion on how to advance job-creation initiatives and urban renewal in the city. Among those present were assisstant managers George Redmond and Seán Haughey. It was at this meeting that Redmond established from comments made by Pádraig Flynn that Gilmartin had acquired O'Callaghan's interest in Neilstown and was in a strong position to successfully develop his planned retail centre at Quarryvale. At this time Gilmartin had agreed, subject to contract, to purchase 68 acres in the townland of Irishtown from Dublin City Council and a further 12 acres in the townland of Woodfarm from Dublin County Council as part of his final assembly of the land bank for Quarryvale. He had agreed a price of £40,000 per acre for the lands, amounting to £2.7 million for the Irishtown lands and £481,600 for the Woodfarm parcel—with Michael McLoone, who was handling the sale on behalf of both local authorities.

The proposed land disposals required the sanction of the city management and the city council. As the deal was being finalised McLoone learnt that Redmond had alerted a rival developer, John Corcoran of Green Property (who was developing the retail centre at Blanchardstown), of Gilmartin's bid and encouraged him to tender for the same lands. McLoone told Gilmartin of the attempt to block the deal they had agreed and also of Redmond's intention to work for Green Property on his retirement some months later, in June 1989. During a meeting of the county council Redmond and Lawlor spoke openly of alleged 'cosy deals' in which Gilmartin had engaged with city officials in respect of the Irishtown lands. All this conspired to cause major delays for Gilmartin.

To compound his difficulties, Gilmartin was also facing problems in getting access for his professional advisers to the relevant officials of Dublin County Council. In his capacity as the most senior official responsible for, among other things, road planning, Redmond directly controlled access for developers and their advisers to the engineers in this department. As Gilmartin had rejected the demand by Lawlor that he and Redmond be paid £100,000 each for their assistance, it seemed that he was to pay a price for his refusal.

A meeting was arranged for 10 a.m. on 22 February 1989 to discuss the road issues at Quarryvale with the council engineers. Gilmartin assembled his team at the Gresham Hotel across the road from the council offices in O'Connell Street in preparation for the consultation there. When he phoned to confirm their imminent arrival he was told by Redmond that no such meeting had been scheduled. Redmond then put the phone down. When Gilmartin phoned Redmond's office back, the secretary who answered said that a number of road engineers had been waiting for Gilmartin but had left when he and his team failed to turn up. An incensed Gilmartin, with his architect, went across to the council offices and confronted Redmond, who told them to leave his office.

Gilmartin then contacted Seán Haughey, the other assistant city and county manager, who was of equal rank to Redmond within the council hierarchy as well as the Taoiseach's brother and a man Gilmartin regarded as 'very straightforward and honest'.

Following an intervention by Seán Haughey, another meeting was arranged in Redmond's office for the same afternoon. As he arrived for the meeting, Gilmartin met an agitated Haughey, who said to him: 'There are so many games going on here, somebody has to do something.' He then witnessed a confrontation between Haughey and Redmond in the latter's office.

'Mr Haughey went in and he asked Mr Redmond, "What's your game?" (in stronger language) and Redmond's answer was, "Ask your brother," and Mr Seán Haughey's response was "I'm not my so-and-so brother's keeper, and George, your game is going to stop, I can assure you."' Again the reference to Charles Haughey might have rung some alarms with Gilmartin, but he did not associate the comment with the Lislary land row involving his sister Chris or indeed the bizarre encounter in Leinster House earlier that month.

At the rescheduled meeting Redmond gave no sign of heeding his colleague's warnings and, according to Gilmartin, was 'acting the clown' and 'making wisecracks.' Redmond was well placed to block Gilmartin from proceeding with his development and thus to deliver on the threat made by Lawlor a year earlier. He could also help his prospective new employer, John Corcoran of Green Property, if he frustrated Gilmartin's plans. (See appendix 1, paragraph 6.)

Arising from the latest shenanigans in relation to the land deals and the aborted meeting with the road engineers, Gilmartin, within days, met Seán Haughey and then the city and county manager, Frank Feely, to describe during a three-hour meeting the problems he was having with Redmond, Lawlor, Hanrahan and others. They agreed that the complaints should be brought immediately to the attention of the responsible minister, Pádraig Flynn, which was done at a meeting on 28 February.

Following a consultation between Flynn and the Taoiseach, and discussions involving the Minister for Justice, Gerry Collins, and the Attorney-General, John Murray, the Gardaí were asked to investigate Gilmartin's complaints as part of an inquiry already in progress into separate allegations of planning irregularities in Dublin.

The Garda investigation into Gilmartin's complaints began on 3 March 1989 on foot of a briefing provided by the then secretary of the Department of Justice, Des Matthews, to the investigating officers, led by Chief Supt Hugh Sreenan and Supt Thomas Burns. Their investigation was based on the allegation that Tom Gilmartin was asked for cash payments of up to £100,000 each by George Redmond, Liam Lawlor and Finbarr Hanrahan, among others, and on the demand for £5 million made outside the meeting with ministers in Leinster House.

Chief Supt Sreenan interviewed Gilmartin by telephone at his Luton home on three occasions during March, on the 4th, 9th and 25th of the month. Accompanied by Supt Burns, he spoke to Frank Feely and Seán Haughey during the same month, while Burns and another investigating garda interviewed Owen O'Callaghan in Cork in early April. Later in the year Sreenan and Burns interviewed two Arlington executives, Ted Dadley and Raymond Mould, before the final report was submitted to the Department of Justice and the minister, Ray Burke, in May 1990.

In the three contemporaneous records of Sreenan's telephone interviews with Gilmartin, only that of 9 March refers to the demand for £5 million made of Gilmartin after his meeting in Leinster House with the Taoiseach and his ministers. There is no reference to the £5 million in the final report. The Garda investigation was marked by a high degree of confusion and extremely inadequate note-taking of evidence. At one point Sreenan attributes the demand for £5 million to Lawlor, even though Gilmartin did not mention any names over the phone and at any rate had always insisted that the approach came from a man he could not identify. Sreenan accepted later that his notes of this conversation were 'bitty' and 'disjointed.'

It was not, however, because of the lack of thoroughness of the investigation that Gilmartin lost complete faith in the Garda inquiry. A day or two after his first chat with Sreenan on 4 March he received a phone call at home. A man who introduced himself as 'Garda Burns' told Gilmartin that the complaints he was making were not welcome and that he should go back to where he came from. The words, as recalled by Gilmartin, were that he should 'fuck off back to England.' He was told that similar investigations into allegations had resulted in those wrongly accused emerging with their reputations unscathed.

From the brief conversation, Gilmartin surmised that the caller had knowledge of the confidential matters he had discussed with Chief Supt Sreenan a few days earlier. Despite the coincidence of surname, there was no suggestion that the caller was Supt Burns, who did not speak to or have contact with Gilmartin during the investigation.

Soon afterwards Gilmartin told the gardaí involved that he did not wish to co-operate any further with their inquiry. (See appendix 1, paragraph 7.)

The investigating gardaí did not interview Liam Lawlor during the inquiry, and also failed to question Redmond or Hanrahan in relation to Gilmartin's claims, despite the serious allegations made against them. Conflicting claims were made about the interview undertaken by Supt Burns with Owen O'Callaghan, during which, the garda claimed, O'Callaghan said that he would ask Gilmartin to co-operate with the inquiry. Burns recorded a telephone call from O'Callaghan on 18 April to inform him that Gilmartin was not prepared to discuss the matter further. Gilmartin insisted that O'Callaghan had never asked him to co-operate but on the contrary had told him that he was 'shooting himself in the foot' by going to the Gardaí. 'This is not the way business is done in Ireland,' Gilmartin said he was told by O'Callaghan.

During their interviews with the Garda investigators in November 1989 in London neither Dadley nor Mould admitted to making a series of payments to Liam Lawlor, even though (unknown to Gilmartin) they had paid £33,000 seven months previously to an account used by Lawlor in the name of Economic Reports Ltd. This final consultancy payment to Lawlor was made after the Arlington directors had decided to terminate their business in Ireland. It brought the total given to Lawlor by Arlington to £75,000, including the monthly amounts paid to him by Gilmartin and then reimbursed by the company. Gilmartin had stopped making the payments after Lawlor walked into the Bank of Ireland in Blanchardstown in March 1989 and instructed the manager, Paul Sheeran, to pay him £10,000 from Gilmartin's account. When contacted, Gilmartin told Sheeran not to make any such payment to Lawlor and refused to give him any more hand-outs.

In refusing to confirm to the Garda investigation that they had paid anything to Lawlor, Mould and Dadley clearly felt it preferable to withhold any information that might implicate them in a controversy and a possible criminal investigation in Ireland. (See appendix 1, paragraph 8.)

Despite the failure to question Redmond in respect of the Gilmartin allegations, the final Garda report concluded that there was no evidence to suggest that the now retired assistant city and county manager 'has committed any crime.' It also said that 'no evidence of criminal conduct by Mr Liam Lawlor TD had emerged in the investigation. Where verbal allegations have been made, they have been found wanting . . . Gossip and rumour abound in Ireland and many an innocent, defenceless person has had his good name tarnished as a result. Therefore, it was an important part of this enquiry to delve fully into the allegations made by Thomas Gilmartin and others concerning Mr Liam Lawlor TD . . . [who] emerges from this enquiry with his good reputation unscathed.'

There is no mention in the final report of the demand for £5 million made of Gilmartin in Leinster House or of several other complaints made by him. (See appendix 1, paragraph 9.)

The reference to Lawlor and Redmond and their apparent high standing in the community was particularly ironic, as both would later be exposed as central to corrupt rezoning activities around Dublin. Clearly the Garda inquiry left a lot to be desired. Its failure also ensured that the corrupt practices it was set up to examine could continue unabated for years to come. Lawlor's status as an elected and influential politician most probably influenced the decision not to subject him to Garda interview and allowed him to continue his self-serving interference in the planning process and other illicit activities for years to come.

Chapter 5 ～

'THEY'LL TAKE YOUR MONEY AND THEY'LL STILL DO NOTHING FOR YOU'

Among the national politicians with whom Gilmartin had most contact was the Minister for the Environment, Pádraig Flynn, with whom he and his professional adviser, Richard Forman, had discussed as far back as November 1987 the issue of tax designation for the part of the ill-fated Bachelor's Walk site not already covered by the urban renewal scheme.

During 1988 Flynn maintained regular contact with Gilmartin. He was familiar with Gilmartin's plans for Quarryvale, while he was also receiving information from Liam Lawlor and others about the potential developments in west county Dublin. By early 1989 Gilmartin was pursuing the possibility of obtaining urban renewal designation or enterprise zoning for the Quarryvale site; and while he did not believe he required either for commercial success, he was discussing this with various people, including his political contacts. Their relationship was such that Gilmartin was comfortable enough to tell Flynn at a meeting on 22 February 1989 of the outrageous demands for money made of him, including those by George Redmond and Liam Lawlor, which led to the Garda inquiry.

When Flynn met Gilmartin and Ted Dadley in April the obstacles to progress and the 'games' Redmond was playing were raised again, and the minister confirmed that the complaints were now 'a Garda matter.' Gilmartin complained that while the Gardaí were now involved, no-one in Leinster House appeared to be doing anything about what was going on. In response, and without any apparent sense of irony, Flynn then suggested that a 'substantial donation' to Fianna Fáil 'could help to curb these activities.' Flynn was at the time one of the two national treasurers of the party (the other being Bertie Ahern).

Gilmartin recalled: 'Well, he said . . . the party was—it was in deep problems financially. A figure of £3 million or something in debt was mentioned.' (See appendix 1, paragraph 10.)

As they left the meeting Dadley commented: 'Everybody's looking for money. Déjà vu.'

Although at first reluctant to consider any such donation, Gilmartin had a change of mind as he learnt of Redmond's continued interference in his purchase of the Irishtown lands. Speaking to the chief city valuer, Michael McLoone, in early June, he told him of the various demands made on him for money, including Flynn's request some weeks earlier, and of how the minister had said that giving a donation to the party might help 'smooth out' the problems he was encountering. McLoone's immediate response, he said, was to exclaim, 'They'll take your fucking money and they'll still do nothing for you,' and he warned Gilmartin against making any such donation.

Gilmartin, however, was desperate to remove the obstacles that were threatening to ruin him financially, and despite McLoone's warning he resolved to make a donation. He phoned the minister's private secretary, Gerry Rice, to arrange an appointment, which was duly set for Flynn's office in the Custom House. When Gilmartin arrived for the early evening meeting Flynn appeared to be rushing off. Gilmartin told him he wished to make a donation to Fianna Fáil. He had first considered a donation of £20,000 but thought it was too small and then decided that £50,000 would be appropriate in the circumstances. 'So I actually left McLoone's office and I went in and I told Mr Flynn I'd decided to give the party a donation. So he was in a hurry. He was packing his briefcase. He said there was "a car waiting for me." He was in a great hurry, and he was standing behind the desk. So I wrote out the cheque and I asked to whom did I make it payable . . . and he said, "Oh, leave it, leave it on the desk." So I left it on the desk.' The payee section on the cheque was left blank.

As Gilmartin had not brought his chequebook with him, he had stopped in the Bank of Ireland branch in College Green and arranged through a phone call to Paul Sheeran in Blanchardstown to obtain a blank cheque, which he then signed in Flynn's office. The cheque for £50,000—the approximate equivalent of the annual salary of a Government minister—was debited to Gilmartin's personal account.

'All I wanted was to give some chance to the scheme getting off the ground,' Gilmartin said of the reason for the donation. 'After all, it was creating twenty thousand jobs. I risked everything to put it there, including my name. And it had been suggested to me by a Government official that I had to pay to get justice, so I felt I had no option but to do that.' (See appendix 1, paragraph 11.)

The £50,000 was lodged to the personal account of Pádraig Flynn and his wife, Dorothy, in Allied Irish Bank, Castlebar, on 7 June 1989. The address for this account was stated to be 3 Northumberland Road, Chiswick, London, which indicated that it was a bogus non-resident account set up in 1986 to avoid deposit interest retention tax—a common practice by thousands of bank depositors in Ireland at the time. Between 1987 and 1993 the Flynns had opened three non-resident accounts, into which they lodged more than £155,000, using addresses in London and, after Flynn became a member of the EU Commission, at Avenue Jules César, Brussels. (See appendix 1, paragraph 12.)

Later in 1989 the Flynns gave two sums of £25,000 in cash to their daughter, Beverly Cooper Flynn, an employee of National Irish Bank, which she used to purchase offshore unit-trust investments for her parents. With the proceeds of these investments Dorothy Flynn was in a position to spend £45,000 on 100 acres of forestry land at Cloonanass, county Mayo. She benefited from an annual premium of slightly over £7,000, equal to £140,000 over twenty years, given to farmers who grew trees on their land, provided they derived at least a quarter of their income from farming. Dorothy Flynn, by her own admission, never farmed the lands 'in any meaningful way.' (See appendix 1, paragraph 13.)

When Flynn accepted the cheque a general election campaign was coming to a climax, and for this reason he made his excuses before terminating his brief meeting with Gilmartin. He must have been fully aware of the consequences of his action and of the context of Gilmartin's decision to make the donation, given that he had passed on details of the developer's complaints three months earlier to his Government colleagues, the Taoiseach and the Minister for Justice, who in turn had instigated a Garda inquiry into them. Flynn issued no receipt and apparently did not inform the Taoiseach, his fellow-treasurer or other party officials about the huge payment he had solicited from the developer.

For Gilmartin, it appeared that his large donation to Fianna Fáil was not having the desired effect, and he was becoming increasingly concerned at the delay in closing the purchase of the local authority lands at Quarryvale. Because of Redmond's intervention with Green Property and his and Lawlor's vocal objections to what they described as the 'cosy deal' by Dublin City Council with Gilmartin, the sale of the Irishtown lands had been put out to tender again. On 19 May 1989 Gilmartin had put in a bid of £5.1 million (just over £70,000 an acre, compared with the previously agreed £40,000 per acre), along with a deposit of £255,000. A bid by a subsidiary of Green Property was significantly lower, and a week later Gilmartin's tender was approved by a senior official of the city council, subject to agreement by the city council itself. Although the deal appeared to be progressing satisfactorily on this occasion, despite having cost a substantial amount more than earlier agreed (and more than other parcels of land in the area), McLoone continued to warn Gilmartin that Redmond and Lawlor were still interfering with the purchase and attempting to 'shaft' him.

Asked by McLoone whether there was anyone with political influence whom he could trust, Gilmartin thought of Bertie Ahern, the Minister for Labour, whom he had met previously. The Bachelor's Walk development backed by Arlington was in Ahern's Dublin Central constituency, where he had already constructed one of the most powerful political organisations in the country, humorously dubbed the 'Drumcondra Mafia', and not much of consequence happened there without his knowledge.

'It was suggested that if I knew someone in government I could trust I should contact them. I subsequently decided to contact Bertie Ahern . . . as I had previously spoken with him on a number of occasions and found him approachable and very supportive of the development plans for Bachelor's Walk. I had met Mr Ahern on two prior occasions. To the best of my recollection, the first meeting took place in the autumn of 1987 in Mr Ahern's office in the Department of Labour building in Mespil Road. At this meeting we discussed the plans for the Bachelor's Walk development. Mr Ahern was affable and approachable and he was very supportive of my plans. The next meeting I had with Mr Ahern was in October 1988 . . . in Mr Ahern's constituency office located above Fagan's public house in Drumcondra.'

Now he was about to find out whether Ahern could deliver on his expressions of support for his plans.

Although it was the middle of a general election campaign, Gilmartin made contact by phone with the busy politician and outlined his complaints in relation to the purchase of the Irishtown lands and the behaviour of Redmond and Lawlor. Ahern listened and said he would see what he could do. A few days later Councillor Joe Burke, a friend and political associate of Ahern, arrived in Gilmartin's office in St Stephen's Green, where he heard of his concerns and promised to assist. Burke was a member of the Planning and Development Committee of the city council, which at its meeting of 26 May had recommended the approval of Gilmartin's tender for the lands before it went on to the full city council for a final decision.

A few days after their meeting Burke phoned Gilmartin to inform him that the council meeting had approved his tender at its meeting the previous day, 12 June, and said he should have no further problems. On 19 June the city's law agent told Gilmartin that his tender had been accepted, and he requested the deposit of £255,000 pending the completion of the conveyance and other legal details of the sale.

A day later Gilmartin phoned Ahern to thank him for the assistance he had received from Joe Burke in relation to his successful bid for the Irishtown lands. He recalled that during the conversation Ahern mentioned a fund-raising event that Fianna Fáil was organising in the Reform Club in London the following November. He said the party's finances were 'in a bit of a state' and asked Gilmartin whether he would consider making a donation to it. Gilmartin told Ahern that he had already given £50,000 to Pádraig Flynn for Fianna Fáil. (See appendix 1, paragraph 14.)

Following the election Fianna Fáil was in a position to form a Government with the help of the Progressive Democrats, the party led by Des O'Malley, a former Government colleague turned arch-enemy of Charles Haughey. Haughey resumed his role as Taoiseach, and Flynn (Environment), Reynolds (Finance), Burke (Communications and Justice) and Ahern (Labour) were among those he reappointed as ministers. Ray MacSharry had resigned from the Government late the previous year to take up the position of Ireland's EU commissioner.

Among the disastrous results for Fianna Fáil in the election was the loss of the Sligo seat held by MacSharry. The election had been hastily called by Haughey after the Government lost crucial votes in the Dáil, including one critical of Liam Lawlor. A reluctant Lawlor had been forced by Haughey to resign from the Dáil committee on state-sponsored bodies because of a conflict of interest arising from his commercial relationship with the 'beef baron' Larry Goodman. Lawlor was involved in a Goodman company that wanted to purchase the state-owned Irish Sugar Company, for which the committee had supervisory responsibility. The Government subsequently lost a Dáil vote on the controversy.

––––

Some months later Arlington executives attended the November fund-raiser in London to which Gilmartin had been invited by Ahern. The room in the Reform Club was busy, with London-Irish businessmen taking up the opportunity to meet Government ministers from Dublin, including Ahern and Flynn. After speeches about the healthy prospects for the economy under the direction of the new Government, Flynn approached Ted Dadley of Arlington Securities and asked for a donation 'for the boys,' which Dadley took to be a reference to Fianna Fáil. After he had discussed it with his colleague Raymond Mould, the request was rejected. Dadley later described relations with the Irish ministers at the event as being effectually 'terminated' after this refusal.

For unexplained reasons, Gilmartin was asked by Flynn not to attend the function and instead to meet him in a nearby restaurant. After waiting a considerable time Gilmartin met Flynn when the somewhat flustered politician arrived, only to spend the time evading any questions he was asked about the fund-raising event. It was only later that Gilmartin realised that the reason he was not invited to the Reform Club when the Arlington executives were asked to contribute to 'the boys' was that he might have informed them about his substantial donation to Fianna Fáil earlier in the year. 'They were probably worried that I would advise Mould and Dadley that I had already made a donation to the party,' Gilmartin said, 'which would have made them less likely to contribute. I did not particularly want to be there, but later I realised that is probably the reason Flynn asked me not to go.' The minister, of course, would also have been conscious of the fact that the donation to the party from Gilmartin had ended up in his wife's bank account and not where it was intended to go.

Relations between Gilmartin and the various politicians and officials he encountered were not going particularly well either as the autumn of 1989 approached and his efforts to complete the assembly of lands at Quarryvale continued. His progress was made easier with the retirement of George Redmond in June, although Liam Lawlor, re-elected to the Dáil the same month, continued to shadow him, with a tendency to surface at unexpected moments during Gilmartin's visits to Dublin.

However, his most immediate challenge was to raise the finance to allow him to complete the various land purchases remaining, having already spent £4.4 million of his own funds, which were now rapidly being depleted. He was also approaching the deadline for payment of the second tranche to Owen O'Callaghan for the Neilstown lands, which had been agreed in early 1989.

After Bank of Ireland declined to lend him the money he needed, in December 1989 Gilmartin contacted Eddie Kay, senior manager of Property and Construction in AIB's Corporate Commercial Division, with a view to negotiating emergency funds to complete the land purchases. Kay had a long association with Owen O'Callaghan and had been arranging loans to him since 1983. He was also acquainted with Lawlor, for whom he organised a loan to buy land adjacent to Lawlor's home, Somerton House, outside Lucan, in the 1970s. These relationships were unknown to Gilmartin. He told Eddie Kay that his company, Barkhill, required a short-term loan facility of £9 million to complete the land purchases while he was seeking other equity partners or investors to help finance the Quarryvale project. Arlington Securities was prepared to invest up to £10 million, and he had, with Richard Forman, extensive contact with other prospective investors, including the British financial giants Norwich Union and the London and Edinburgh Trust.

While the guarantee of financial backing was there from the investors, Gilmartin could gain access to it only after rezoning was secured. He also said that he was confident the site would be granted tax designation and that he had contact with the Minister for the Environment and other ministers in that regard. A loan facility of £8½ million was agreed, subject to strict conditions, including that the payment of £1.35 million to O'Callaghan would be deferred until the tax designation was confirmed. The AIB loan was due for repayment by August 1990, six months after it was granted, adding considerably to the pressure on Gilmartin. Crucially, the lands already acquired by Gilmartin and other assets he controlled were put up by him as collateral for the loan.

After these early dealings with AIB, Gilmartin claims to have been told by senior bank executives, including Eddie Kay's assistant manager, Jim Donagh, that he should take O'Callaghan on as a partner, as he had better 'political clout'. Gilmartin had noticed that on occasions when he visited the AIB Bankcentre in Ballsbridge, O'Callaghan and his architect, John Deane, were also present, and as 1990 went on he became convinced that there was more to the relationship between his bankers and the Cork developer than met the eye.

Richard Forman, who accompanied Gilmartin to meetings in Dublin, including those with the bankers, identified from an early stage an 'aggressive attitude' on the part of its officials towards their new client. Some of the bank's officers, he said, 'appeared to take an aggressive attitude and started to dictate how matters should proceed, as though they, not Tom, were the shareholders in Barkhill. I was aware also of Tom's getting demands to attend meetings at the bank at short notice, the sole purpose of which appeared to be to abuse him. The whole thrust of the bank's attitude appeared to be designed to force Mr Gilmartin to pass over equity and control to Mr Owen O'Callaghan. It appeared that the bank [was] discussing Barkhill's business with Mr O'Callaghan, even though he had no involvement with the company. I recall as an example of this attending the bank with Tom to find Mr O'Callaghan was also present, although neither Tom nor I had invited him.'

Gilmartin shared this view, though he always insisted that only some AIB officials acted as described by Forman while others with whom he dealt acted with integrity and in a totally professional manner.

At a public presentation in early July 1990 to potential investors, Government and local authority officials and the media, an elaborate model of the Westpark scheme (as it was then called) was unveiled in the Berkeley Court Hotel, Dublin. Accompanied by a thirty-page brochure, it described Gilmartin's plans for a 'high-quality regional shopping centre' and 'new leisure, sport and entertainment facilities for use by local people and those who travel longer distances to visit the centre,' as well as 'a major Business Park' on the 820-acre site. It promised €750 million of investment capital and up to twenty thousand jobs when fully operational.

Despite the scale and ambition of the project, Gilmartin detected a barely disguised hostility to his proposal among some of the audience, while the atmosphere with some of his bankers continued to sour. He also suspected a degree of orchestration in what he considered the negative media coverage of the event, which was intended to generate enthusiasm and essential public and financial support. He also discovered that his purchase of local authority lands at Fonthill Road, across the road from the Quarryvale site, which he had earmarked for a potential hotel development, had been frustrated by the intervention of the Industrial Development Authority. The IDA, already carrying a surplus of commercial properties on its books, had suddenly declared an interest in some of the available sites around Quarryvale. In fact Liam Lawlor, without Gilmartin's knowledge, was in correspondence with senior IDA officials at the time concerning its possible purchase of lands in the area after contacts between O'Callaghan and the Minister for Finance, Albert Reynolds, on the issue. It did not subsequently purchase the lands.

Following the less than successful launch, a somewhat disillusioned Gilmartin prepared to close down his Dublin office, following Arlington's decision to abandon the Bachelor's Walk scheme and to withdraw from its Irish investments because of the seemingly intractable delays it encountered. From then on Gilmartin commuted from England to carry on his business in Dublin.

As he packed up his belongings one evening to prepare to return to Luton he had an unexpected visitor in the person of Ahern's friend Councillor Joe Burke. Burke had maintained an infrequent contact with Gilmartin since he was involved in assisting with the acquisition of the Irishtown lands a year previously. Following a litany of complaints about the obstacles he had faced trying to get Quarryvale off the ground, a frustrated Gilmartin said he would 'pay a fucking half million to get out of here' if he got back his total investment, which was more than £5 million at that point. Burke asked, 'Would you?' Gilmartin said that Burke then asked whether he would pay half a million pounds, as 'Bertie Ahern was looking after' him. 'It wasn't a demand, it was talking about £500,000. Whether I would pay it. It wasn't a question like Lawlor [would ask], 'Hand me, you know, £100,000.' This wasn't a demand like that. It was what I call typical Donegal fashion, talking in circles. Talking around the half a million.' During the conversation with Burke the phone rang and

Barry Boland, who worked for Arlington in Dublin, asked Gilmartin to turn off the lights in the office before he left for England.

It was then, according to Gilmartin, that Burke asked him if he would meet Bertie Ahern and offered to take him to the airport. On the way, Burke said, they could call in to meet Ahern. Gilmartin described how Burke brought him in a pick-up truck to two pubs in north Dublin, close to the airport road. 'We then made arrangements to leave the office, and Mr Burke gave me assistance to take the Quarryvale model, which I was putting into storage. Burke then drove to Fagan's pub [in Drumcondra]. I recall that Mr Burke was in the pub for about twenty minutes. When he came out he told me that Mr Ahern was not inside but he thought he might be in another pub. I recall Mr Burke then driving to another pub located in the vicinity of Beaumont Hospital. Again I remember Mr Burke going inside and being in the pub for about ten minutes, while I waited outside in his pick-up truck. When Mr Burke came out he told me Mr Ahern would be there very shortly. However, I was very anxious at that stage that I could miss my flight back to Luton. I told Mr Burke I had a commitment to attend a meeting the following morning which I could not miss, and I had to insist that he drive me immediately to the airport. Mr Burke tried to persuade me to wait for Mr Ahern's arrival, but when I refused to do so Mr Burke got very upset.'

However comical the image of Gilmartin being trailed around to two of Ahern's known haunts—Fagan's, above which he had his constituency office, and Beaumont House, owned by his friend Dermot Carew—the notion, however misplaced, that he was facing yet another apparent request for a huge sum of money on behalf of yet another politician, and one whom he believed he could trust, shattered what little faith Gilmartin had left in the Irish political system. (See appendix 1, paragraph 15.)

————

Soon after this latest demand Liam Lawlor made an unexpected entry at a lunch meeting hosted by Gilmartin for some prominent potential investors from Britain in Finnstown Country House Hotel, Lucan, where Lawlor proceeded to scare off the business people by referring to the area surrounding Quarryvale as 'bandit country'. The only way in which Lawlor could have discovered where and at what time Gilmartin was lunching with the visiting investors was from a bank executive whom Gilmartin told of his whereabouts less than an hour earlier. Richard Forman, who was at the lunch, recalled how Lawlor suddenly arrived and introduced himself to the visitors, including Ian McGregor of the Herron Group and his agent, Harvey Conning, as they sat in the hotel having completed a site inspection of the Quarryvale lands. Forman said that attracting investment to Ireland from leading British finance houses such as Herron was difficult enough, as there was a 'prejudice in England' because of the conflict in the North, but Lawlor's unexpected intervention frightened off whatever prospects there were of a successful outcome of the visit. He said Lawlor's description of the west Dublin area as 'mad-dog and bandit country' played a major part in the decision of the investors concerned to withdraw from negotiations to become involved in the Quarryvale scheme. 'Liam Lawlor sowed the seeds of doubt in terms of the market-place generally and the locality specifically,' said Forman.

Gilmartin claimed that he was told by O'Callaghan on a number of occasions that Lawlor was 'on his payroll,' and the politician's constant disruption and use of dirty tricks to discredit him in front of potential investors was a source of irritation and frustration to Gilmartin.

Following meetings with AIB officials and with O'Callaghan and Deane in London in early September 1990, Gilmartin informed the bank that O'Callaghan had expressed a keen interest in discussing a joint venture or other type of involvement in Quarryvale, though he first wanted payment of the £1.35 million he was owed for the Neilstown site. Meanwhile, in what Gilmartin believed was a tactic to apply further pressure, O'Callaghan obtained planning permission during the same month to develop a town centre on the Neilstown land. Gilmartin was resisting O'Callaghan's efforts to take a stake in Quarryvale unless he was prepared to make a significant investment of his own funds.

White knights, in the form of the English businessman Derek Saunders and the Cork businessman Peter Kearns, a friend of Gilmartin's, who were partners in SK Computers, emerged with an offer to AIB to put £20 million on the table, which could be used to complete the assembly of the Quarryvale lands, pay O'Callaghan his money and clear the debt to the bank. In the event, Saunders was forced to withdraw his offer, as he had run into difficulty in raising the finance.

When Gilmartin once again raised his complaints in the course of his discussions with the Dublin property consultant Colm Scallon he was brought to the head office of Fianna Fáil in Lower Mount Street to meet the party's national organiser, Seán Sherwin. Scallon was appalled by what he thought were horrendous and disgraceful demands made to Gilmartin for money by Lawlor and others, while Sherwin said he was astounded and shocked when informed of the demand by Councillor Finbarr Hanrahan for £100,000. He also heard Gilmartin describe how he had given a donation for the party of £50,000 to Pádraig Flynn the previous year. Sherwin subsequently enquired from the party fund-raiser, Paul Kavanagh, whether the payment to Flynn had been received by the party and was informed that there was no evidence in the accounts of any such donation. Remarkably, and despite the scale of the donation that was hidden from party officers, neither Sherwin nor Kavanagh approached Flynn about the reported donation or raised it with the party leader, Charles Haughey. (See appendix 1, paragraph 16.)

Gilmartin also repeated his complaints about the low standards in business and political life in Dublin during his discussions with O'Callaghan, only to be met with an attitude of cynicism or disbelief. On one occasion he told O'Callaghan that the only politician who had delivered anything positive for him was Bertie Ahern when he intervened, at Gilmartin's request, with Dublin City Council during his purchase of the Irishtown lands in 1989. According to Gilmartin, he was flummoxed when O'Callaghan laughed and told him that the intervention had cost O'Callaghan £50,000, which he paid Ahern to ensure that Green Property would not get its hands on the land. Gilmartin claimed he was told by O'Callaghan that he paid Ahern at a football match, which he assumed, wrongly, was the Cork v. Mayo GAA final in September 1989. (This story was later the subject of some debate at the planning tribunal.) He later learnt that O'Callaghan and Ahern may have attended an international soccer match at Lansdowne Road on 11 October 1989. Either way, he was told that Ahern was 'in the pay' of O'Callaghan and that Ahern's assistance with the acquisition of the Quarryvale lands was a favour for which he was richly rewarded.[a]

By late November 1990 the noose was tightening around Gilmartin's neck as AIB threatened to call in its loan of more than £9 million, while O'Callaghan was pressing for his £1.35 million, and significant lands at Quarryvale had yet to be purchased. His attempt to secure outside investors had run into the ground, and AIB had made it clear that it 'considered it important that O'Callaghan is now brought in on the overall Barkhill project.'[b]

While O'Callaghan conceded that the Quarryvale site was superior to the one he still controlled at Neilstown, he was in the driving seat, as AIB was informing him that it had lost confidence in Gilmartin's ability to bring the project to fruition. The bank's strategy, now explicit, was to sideline Gilmartin and arrange for O'Callaghan to take a significant stake in Barkhill. O'Callaghan was seeking an equity stake of 25 per cent and control of the daily decisions in relation to the project, for which he said he could 'deliver on site rezoning/planning and designation.'[c]

The potential ability of O'Callaghan and his business partner John Deane to deliver what were essentially political decisions was underlined by a reference they made in another phone call on the same day to Eddie Kay to a function due to take place later that week. This was the Fianna Fáil president's dinner, a highlight of the party's annual calendar, where O'Callaghan said he expected to be asked about progress at Quarryvale by, among others, Pádraig Flynn, Albert Reynolds, Brian Lenihan (senior) and Liam Lawlor. It was another example of O'Callaghan letting people know of his extensive political contacts and influence.

Under the increasing financial stress Gilmartin reluctantly engaged in discussions on the 'heads of agreement' to allow for O'Callaghan's participation in Barkhill—Gilmartin's Quarryvale company—and signed a proposal to give him a 25 per cent stake in the company in return for an additional loan facility from AIB. The deal, agreed on 14 December, allowed for the participation of his new partner and two or three AIB personnel on the board of the company, as nominees of the bank, as well as an option whereby Gilmartin could terminate the deal if he paid his outstanding debts to O'Callaghan and the bank by 10 January 1991.

Gilmartin signed a faxed copy of the deal at his home in Luton without taking any legal advice, a factor that made its status somewhat dubious. The deadline for accepting the terms or paying his debts was subsequently extended to 31 January.

Chapter 6 ∿

'THE NIGHT OF THE LONG KNIVES'

The bank agreement was soon overtaken by events. Gilmartin was informed by Councillor Colm McGrath, with whom he had occasional contact, that he was about to table a motion in Dublin County Council that the lands at Quarryvale be rezoned, and that he was confident it would enjoy cross-party support at the meeting to review the Dublin Development Plan in February 1991. From his own contacts with other councillors, including Seán Gilbride, Tommy Boland (chairperson of the council) and Liam Lawlor, Gilmartin was aware that there was strong support for the rezoning of Quarryvale.

Meanwhile AIB was piling pressure on Gilmartin to discharge his obligations to it and O'Callaghan or reach an acceptable arrangement with them that would 'facilitate this rezoning process,' which, it said, was critical for the development of the plan for a shopping centre at Quarryvale. Three days before the deadline for submitting the motion, on 15 February, AIB called in its £9.35 million loan to Barkhill, further coercing Gilmartin into signing re-drafted 'heads of agreement'.

The draft agreement was faxed to Gilmartin at his home in Luton on the evening of 15 February, with instructions that if he did not sign it the rezoning motion would not be lodged. Councillor McGrath phoned him to say he was being advised not to submit the motion until Gilmartin signed the agreement, while Councillor Gilbride also phoned to give him the same message. Jim Donagh of AIB and Owen O'Callaghan also told him to sign or lose the opportunity to have the lands he had so painstakingly and expensively acquired, rezoned.

Describing the experience as the 'Night of the Long Knives', Gilmartin complained that he had been threatened 'with everything bar execution.' Eventually, after a consultation with his solicitor, Seamus Maguire, he signed the agreement and faxed it to AIB shortly after 9 p.m.

The manner in which Gilmartin was forced to sign an agreement that effectually ceded control of his company in order to advance the rezoning of the Quarryvale lands was unprecedented, involving as it did the bank, several councillors, and O'Callaghan and Deane. Under its terms O'Callaghan was to receive 33 per cent of the equity in Barkhill, while he and Gilmartin were to find an outside investor to buy a further 33 per cent for £4 million by the end of March 1991. (See appendix 1, paragraph 17.)

Central to devising the political and zoning strategy for O'Callaghan was Liam Lawlor. With his and McGrath's assistance, a motion was submitted to the county council that the town-centre zoning on the Neilstown site be removed and replaced with industrial zoning, thus facilitating the retail development at Quarryvale. The rezoning vote was expected in May, and the stakes were now considerably higher: professional advisers estimated that the site would have a value of £20 million if rezoned. O'Callaghan was aware that this value would make it possible for Gilmartin to cover his debts, buy out his partners, and proceed with his plans unencumbered by what Gilmartin considered were his hostile bankers and his developer rival. It was not in O'Callaghan's interests to allow the rezoning to proceed without ensuring that he was going to succeed in ultimately gaining control of Barkhill. At the same time he did not wish to damage the good relations he had established with councillors to ensure their continuing support. With Lawlor already on side, he decided to avail of the services of another astute political dealer and public relations expert: Frank Dunlop.

A former Fianna Fáil and Government press secretary in the 1970s and early 80s, Dunlop had moved into the world of public relations with the influential Murray Consultants in 1986 before forming his own company in 1989. He had extensive contacts in the party, having worked closely with the former Taoiseach Jack Lynch and his successor, Charles Haughey. Indeed with Haughey, Lawlor and the party adviser P. J. Mara he had travelled the length and breadth of the country as Haughey sought to rehabilitate himself following the Arms Trial controversy of 1970–71 and his years of political exile during the 1970s.

Dunlop (known as Pirelli to associates and some media contacts) specialised in lobbying politicians and used his extensive contacts within the political world to benefit his mainly corporate clients. (Both Dunlop and Pirelli are well-known tyre manufacturers.) When he first heard of Tom Gilmartin and his plans for Dublin, Dunlop wrote to him to offer his services. His reputation as a 'political bagman' for Fianna Fáil preceded him, however, and Gilmartin spurned the offer, instead employing a recent entrant into the public relations business, Eileen Gleeson, to promote his schemes. Gilmartin had heard of Dunlop from others in the property business in Dublin, who warned him to stay clear of him because of his association with questionable political and financial deals. Dunlop did send Gilmartin newspaper extracts relating to the Garda investigation into planning matters in 1989, presumably to prove his *bona fides*. But Gilmartin did not respond or engage with him.

Shortly after establishing his own public relations firm, Dunlop and Associates (later Frank Dunlop and Associates), Dunlop set up a Channel Islands company, Sheafran Ltd, in late 1989, later renamed Shefran (a blending of Dunlop's first name and that of his wife, Sheila). He formed another offshore company, Xerxes Consult (Jersey) Ltd, in early 1990. Gilmartin recalled observing Dunlop (recognising him from television images broadcast during his time as Government press secretary) with Owen O'Callaghan and Bertie Ahern during a visit to Leinster House in 1989 but did not meet him in connection with the Quarryvale project until April 1991, less than a month before the rezoning vote. The circumstances of this meeting did nothing to convince him that the advice he received to stay well clear of Dunlop was incorrect.

The encounter took place on 25 April 1991 after Gilmartin was called to the AIB Bankcentre for a meeting. There he met O'Callaghan and banker Eddie Kay, who suggested that Gilmartin go to the Dáil for a meeting with some politicians. O'Callaghan then brought Gilmartin to Buswells Hotel, where they met Liam Lawlor. Instead of bringing them to meet senior politicians, however, as Gilmartin had expected, Lawlor brought the two men through Leinster House to the exit at Merrion Square on the other side of the complex and from there to nearby Upper Mount Street and the offices of Frank Dunlop and Associates.

Gilmartin recognised Dunlop, who was sitting at a desk in an office at the front of the building, but they were not introduced. Lawlor and O'Callaghan walked to a back office, followed by Dunlop, while Gilmartin was left sitting in the outer office, where he heard what he thought were angry exchanges from the other room. After a prolonged wait the increasingly impatient Gilmartin left the building in disgust, only to be followed down the street by an irate O'Callaghan, who wanted to know where he was going. Gilmartin told O'Callaghan he was being 'set up' and that he had had enough of the 'games' that were going on, to which Gilmartin says O'Callaghan replied: 'No unionist is going to build on that site'—an apparent reference to Taggarts, the Belfast architects employed by Gilmartin for the Quarryvale development. (Taggart was from a Protestant background but was not aligned with the unionist or any other political culture.) As they argued, Dunlop arrived in a car and, with O'Callaghan, convinced Gilmartin to accept a lift back to Ballsbridge, where he was staying at the Merrion Road guesthouse of his friend and former bank manager Paul Sheeran.

During the short car trip Dunlop berated O'Callaghan for leaving him alone with Lawlor, who, he said, had demanded £100,000 from him (and that Lawlor had claimed he was promised). 'Dunlop was fuming and said that he thought Lawlor was going to hit him. He wanted £100,000 but had received only £40,000 of what he said he was owed. O'Callaghan laughed at Dunlop and said that he "would try and square it" by giving "a bit more" to Lawlor . . . It was obvious that they wanted me in the offices for a reason, but that was never explained. The bank had contacted me to meet Lawlor on the basis that he was to introduce me to some senior politicians in the Dáil. Clearly it was a set-up.'

It also became evident to Gilmartin after his meeting with Dunlop that the latter had been in contact with O'Callaghan and Lawlor for some time before he arrived at the office in Mount Street. It seemed to Gilmartin that Dunlop was already on O'Callaghan's payroll, as was Lawlor, but it was not clear what their role was in relation to his Quarryvale development. He had made it plain to O'Callaghan that he wanted nothing to do with either the lobbyist or the politician, who he had good reason to mistrust.

During this period Lawlor was suspected by Gilmartin to be the instigator of yet another sinister incident. He was asked by Eddie Kay of AIB to attend a meeting of community leaders in the west Dublin area with O'Callaghan. He travelled by taxi to the Finches pub in Neilstown. Instead of meeting a group of residents Gilmartin was confronted in the pub by a man, accompanied by two others in dark glasses, who claimed to be the local Sinn Féin representative. 'We arrived into a pub . . . There was one or two people at the bar. We went over and sat at a table and I asked Mr O'Callaghan, "Where are those residents I'm supposed to meet?" and he says, "Well, just wait, just wait." So we waited about five minutes or more, I'm not quite sure of the time. And then three people arrived . . . Two of them had dark glasses on them, they had dark sun-glasses on them. They walked over and sat at a table looking at me, but just looking in my direction, and then one came over and sat at our table. So I asked Mr O'Callaghan, "What is this about?" and he says, "Oh, well, listen." So this gentleman said to me, "I am the Sinn Féin representative for this area," and he said, "You are on our patch."' Gilmartin replied to the man in dark glasses that he did not give a fuck who you are.'

The man claiming to be the local Sinn Féin representative then told Gilmartin that 'the boys' had a file on him, arising from his previous involvement with the Clandeboye retail development in Bangor, county Down. Taking these comments as an implicit threat to take his business elsewhere, Gilmartin got up and walked out of the pub.

As they returned to the city in a taxi he confronted O'Callaghan, who had moved away before the exchange in the pub took place, about the meeting. O'Callaghan's response was that Gilmartin should heed what he was told. Gilmartin subsequently came to the view that Lawlor had orchestrated this meeting and the hostile attitude that, he believed, was displayed towards him at the encounter. He may, however, have been reading too much into the comments made to him in the pub and attributing motives to those present that were not soundly based. He was convinced, however, that Lawlor had a hand in setting up the encounter. (See appendix 1, paragraph 18.)

Before the rezoning vote on 16 May, AIB executives were aware that Dunlop's role was to assist with the 'advancement of zoning on the site' as well as 'to advise on media issues,' and that he did not come cheap. Large payments were being made to Frank Dunlop and Associates by O'Callaghan to cover Dunlop's fees and expenses, while even larger amounts were being paid to Shefran Ltd, including some £100,000 between May and June 1991. Though Gilmartin was not aware of it, the purpose of the use of Shefran in connection with Quarryvale was to facilitate the receipt of substantial funds from O'Callaghan from which corrupt payments could be made to councillors. It was also to conceal from Gilmartin that such funds were being provided to Dunlop, and their scale.[d]

With local elections looming in June 1991 there was fertile political ground for Dunlop to plough as he and O'Callaghan sought, successfully, to convince a majority of councillors to agree to rezone the Quarryvale lands as categories D (major town centre) and E (industrial) and to move the existing zoning from Neilstown. The motion by Colm McGrath, and his amendment to limit the scale of the Quarryvale development to that provided for Neilstown in the 1983 development plan, in deference to the concerns of some councillors over the scale of the proposed retail centre, were comfortably carried.

During the election campaign Dunlop dispersed tens of thousands of pounds to various candidates, including the £40,000 to Lawlor, from a 'war chest' he accumulated in Shefran Ltd and other accounts, the money being provided by O'Callaghan and other property developers whose interests the lobbyist represented. A number of councillors benefited from these improper contributions. One Fine Gael politician, the late Tom Hand, had demanded, unsuccessfully, no less than £250,000 from Dunlop, which he insisted should be lodged in an Australian bank account on his behalf. (See appendix 1, paragraph 19.)

Dunlop's generous contributions were not enough, however, to save the seats of many of those he assisted financially. Up to a third of the councillors, including Lawlor and several other Fianna Fáil members, lost their seats amid public revulsion at perceived irregularities in the planning process, following a fierce public campaign by Green Property aimed at politicians who supported the Quarryvale rezoning. By this time O'Callaghan, through his company Riga Ltd, had expended some £230,000 in relation to what it called 'Westpark expenses' associated with Quarryvale, including the money given to Dunlop for dispersal to politicians, which he clearly hoped to recoup when he finally got control of Gilmartin's company, Barkhill.

Yet further 'heads of agreement' were put to Gilmartin in the wake of the successful rezoning vote, providing for a loan of £3 million to Barkhill Ltd from AIB and a further £1 million from Riga Ltd. The revised shareholdings left Gilmartin with a 33.5 per cent stake, Riga with just over 44 per cent, and AIB with just over 22 per cent. It was stipulated that the loan facility could be used only for the completion of land purchases at Quarryvale, unless Tom and Vera Gilmartin agreed otherwise. Gilmartin did not accept such a dilution of his shareholding and rejected the proposal. Over the summer he continued to play hard ball with his bankers, insisting that he would accept no less than an equal 40 per cent share if O'Callaghan was to come on board. He also rejected a suggestion that O'Callaghan's favoured architect, Ambrose Kelly of Dublin, would replace the Belfast firm Taggarts on the development.

———

Gilmartin soon realised that he had no choice but to accede to a new shareholders' agreement. One of the reasons was the fact that his companies and business history had unexpectedly come to the attention of the Inland Revenue in Britain. He had previously settled his tax affairs for £120,000 (sterling), arising from a property deal he had completed in Milton Keynes. However, the Inland Revenue was now pursuing him for a far greater sum, almost £7 million, and he mentioned to AIB officials that he was facing a tax demand that he did not owe.

Soon after this conversation he read about his so-called tax difficulties in the *People*, an English tabloid newspaper, and the story of his supposed tax problems was soon doing the rounds in Dublin. However these difficulties became known, Dunlop spoke of them in discussions with various politicians, including Councillor Therese Ridge of Fine Gael, while a senior AIB executive, David McGrath, had referred to the possibility that Gilmartin 'could perhaps be made bankrupt in the UK' during a discussion in the offices of William Fry, solicitors, in Dublin on 31 May 1991.

In fact Gilmartin did not owe anything close to that amount in outstanding taxes, but he heard that a plot had been hatched to discredit him by spreading unfounded rumours about his tax status. Wherever it came from, it put Gilmartin and his family under severe financial stress at a time when he was desperately trying to retain control of his company. 'I had informed AIB that I had a settlement agreed with the Inland Revenue for £120,000 in relation to a property deal in Milton Keynes. The next thing the newspapers in England had a headline "Tom's tax problems," with a photo of me and a claim that I owed £7 million plus penalties. When the media called to my home Vera opened the door and was knocked to the ground. The Revenue came looking for up to £14 million, and I was made bankrupt by the courts in 1992. They seized my car and other assets in front of my wife and children.

'They then realised their mistake and told me they had been misled with information from Dublin. I didn't owe them anything but the £120,000 we agreed. They offered me compensation for their mistake, which I refused. But that destroyed any chance of keeping control of my business in Ireland. I could not even afford the price of an air fare to attend board meetings of Barkhill. On one occasion O'Callaghan offered to pay my fare with money he had taken from my company. My family suffered terribly at this time. I learnt later the whole plan was hatched in Dublin.'

Being made bankrupt in England had a profound effect on Tom Gilmartin and his family. Vera, until then a mobile and hard-working wife and mother, was placed under extraordinary stress as she tried to look after the home without even being able to draw social welfare benefits. She would gather pennies where she could in order to buy at least some food, but the family occasionally had nothing in the fridge despite her best efforts. The unrelenting ordeal triggered a marked decline in her health, her multiple sclerosis gradually overcoming her.

Tom Gilmartin was at what would be the lowest point in his life. Though his position was a result of the wrongdoing of others, he felt a sense of guilt and shame that he was unable to provide for his family or prevent the stress that would lead to his wife's collapse. His son Thomas, then still at school, gave what he had saved up over previous years, including his Holy Communion money, to help his parents. Gilmartin recalled that he wept privately at his son's gesture. Family members in Ireland and others to whom Gilmartin had been generous over the years also sent some money to help out. For Tom Gilmartin, every day was now a living nightmare.

It took three years for Gilmartin to emerge from the bankruptcy process that he insisted was never justified in the first place, as he did not owe the sum demanded by Inland Revenue. Indeed, he claimed that a senior Revenue official confirmed to him that the claim was based on information from sources in Dublin, which was never verified.

On 13 September 1991, as the tax scandal was breaking in Britain, a distressed Gilmartin signed the latest shareholders' agreement, giving him and O'Callaghan a 40 per cent shareholding each and AIB the balance of 20 per cent, under threat from its executives that the bank would wind up Barkhill unless he put his signature on the document. Under the deal the assets of O'Callaghan's Merrygrove Estates, which owned the

Neilstown lands, were transferred to Barkhill, while O'Callaghan and an AIB official, Barry Pitcher, joined Gilmartin on the company's board. Barkhill also received a £3 million loan facility as part of the agreement.

It was a crucial blow to the embattled Gilmartin, who believed that O'Callaghan and Deane were taking over his company, with the aid of the bank, without making any significant financial contribution to it. For his part, O'Callaghan could now continue with his lobbying and other activities to advance the Quarryvale project in the knowledge that any expenses incurred by his company, Riga, would be reimbursed by Barkhill. Among those costs were payments of £10,000 each, in September and October 1991, to Liam Lawlor and Colm McGrath, respectively, authorised by AIB and made without Gilmartin's knowledge but yet identified in the company accounts as money paid to him. In this instance the bank was in effect colluding with O'Callaghan in illicit payments to politicians while charging them to Gilmartin.

O'Callaghan did not reveal the identity of the recipients of these 'political expenses' in correspondence with the bank, which in turn did not record details of them in any internal AIB memoranda. The payments were also in breach of the terms of the £3 million loan facility agreed in September, which required that funds drawn down 'may only be used . . . for the purpose of the purchase of properties.' Information concerning the payments was also withheld from the Barkhill accountant, Leo Fleming of Deloitte, who was engaged by Gilmartin to audit the company accounts. (See appendix 1, paragraph 20.)

While Gilmartin was aware that Frank Dunlop and Associates was receiving payments from Riga Ltd that were reimbursed by Barkhill, he remained completely unaware of the identity of the interests behind Shefran, or its purpose, even though significant round-figure and VAT-free invoiced claims from that entity were coming to his attention by late 1991. When Riga provided Barkhill with its £1 million loan promised under the shareholders' agreement, it debited the £230,000 in 'Westpark expenses' paid by O'Callaghan between January and May 1991 in relation to Quarryvale, including the £80,000 given to Dunlop through Shefran. A further £70,000, in two sums of £40,000 and £30,000, was paid to Shefran in April and June 1992, which again was reimbursed by Barkhill. (See appendix 1, paragraph 21.)

The invoices submitted to Riga Ltd for these payments coincided with the reactivation of the Quarryvale rezoning issue when the county council was to begin its second-stage review of the development plan. Both payments were made directly by AIB from the Barkhill loan account, at Riga's request. They followed a discussion with AIB executives in March 1992 when O'Callaghan estimated that a total of £150,000 would be required if the final rezoning of Quarryvale was to succeed.

By April 1992 Dunlop was operating no less than four accounts, including one in the name of Shefran Ltd at AIB, College Green, where he had an arrangement with its manager, John Aherne, to facilitate the cashing of cheques. Aherne had assisted with the opening of another account at the Terenure branch of AIB, Rathfarnham Road, where he lodged the £80,000. From this account, which became known as the 'Rathfarnham' account, funds could be drawn without Dunlop setting foot in the branch. He also had an account with Irish Nationwide Building Society and another in the name of Xerxes Consult (Jersey) Ltd at Midland Bank Trust in Jersey. Between April 1991 and January 1993 Dunlop was paid £150,000 through Shefran, while Frank Dunlop and Associates received more than £100,000 from Riga or Barkhill.

Another vote on the Quarryvale development was imminent in Dublin County Council in December 1992, requiring several weeks of lobbying by Dunlop and O'Callaghan, while a general election was called on 5 November.

As well as his continuing role as lobbyist for O'Callaghan and other developers, Dunlop was appointed director of publicity for the Fianna Fáil election campaign. The general election provided an excellent cover for the lobbying of politicians before the vote on the further rezoning of Quarryvale. In late October, O'Callaghan asked AIB to release £40,000 in additional funds from Barkhill for the campaign. He informed the bank that he had also 'injected' some £85,000 'into the situation,' according to a memo made on 1 December by an AIB executive, Michael O'Farrell (who had taken over the handling of the Barkhill account for AIB from Eddie Kay in August). 'He [Mr O'Callaghan] is confident a decision will be made one way or the other . . .' the memo says. 'It is very tight . . . His lobbying continues and he indicated that he had injected £85,000 into the situation from O'Callaghan Properties.'

The O'Callaghan injection included a sum of £70,000 sent through an inter-bank transfer in the middle of the election campaign from Riga to Dunlop's war chest in the 'Rathfarnham' account on 19 November, from which Dunlop immediately withdrew £55,000 in cash. It also included amounts of £10,000 and £5,000, which O'Callaghan paid to the Cork Fianna Fáil TD Batt O'Keeffe and a party colleague in Dublin, Councillor G. V. Wright. He was also paying Councillor Seán Gilbride a retainer of £3,500 per month after the latter took a sabbatical from his teaching job to help with the Quarryvale rezoning campaign. Gilbride was a politician from county Sligo whose family was well known to the Gilmartins. Because of this he was one of the first whom Gilmartin had contacted for advice when he had arrived in Dublin. The disbursal of money by Dunlop and O'Callaghan to councillors and more senior politicians during the general election campaign, and before the Quarryvale rezoning vote, was done with a degree of knowledge on the part of AIB, which had released £40,000 for this purpose.

A number of councillors who were also general election candidates were the beneficiaries of this largesse, including Pat Rabbitte (then of Democratic Left), who received £2,000 from Dunlop, and G. V. Wright of Fianna Fáil, to whom Dunlop gave £5,000 in addition to O'Callaghan's contribution of the same amount. After the election Democratic Left sent a cheque for £2,000 to Dunlop and explained that Rabbitte and his party colleagues on the council were concerned that it was inappropriate to retain the donation because of the fact that, as councillors, they would be voting on matters in which Dunlop had an interest.

Dunlop also claimed to have given £5,000 to a Fine Gael election candidate, Liam Cosgrave (junior), at a church car park in Blackrock, county Dublin, on 11 November 1992, even though Dunlop was then heading the publicity campaign for Fianna Fáil!

Liam Lawlor was among the main beneficiaries of the payments, receiving a contribution of £25,000 from Dunlop, who was provided with a false invoice by Lawlor in return. There was also evidence that the more senior political figures meeting Dunlop and O'Callaghan during this period in relation to Quarryvale, and a stadium project they were promoting on the Neilstown lands, also benefited from the funds being disbursed by O'Callaghan. In particular, the draw-down of £55,000 in cash by Dunlop on 10 November 1992 coincided with the launch of the Fianna Fáil election manifesto, when he was in direct contact with senior ministers of the outgoing Government who were also candidates. In a letter to the Taoiseach, Albert Reynolds, on 17 November, O'Callaghan wrote that he had given support 'in excess of six figures' to the party, as 'it is vital for the country that we have a Fianna Fáil controlled

Government.' He enclosed a cheque for £5,000 with the letter.

Significant amounts of the improper payments to politicians were being funded by Barkhill Ltd and Gilmartin, without his knowledge and even though he had objected, and continued to object, to AIB about any involvement of Dunlop in his affairs. He was still concerned at payments he was asked to authorise in relation to Quarryvale and only approved, at the bank's request, various payments to Shefran Ltd many months after they were made. His authorisation of a number of such payments on 9 October 1992 came just as he was made bankrupt in Britain as the result of the false information provided to the Inland Revenue by, he suspected, unknown sources in Dublin during 1991. He also raised questions concerning the large fees being paid to Dunlop's company Frank Dunlop and Associates, while his suspicions concerning those behind Shefran deepened. The true ownership of Shefran was not disclosed in company documents filed offshore. (See appendix 1, paragraph 22.)

Following the election on 25 November 1992 a weakened Fianna Fáil under Albert Reynolds re-entered Government in a coalition with a resurgent Labour Party led by Dick Spring.

For Gilmartin, who took no part in the election campaign, the focus was now on 17 December, when a special meeting of Dublin County Council would review objections and representations made in relation to the changes in the 1991 draft development plan for Dublin. On 16 May 1991 a majority of councillors had agreed to zone Quarryvale as categories D (major town centre) and E (industrial) at a special meeting. There was now a threat to alter the zoning because of continuing objections to the site and the scale of the proposed development, and suggestions that its size should be capped. Thus a second vote, in December 1992, was crucial to the survival of the project.

In addition to Gilmartin's difficulties with the bank and O'Callaghan, as well as the unexplained sums going to Dunlop and Shefran, he objected to the proposed 250,000-square-foot retail cap being proposed by O'Callaghan, which he believed would further diminish his equity in the project. He was also angry that information relating to his bankruptcy was published in the *Sunday Business Post* before the vote, and he took exception to a report in that paper that, he said, suggested that he had no interest in the lands at Quarryvale. It was not hard to draw the conclusion that the source of the information used by the journalist in question was Dunlop or O'Callaghan, or both.[e]

On the day of the crucial council vote Gilmartin was invited to a meeting in London with an AIB executive, David McGrath, with whom he had previously clashed, and Eddie Kay, with whom he had a more civil relationship and who was asked by the bank to accompany his colleague for this reason. The invitation followed a heated, and unrecorded, conversation between Gilmartin and another AIB official, Mary Basquille, during which he had threatened to go to the press with complaints in relation to issues surrounding the Quarryvale project. The ostensible purpose of the trip to London was to assuage his fears and to ensure that he did not alert the media, as threatened, in case he might 'wreck the entire project and bring it down,' as Eddie Kay later described it. What actually happened was, in Gilmartin's view, a 'stunt' to keep him engaged in London so that he would not interfere with the vote of Dublin County Council that evening.

Gilmartin arrived first at the hotel at Heathrow Airport, where he then met Eddie Kay as arranged, but it was several hours before David McGrath turned up, even though the two officials had travelled together on the same morning flight to London. The bankers then held him in discussion for a lengthy period.

Gilmartin had intended to phone some councillors to try to postpone or delay the vote as soon as he got home to Luton, because of his disagreement with the proposal to cap the development at 250,000 square feet. By the time he was able to make the call, however, the county council offices in Dublin, and the central switchboard, were closed. When he phoned the number of the Fianna Fáil rooms at the county council he found that the telephones were being manned by O'Callaghan's solicitor, John Deane. His efforts to reach sympathetic councillors who might have agreed to postpone the vote were unsuccessful, he claimed. 'I suddenly realised that the main reason for McGrath being late—or that was my opinion—was to stall me until after the council offices were shut, so when I did try to get through the person answering the phone was John Deane.' No memos or notes were retained by the bank in relation to the London meeting. (See appendix 1, paragraph 23.)

On the same day as the council vote an independent councillor, Gus O'Connell, who opposed the development, was invited to go on a working visit to England on behalf of his employer, the training agency FÁS. Coincidentally, the trip followed a telephone conversation between

Owen O'Callaghan and a FÁS director, John Lynch, a few weeks earlier. His absence meant that O'Connell could not register his opposition to the proposal. Lynch at the time was chairman and chief executive of An Bord Gáis, while O'Callaghan was a director of the same state-sponsored company. The tribunal later found that Lynch did not orchestrate the involvement of O'Connell in the trip. (See appendix 1, paragraph 24.)

At the council meeting the Quarryvale zoning was revised to categories C (town or district centre) and E (industrial), subject to a cap on the retail space of 250,000 square feet, an outcome that further angered Gilmartin. His disillusionment with his board partners continued unabated as he complained that he had not been consulted on important decisions and of the 'blackmail and corrupt practices' that resulted in his losing control of Barkhill Ltd through the shareholders' agreement. He was also questioning the AIB officials Basquille and O'Farrell about the purpose behind the Shefran payments, and getting little or no response to his queries.

While he missed monthly board meetings in early 1993—not least because of difficulties raising the air fare to attend them—Gilmartin complained at those he did attend in April and June about the Dunlop and Shefran payments and the lack of documents that he required for his auditor, Leo Fleming, particularly in relation to the two payments of £10,000 taken from his account and paid to Liam Lawlor and Colm McGrath in 1991. The payments were wrongly attributed as expenses incurred by Gilmartin.

Fleming believed that the incorrect attribution could have been based on information provided by Aidan Lucey, Riga's bookkeeper. Lucey, who managed the accounts for Riga Ltd and O'Callaghan Properties, denied that he had informed the auditor that the two amounts of £10,000 were expenses incurred solely by Gilmartin. The amounts had been reimbursed to O'Callaghan's personal account, though they rightly belonged to Barkhill Ltd. (Tribunal transcript, day 832, question 810.)

The bank's difficulties in containing Gilmartin's threat to go public with his complaints were compounded by a series of articles on corruption that appeared in *The Irish Times* in July 1993, which reported that the Minister for the Environment, Michael Smith, had asked the Garda Commissioner to investigate urgently 'the reports of money changing hands' at Dublin County Council in respect of rezoning motions. The bank, and Michael O'Farrell in particular, was well aware that some £250,000 had been provided to Frank Dunlop through his companies over the previous two years, most of which was spent on so-called lobbying in respect of the rezoning of Quarryvale. There was clearly danger for the bank coming down the tracks. (See appendix 1, paragraph 25.)

Even so, O'Farrell never bothered to ask O'Callaghan whether he was involved in making any such corrupt payments to councillors as referred to in *The Irish Times* articles, or whether Dunlop had done so on his behalf. It would have been inappropriate, in his view, to ask such a question of such an upstanding customer and a man whom only months previously he had described (in the report of the bank's Credit Committee of 18 August 1992) as 'probably the most respected and capable shopping centre developer in Ireland,' whose involvement in Barkhill 'is undoubtedly very helpful to us . . . and through his efforts it is probable that the site value will be substantially enhanced, thereby protecting our exposure.' Indeed there was no reference to the *Irish Times* articles in a memo of a meeting between O'Farrell, his superior David McGrath, Donal Chambers (AIB general manager of corporate and commercial) and O'Callaghan held on 28 July, very soon after they were published. (See appendix 1, paragraph 26.)

Dunlop and Shefran continued to pull in huge payments in fees and expenses as well as for disbursement to politicians; but the justification for much of this income from O'Callaghan was complicated by the work they were doing on promoting the stadium project on the Neilstown lands with Liam Lawlor and Ambrose Kelly. Dunlop also assisted unsuccessful general election candidates and councillors, including Therese Ridge, Michael Joe Cosgrave and Liam Cosgrave (junior) of Fine Gael as well as Anne Ormonde and Don Lydon of Fianna Fáil in the campaign for the Seanad in early 1993. O'Callaghan went so far as to finance the transport of Ridge by plane to and from Cork and by car to Kerry and Limerick to lobby councillors and other members of the Seanad electorate.

Many councillors had by this stage done very well out of Quarryvale and Dunlop. By April 1993, Seán Gilbride (Fianna Fáil) had collected a total of £17,250 in his monthly 'sabbatical' payments from O'Callaghan. Finbarr Hanrahan (Fianna Fáil) was also well rewarded for his efforts on the developer's behalf, with a donation of £2,000 to £2,500 during the November 1992 election. John O'Halloran, who lost the Labour

Party whip over his support for the Quarryvale rezoning and became an independent councillor in 1993, also received varying amounts, including a sum of £5,000 between 1991 and 1993.

O'Callaghan also assisted other councillors to obtain lucrative insurance and other contracts with the Quarryvale development. Colm McGrath received £30,000 directly from O'Callaghan between 1991 and 1993 and also obtained a valuable security and plant-hire contract on the site, while Colm Tyndall of the Progressive Democrats supplied insurance services for O'Callaghan, and John O'Halloran opened a canteen at the development during the construction phase.

O'Callaghan did not attempt to disguise his financial assistance to councillors. Following a meeting of the board of Barkhill during this period he showed Gilmartin a cheque for £10,000 he had made out to Colm McGrath. He was bringing the impoverished Gilmartin by taxi to Dublin Airport when he began to boast of his control over the councillors, including McGrath, whom he had arranged to meet in order to hand over the payment. When they reached the airport O'Callaghan asked Gilmartin to stay out of sight, as he did not want the councillor to see them together before he handed over the cheque.

But it was not only junior politicians who were continuing to enjoy the largesse: O'Callaghan and Dunlop were engaging with others at the higher end of the political food-chain as they pursued their ambitious plans for Quarryvale and Neilstown. In September 1993 Frank Dunlop was carrying a sum of £25,000 in cash when he met an unidentified politician in Power's Hotel in Kildare Street, near Leinster House, according to his own diary records. When he was later asked who the man was he claimed he could remember the amount of money, and its source, but for the life of him could not recall the politician's identity! (See appendix 1, paragraph 27.)

The final zoning of the Quarryvale development was confirmed at a special meeting of the county council on 19 October 1993, and cash payments to politicians in respect of that aspect of the project were no longer necessary. On 10 December the 1993 development plan for Dublin was adopted, a few weeks before the county council was broken up into three separate local authorities: Fingal, Dún Laoghaire-Rathdown and South Dublin. The retail cap remained, but O'Callaghan expressed his confidence that in time it would be lifted by the incoming management of South Dublin County Council. The effect of the cap was to reduce the potential value of the development, and to dilute the value of Gilmartin's shareholding.

For Gilmartin, the zoning decision was a mixed blessing. The ambitious Quarryvale project was still on track, but he was not in control of it and was effectually sidelined from its management. He had witnessed some of the unorthodox political dealings that Owen O'Callaghan was involved in, and indeed bragged about, but had only a partial view of the scale of the operation in which his business partners were engaged to ensure that the massive multi-million retail proposal would be realised.

It is necessary to examine how the stadium planned for the Neilstown site progressed in order to grasp the extent of the political manoeuvring that ensued behind Gilmartin's back. Even though he held a stake in the lands involved, he was deliberately excluded from the stadium project, not least because it involved more than a hint of high-level intrigue.

| 'THE BIG ONE'

I n December 1992 the Ambrose Kelly Group lodged a submission with Dublin County Council on behalf of O'Callaghan Properties for the development of a national soccer stadium on the Neilstown-Balgaddy lands. The proposal, for which Liam Lawlor took credit, had begun in 1991 as a ruse to ensure that the rezoning of Quarryvale remained uncontested by convincing local representatives and community leaders that there would be a significant investment in the Neilstown lands, bringing employment and economic activity to the depressed north Clondalkin-Balgaddy area even if the people of the area were not to get their long-promised town centre. Once Quarryvale got the go-ahead, the stadium scheme could be quietly dropped.

But a dramatic change in political circumstances in early 1992 convinced O'Callaghan that the proposal might actually attract enough financial support from the Government to make it commercially viable. The shareholders in Leisure Ireland Ltd, the company incorporated to develop the plan, each with a 25 per cent stake, were Frank Dunlop, Owen O'Callaghan, Ambrose Kelly and Liam Lawlor. Lawlor's involvement was not disclosed in company records, for fear of alienating political support from those already aware of his shady dealings. Details of the stadium plan, and Lawlor's involvement, were not provided to Tom Gilmartin, even though he was a 40 per cent shareholder in Barkhill Ltd, which owned the land on which the stadium was to be built (through its control of Merrygrove Ltd, in which the site was vested). Far from it being just a ruse, Dunlop was so excited at the prospect of striking it rich through the project, of which he was appointed chairman, that he referred to it as 'the Big One' in his diary entries of the time.

The election as Taoiseach of his friend and ally Albert Reynolds encouraged O'Callaghan. Reynolds had replaced Charles Haughey as Taoiseach and leader of Fianna Fáil in February 1992 after an upheaval within the party. Haughey stepped down after a television appearance by a former Minister for Justice, Seán Doherty, in which he alleged that Haughey was complicit in the illegal phone-tapping of prominent journalists in the early 1980s. Gilmartin claimed that O'Callaghan had informed him of the moves against Haughey, who was himself embroiled in a succession of business scandals over the previous few years, and of his support for Reynolds to replace him.

A few months after Haughey sacked him, Reynolds—with Pádraig Flynn's support—led another heave against the leader and forced him to resign. There were suggestions of other reasons why the 'Boss' finally acceded to pressure from Reynolds, Flynn and other senior party figures, including the belief that his opponents in the Government had discovered his misappropriation or misuse of party leader's funds that were subsequently revealed.

Among those reappointed to the Government were Bertie Ahern, whose own leadership ambitions were frustrated in the divisive contest to succeed Haughey but who now became Minister for Finance, and Pádraig Flynn, who became Minister for the Environment, even though the national organiser of Fianna Fáil, Seán Sherwin, had informed the incoming Taoiseach about the £50,000 Flynn had taken from Gilmartin and had not passed on to the party. Ray Burke, who also kept large donations intended for the party during the 1989 election campaign, was not so lucky and was dropped from the cabinet.

O'Callaghan advised Louis Kilcoyne, a prominent figure in the Football Association of Ireland, that 'the present political situation may be even more favourable to our proposal than the past.' O'Callaghan was so confident of support from the Reynolds Government that he costed the proposal for a 40,000-seat stadium at £32 to £35 million, with £10 to £15 million in support from the Government and the balance provided by the developers and the FAI.

The project suffered a setback when the FAI withheld its support, for financial reasons, and a new concept of an 'all-purpose national stadium', including the possible future participation of the FAI, was devised. Following an introduction by Reynolds, a source of finance for O'Callaghan emerged in the form of a Los Angeles broker, Bill O'Connor of Chilton and O'Connor, which specialised in creating municipal bonds for sale on the financial market. O'Callaghan and Dunlop held meetings during April and May with various senior political figures, including Reynolds and his new Minister of State for Youth and Sport, Liam Aylward, the Minister for the Environment, Michael Smith, and the recently installed Minister for Finance, Bertie Ahern.

At this point Houston Sports Association, a company with experience in building sports stadiums, was engaged on the recommendation of Chilton and O'Connor and began to prepare plans for a potentially larger-scale multi-purpose development, financed with the help of National Lottery funds underwritten by the Government. There were also discussions with Government ministers about the prospect of obtaining a lucrative tax designation for the stadium site.

After months of intense activity involving discussions with Bill O'Connor on financing sources, a feasibility study by the accountancy firm Deloitte and Touche, consultations with potential users, including the FAI and entertainment companies, and further talks with Reynolds and Ahern, the project finally had its public launch on 10 September 1992, with a planning application submitted by Merrygrove Ltd a month later. Following subsequent discussions with the Labour Party after the November election, a commitment was included in the Programme for Government for a capital project 'to support the building of an indoor National Sports Stadium.' The existence of the stadium plan, along with the generous disbursements by Dunlop and O'Callaghan, played a significant role in convincing councillors to support the second vote to retain the Quarryvale rezoning at their December meeting.

Reynolds went on to publicly intervene with the Dublin city and county manager to speed up the planning process after complaints from O'Callaghan over questions by council engineers about the capacity of the road network to handle traffic to the stadium site. Reynolds also met Bill O'Connor in early March 1993. The meeting was arranged after the Irish Consulate in Los Angeles was asked by Niall Lawlor, son of Liam Lawlor and an employee of Chilton and O'Connor, to add his boss to the guest list for the official reception for the Taoiseach who was in the US for the annual St Patrick's Day visit. Reynolds also visited the offices of the brokerage in Los Angeles in August, where he met O'Connor and Kevin Burke, the principals of the firm.

The decision to grant planning permission was made in August 1993, while further commitments were obtained from the Government over potential funding of £5 million per year for ten years from National Lottery funds.

'The Stadium was permitted and the site approved by the Dublin council on August 24,' Kevin Burke wrote to a potential investor in early

September. 'We have been formally retained by the developer to senior manager [*sic*] this transaction. The Taoiseach Mr Reynolds was recently in our offices here in Los Angeles and we are very confident that the level of support which the Republic of Ireland has committed will create a very attractive security.'

With O'Callaghan in regular discussions with Reynolds, and Dunlop meeting Ahern frequently during the autumn of 1993—all of which meetings were unrecorded and held without the presence of officials—as well as the firm commitment in the Programme for Government to build a national sports stadium, it was evident to their bankers and professional advisers that the project enjoyed support and encouragement at the highest political level, including offers of tax designation and lottery funds. Both ministers were given the detailed, and confidential, feasibility study prepared by Deloitte and Touche, which referred to a capital cost of £60 million for the stadium being offset by 'government support' in order to reduce the level of borrowing and allow for debt-servicing and repayment over fifteen years.

In early December, Dunlop wrote to Ahern asking for an early meeting to discuss the proposals. The month of March, with the annual political pilgrimage to the United States, is a particularly busy one for senior Irish politicians, and for Reynolds and Ahern 1994 was no exception. Among their concerns was the party's massive debt, the political challenges of coalition government with the Labour Party, and potentially dramatic developments in the North as the British government and the IRA made moves towards peace negotiations.

Several months earlier Ahern, a party treasurer, had recommended to Reynolds that he appoint Des Richardson, a personal friend of Ahern's, to the position of executive party fund-raiser. His task was to address the debt of some £3½ million that Fianna Fáil had accumulated over recent years and that threatened to overwhelm the party unless it could attract an urgent financial injection. Operating out of a suite in the Berkeley Court Hotel in Ballsbridge, separate from the party head office in Lower Mount Street, Richardson prepared a list of potential contributors from the elite circles of Irish business and property. Among the ten individuals asked personally by Reynolds and Ahern in September 1993 to contribute £100,000 each was Owen O'Callaghan, who gave a commitment to pay and also obliged by helping to organise a fund-raising dinner to which leading businessmen in Cork were invited to hear a personal address by the Taoiseach on 11 March 1994.

Reynolds flew to Cork by Air Corps helicopter and returned in the early hours of the morning to Dublin, from where he travelled by Government jet to the United States for the traditional St Patrick's Day meeting with the American president. The fund-raising dinner was held in the home of the businessman Niall Welch, and, according to Richardson, a sum of £50,000 was collected for the party from eight or nine people who attended. O'Callaghan gave a donation of £10,000 to Richardson, part of the £100,000 he had promised and the largest on the night, attributing it in the Riga accounts as 'Quarryvale expenses.'

Richardson addressed the gathering with the help of a speech drafted by Frank Dunlop and collected the money, most of which was left on the dinner table in unmarked envelopes. He lodged two sums of £25,000 to the Fianna Fáil account three days after the event, though the party received no documents identifying the source of the money. The Cork businessmen who donated had apparently no problem with their contributions remaining anonymous and unrecorded in party files. Fianna Fáil's general secretary, Pat Farrell, the Minister for Agriculture, Joe Walsh, and a member of the party's fund-raising committee, Roy Donovan, also attended the function. The guests included the property developers Michael O'Flynn (who said he made no contribution) and John Fleming, Ed McNamara, John McCarthy and Noel C. Duggan. Eight substantial cash contributions of between £5,000 and £10,000 were made. However, there were no detailed records of the individual donors and no receipts issued. The party did receive a bill from Richardson for a breakfast meeting he had with Welch and Ahern in a hotel in Dublin a few days before the dinner, which referred to the Cork function.

But that was not all. After a board meeting at AIB head office, O'Callaghan told Gilmartin of the dinner party in Cork. According to Gilmartin, O'Callaghan said he gave the Taoiseach £150,000 in the bedroom of his house after the dinner. He said O'Callaghan referred to Reynolds leaving Cork by helicopter in the early hours in order to catch his flight to the United States from Dublin. (See appendix 1, paragraph 28.)

Whether he misheard or misinterpreted O'Callaghan's description of this event, the venue and how the funds were raised and distributed, Gilmartin was again left in no doubt that O'Callaghan wielded considerable influence at the highest levels of government. Bringing the country's top politician to Cork the day before he was to take a tiring trip to the United States was a fairly impressive illustration of O'Callaghan's relationship with Reynolds, leaving aside the issue of who ultimately benefited from his generosity and that of his fellow-guests.

On 11 March, the day of the dinner, Ahern was in the United States, where he met Chilton and O'Connor in Los Angeles to discuss their role in the stadium project and its prospects for success and for Bill O'Connor and his partner to assess the level of expected Government support from the Minister for Finance. The meeting allowed the American partners to raise another concern they had regarding a potential commercial rival to the stadium, following information they received of a plan for a sports complex and casino development on the grounds of the disused Phoenix Park racecourse at Ashtown, county Dublin. The casino was being promoted by a Manchester businessman, Norman Turner, and the American firm Ogden Developments. Ahern had reason to be familiar with the proposal, as his friend and party fund-raiser Des Richardson had a business relationship with Turner, while another former school friend, the jeweller Robert White, was also engaged with the project. The party adviser P. J. Mara was acting for the developers as a lobbyist, while other senior politicians were feted by the company promoting the controversial project, which was planning to bring large-scale gambling to one of Dublin's more desirable suburbs.

It is a measure of O'Callaghan's strong connections and financial clout with Fianna Fáil that he had managed to secure a meeting between the Minister for Finance and his American brokers in Los Angeles on the same day that he was sitting down for dinner with the Taoiseach at the private fund-raiser in Cork. Soon after his return from the United States, on 24 March, Ahern met O'Callaghan to discuss a number of pressing issues involving Quarryvale and his stadium project. Among O'Callaghan's immediate concerns was the appointment of the former minister and EU commissioner Ray MacSharry to the board of Green Property, which was seeking a lucrative tax designation for its Blanchardstown retail centre. If granted it would give the development a serious advantage over Quarryvale when it came to attracting anchor tenants. MacSharry, though retired from public life, remained an influential figure within Fianna Fáil and had been asked only months previously by Reynolds and Ahern to follow up some of the 'high net worth' individuals, including O'Callaghan, to whom they had written in September seeking donations of £100,000 for the party. In December 1993, according to MacSharry, O'Callaghan made a commitment to pay the £100,000.

According to Gilmartin, it was during one of his rare attendances at a meeting of the Barkhill board that he raised the contentious matter of the possible tax designation being granted to the rival Blanchardstown Shopping Centre, owned by Green Property. He was concerned that if Blanchardstown received the designation it would attract the type of quality retail investors that were required to make Quarryvale a success. It would give the rival developer a marked advantage, he felt, and damage the commercial prospects of their scheme. Gilmartin later described how O'Callaghan had left the room during the discussion, only to return a few minutes later. He said that at the end of the meeting he was told by O'Callaghan that he had it 'from the horse's mouth' that Blanchardstown would not get the lucrative designation. According to Gilmartin, he was referring to the Minister for Finance, Bertie Ahern, who O'Callaghan told him had received a payment of £30,000 in return for the decision to refuse the designation to the rival centre. Ahern had determined that neither site would be granted tax designation.

It was clear from this and other discussions that Ahern and O'Callaghan were in regular contact, either directly or through Dunlop, in relation to a number of issues, including Quarryvale and the planned stadium. Five days after his meeting in March with O'Callaghan, in response to a question from the opposition, Ahern told the Dáil that he had met Chilton and O'Connor in Los Angeles during his visit to the United States earlier in the month.

During a visit to Ireland in May, Bill O'Connor, accompanied by O'Callaghan and Dunlop, had a meeting with the Taoiseach during which Reynolds asked them to prepare another financing plan for the project. O'Connor also met the chief executive of National Irish Bank, Jim Lacey, at the suggestion of Ahern, to discuss financial aspects of the project. Dunlop had another meeting with Ahern over the same week. With the stadium and Quarryvale projects and indeed other business ventures advancing at a steady pace, including the Golden Island retail centre outside Athlone, for which he was seeking Government support of one kind or another, O'Callaghan delivered on his promise in December to give £100,000 to Fianna Fáil, paying the balance of £80,000 on 21 June (having given £10,000 to the party at the private dinner in March).

He had also contributed £10,000 to the European Parliament election campaign of Brian Crowley, a former Fianna Fáil TD in west Cork. (See appendix 1, paragraph 29.)

Among the other successful fund-raising initiatives organised by Des Richardson was the annual Fianna Fáil tent during the Galway horse-racing festival held each July, a popular and expensive occasion for the country's leading property developers, builders and assorted business interests as they sought to display their support for the party. During the race week Reynolds was presented with the updated financial plan for the stadium at a meeting with O'Callaghan and Kevin Burke at the Connemara Coast Hotel. The stadium, it projected, could be built in thirty months at a cost of £59½ million, with an annual subvention over twenty years of £4.4 million coming from the National Lottery, or £2.7 million if tax designation was granted to the project. At the suggestion of the Taoiseach, a copy of the financial feasibility plan was delivered by Dunlop to Bertie Ahern's office within days of the Connemara meeting, on 28 July. In a letter to Ahern, Dunlop also requested to meet the Minister for Finance. 'I wouldn't mind sitting down with you for ten minutes to discuss the matter before it progresses further,' Dunlop wrote on 2 August in a letter marked 'Strictly private and confidential'.

While Reynolds may have been enthusiastic about the stadium, officials of the Department of Finance, who prepared a note on the costed plan in early September, were distinctly unimpressed. They estimated the annual debt-servicing cost to the National Lottery at £6.3 million over twenty years, though they accepted that this would be offset by operating surpluses from the stadium. They advised the minister that 'there are more pressing needs to be met from Lottery funds in the sports area and elsewhere than earmarking potentially £120 million over 20 years to provide a new National Stadium.' They also made reference to the alternative stadium proposal for the Phoenix Park racecourse site, the promoters of which were also seeking public funds, including EU structural funds. They recommended rejection of O'Callaghan's plan for an all-purpose stadium.

After a breakfast meeting with Ahern in the Davenport Hotel, Dublin, in late October, Dunlop made a hurried trip to New York, where he met Bill O'Connor, who was preparing to come to Dublin for a discussion with Ahern a few days later. On 10 November, O'Callaghan and O'Connor met Ahern to discuss the stadium proposal, notwithstanding the negative appraisal by his department officials, none of whom were present at the discussion. Following their conversation O'Callaghan informed Michael O'Farrell at AIB that the relevant minister had met the American financiers and indicated that the stadium would attract the involvement of both the Football Association of Ireland and the Irish Rugby Football Union, while the proposed Phoenix Park development would not proceed, because of difficulties its promoters would have in obtaining a gambling licence for a casino.

This round of meetings and communications came at a time of considerable political instability, as the coalition Government was rocked by a scandal surrounding a child-abusing priest, Brendan Smyth, and the failure of the authorities to have him extradited to the North, where he was facing serious charges. Reynolds was forced to stand down as Taoiseach and leader of Fianna Fáil and was quickly replaced by Ahern, though the prospect of the party continuing in government with the Labour Party under its new leader remained uncertain.

Bill O'Connor wrote to Ahern on 28 November, just after he had taken over as party leader from Reynolds and the dramatic upheaval within the party. 'I would like to congratulate you on your recent unanimous election as leader of Fianna Fáil. Also thank you for allocating the time to meet Mr Owen O'Callaghan, Frank Dunlop and myself on the financing plan for the National All-Purpose Stadium. We wish you every success in the crucial talks you are embarking upon [to form a Government] and we hope to be in contact with you in the near future to progress the subject.'

Reynolds had resigned on 17 November, and talks with the Labour Party were under way to try to maintain the coalition Government, with Ahern as the new Taoiseach. On the day before the Government collapsed, following the failure of the parties to find agreement, O'Callaghan was in Leinster House for urgent discussions with Reynolds and Ahern on a more pressing matter. He was concerned that a promised tax designation for his Golden Island retail development outside Athlone had not been formally concluded. Along with supportive members of Athlone Urban District Council, O'Callaghan had lobbied the Minister for the Environment, Michael Smith, some months earlier to have the development covered by the urban renewal tax relief scheme, but the final decision rested with the minister. On 14 November, in the dying hours of the Government, Ahern delivered the promised—and lucrative—designation.

Ahern's failure to make a deal with the leader of the Labour Party, Dick Spring, sounded the death knell of the stadium project, though it did not prevent O'Callaghan and his partners from seeking to rescue it in one form or another over subsequent years. The Labour Party instead formed a Government with Fine Gael, led by John Bruton, and the small Democratic Left party.

———

While Gilmartin claimed that he was told by O'Callaghan that he had paid money to Ahern in relation to the Golden Island designation, he was largely unaware of the progress being made by O'Callaghan on his other commercial projects, including the all-purpose stadium—even though he had a material interest in the land on which it was to be built. He was also unaware that payments made in relation to the stadium, in which he had no involvement, had been charged to the Barkhill account. Neither did he realise the level of contact his so-called business partner was having with senior politicians and the scale of financial support he was providing to the party. O'Callaghan had clearly indicated that he was prepared to pay, and indeed had paid, senior politicians in return for their support, but had not disclosed how such payments were made.

Gilmartin's personal and financial difficulties were compounded by the deterioration in Vera's medical condition. On one trip to the local town centre, in August 1994, her legs gave way underneath her, but she managed to reach a payphone by clutching on to a supermarket trolley. Gilmartin and two of his children rushed there to rescue her, but that day marked the end of her independence and a descent into the paralysis that leaves her wheelchair-bound to this day.

| 'HE WAS AN HONEST MAN'

B y early 1995 Tom Gilmartin was in a losing battle for control of Barkhill Ltd and suffering financial hardship while completely oblivious of much of the activity that was going on around him involving O'Callaghan and Allied Irish Banks. In frustration over his failure to elicit accurate information concerning the financial affairs of his company, and over his inability to regularly attend monthly board meetings, he authorised Paul Sheeran to attend and to act on his behalf.

In May 1995, on one of the rare occasions when Gilmartin attended, with Sheeran also present, he launched a tirade of criticism at the other shareholders, bluntly accusing them of fraud and collusion. Sheeran recalled that his friend 'made it very clear as regards bribery and corruption to the other parties [shareholders] concerned.' Gilmartin had described a litany of complaints to his fellow-directors and bank executives Mary Basquille and Michael O'Farrell about their treatment of him and the lack of information being provided to him as a substantial shareholder in Barkhill Ltd, including information about payments to Frank Dunlop and Shefran Ltd. The bank executives insisted that they were at all times motivated by commercial and banking considerations rather than any preference for O'Callaghan. Sheeran intervened and suggested that Gilmartin's anger could be alleviated if he could get some of his investment back, or could at least get money to cover his expenses, which in turn would make it easier for him to participate in the affairs of the company. (See appendix 1, paragraph 30.)

At another board meeting in the AIB Bankcentre an unusual event occurred that led Gilmartin to believe that O'Callaghan was eavesdropping on his conversations. When he left the room during a toilet break he was accompanied by his solicitor, Seamus Maguire. Gilmartin claimed that as they were chatting and preparing to return to the boardroom nearby he heard a loud sound and on turning around discovered O'Callaghan emerging from a broom cupboard in the toilet area. 'We had a break and went into the gents,' Gilmartin recalled, 'and

Mr O'Callaghan had been outside the door talking to someone, and he disappeared when we went out, and he fell out of a broom cupboard . . . We heard this rattling and when I looked . . . he opened the door of the broom cupboard and he fell out of it.' (See appendix 1, paragraph 31.)

Starved of funding, Gilmartin was not present at board meetings when crucial decisions were being made, including one to accept an offer from Grosvenor Holdings, a company controlled by the Duke of Westminster, to buy into the Quarryvale development. This investor's approach was the result of contact made by Gilmartin and Richard Forman with Grosvenor Holdings, one of the largest investors in the British retail and property market. Gilmartin had agreed to help negotiate the Grosvenor investment, despite the breakdown of relations with his fellow-members of the board. O'Callaghan had failed to attract any significant investment, and the bank asked Gilmartin to get the necessary funds, despite his own financial difficulties.

Similarly, the interest in Quarryvale shown by some of Britain's largest retail chains, including Marks and Spencer, Debenham's, John Lewis and Topshop, as well as some of the major Irish retailers, had been prompted by approaches from Gilmartin. This vital assistance, however—which ultimately ensured the success of the retail scheme— did not imply any reconciliation with O'Callaghan or the bank. So frustrated and disillusioned was Gilmartin that he told Basquille that he had considered accepting an offer from a British television company to co-operate with its investigation into planning corruption in Ireland. This followed the publicity surrounding the offer of a £10,000 reward in August 1995 by a Newry solicitor, Kevin Neary, on behalf of two Dublin environmentalists and lawyers, Michael Smith and Colm Mac Eochaidh, to anyone who could provide information that led to a criminal conviction in relation to planning irregularities. Mary Basquille noted in a memo of her conversation with Gilmartin: 'I responded that the bank would be alarmed that any director/shareholder/interested party in Barkhill would take any action which may jeopardise the successful outcome to the company's current development plans and negotiations with anchor tenants. However, he subsequently reverted to his old story of being cheated out of his company and indicated his belief that he will never see any return out of the Quarryvale development.'

With Grosvenor lined up to make a significant investment in the project, and Gilmartin effectually frozen out of the Quarryvale scheme and Barkhill, it was no surprise that O'Callaghan and his partner, John Deane, sensed a bonanza in prospect even before a brick was laid on the site. On 15 November 1995 Gilmartin's solicitor, Seamus Maguire, wrote to Deane and AIB stating that his client was willing to sell his holding in Barkhill because of his financial difficulties, an offer that was duly accepted by the other shareholders. A month later Gilmartin entered negotiations for a buy-out by Riga Ltd of his shareholding but repudiated the 'heads of agreement' presented to him during the discussions.

At a board meeting in February 1996 Gilmartin, accompanied by the new solicitor he had retained, Noel Smyth, confronted his fellow-directors from Riga Ltd and AIB and threatened legal action against them over alleged criminal behaviour. According to a bank memo of the heated discussion, Smyth accused the bank of using duress against Gilmartin, who was an 'oppressed shareholder', and said he had advised his client to take legal proceedings against the other shareholders, during which four or five councillors would be subpoenad to give evidence.

'Tom could be described as naïve or stupid or maybe a combination of both,' John Deane noted Smyth as saying, 'but he was an honest man. He had been treated very badly; the situation regarding some of the matters was criminal. When challenged on use of this word he said he would withdraw the word but did not withdraw the implication contained by such a word, that there had been grave and serious misconduct.'

At a meeting later that month Gilmartin agreed not to interfere in the Grosvenor deal, which was concluded in March, following which his interest was purchased by Riga Ltd for £7.675 million. After years of acrimony and hardship Gilmartin walked away from the company he had formed to do business and help assist with job creation in Dublin, vowing that he never wanted to see the sky over the city again. It was a heartbreaking moment for the man who had fought so hard to keep control of his company and project but had been forced out by a combination of circumstances that he did not fully understand.

By making a settlement, the bank and O'Callaghan had conceded that they were at possible risk of litigation by Gilmartin; but at this point he still did not know the full scale of their activities in relation to his company. He had suspicions concerning Dunlop and Shefran Ltd, though they remained unproved; he knew O'Callaghan was in league with a number of politicians, as the latter could not avoid boasting of his influence in high places; and he had direct experience of intimidation and bullying by senior AIB executives. At the end of the day he was beaten and exhausted from his efforts.

Gilmartin's departure from the scene allowed O'Callaghan to pursue his plans without the constant interference of his former partner and to conduct his business with Dunlop, Lawlor and others unencumbered by the restraint of having to inform his fellow-shareholder. AIB, as described by O'Farrell and Basquille in a memo of May 1996 on Barkhill Ltd, was committed to its 'continued support to enable O'Callaghan obtain zoning and planning,' praising him and Deane for 'being unstinting in their efforts over the past five years' and stating that they 'have been outstanding in their delivery.'

With the stadium project frozen, Frank Dunlop realised that he was unlikely to reap the expected harvest from his 25 per cent stake in Leisure Ireland or Leisure West Ltd for 'the Big One' but continued to press O'Callaghan for £1 million, which he claimed to be due for his efforts on the project and on Quarryvale. (See appendix 1, paragraph 32.)

Following the exit of Gilmartin, Dunlop was on a retainer of £5,000 a month from Barkhill Ltd, while he was also paid £100,000 in early 1997 'for professional services rendered.' Liam Lawlor secured a cut of £25,000 from this latter amount, sending an invoice on the fraudulently obtained stationery of Ganley International, the company owned by the businessman Declan Ganley, with London and Albanian addresses. Lawlor had already received, directly or indirectly, some £81,000 from O'Callaghan between 1991 and 1996. While his political connections at Government level were not what they used be, because Fianna Fáil was in opposition between 1995 and 1997, there was in O'Callaghan's mind a reason to be confident that the party would soon return to its 'proper position' in government. He had good reason to encourage its return following a spat during the summer of 1995, when his efforts to secure state-owned land at Horgan's Quay in Cork led to political controversy, including the demotion of the Minister for Defence and the Marine, Hugh Coveney of Fine Gael, and subsequently a full-blown crisis that contributed ultimately to the resignation of the then Minister for Communications and Energy, Michael Lowry.

The controversy erupted in the summer of 1995 when Lowry alleged that a 'cosy cartel' operated in the purchase of the assets of state-sponsored companies and refused to sanction the purchase by O'Callaghan of three acres of land from CIE at Horgan's Quay along the River Lee. The purchase was subsequently sanctioned but not before Coveney was demoted to the more junior position of minister of state from his senior Government post after it emerged that he had inappropriately sought to get work for his firm of quantity surveyors in Cork from the state-sponsored Bord Gáis, of which O'Callaghan was a board member. O'Callaghan claimed to Gilmartin that he had influenced the resignation of Coveney, an assertion that was in line with others he had made to establish his powerful political connections and patronage, particularly in Cork. Coveney, a popular figure in Cork political and sailing circles, died some years later in a tragic accident.

Among those who defended O'Callaghan in the Dáil over the Horgan's Quay controversy were two of the TDs to whom he had made significant payments over previous years, Batt O'Keeffe and Liam Lawlor. The Cork TD Mícheál Martin, who had received a donation of €5,000 from O'Callaghan in June 1991 during the local government elections, also defended him during the Dáil exchanges. Meanwhile the public-relations advice and lobbying activity required to ensure his ultimate acquisition of the Horgan's Quay lands were provided by Frank Dunlop. Michael Lowry was later forced from office over the revelation that he had accepted financial benefits, including a major house renovation, from the retail millionaire Ben Dunne.

————

After the ousting of Gilmartin, O'Callaghan renewed his links with Bertie Ahern, whom he met again when he visited the Quarryvale site, now being developed as Liffey Valley Shopping Centre, in November 1996. Here, according to Ahern, they once again discussed the stalled stadium project. It was only after Ahern's appointment as Taoiseach following the return to office of Fianna Fáil, now in coalition with the Progressive Democrats after the June 1997 general election, that yet another proposal to build a stadium on the Neilstown lands emerged.

The journalist, broadcaster and former international footballer Eamon Dunphy was informally advising on a project that involved bringing a London soccer club, Wimbledon Football Club, to Dublin, where it would host English Premier League games. Having been asked by the manager of the financially challenged club, Joe Kinnear, another former Irish international, to explore the possibility of moving the club to Dublin, Dunphy approached a number of people for financial backing for the project, including the manager of the rock group U2, Paul McGuinness, and the financier Dermot Desmond, before approaching Owen O'Callaghan when he heard of the latter's plan to build a stadium at Neilstown.

The two men became friendly, and Dunphy's connections with the FAI and senior figures in English soccer were potentially helpful to O'Callaghan with the Neilstown project. Dunphy spent a considerable amount of time assisting O'Callaghan, including meetings with the owner of Wimbledon, Sam Hammam, a native of Lebanon. As it turned out, the Wimbledon project foundered as Hammam turned his attention to other sites in Britain. In the course of their meetings and discussions on the project, O'Callaghan complained to Dunphy about the difficulties and cost of doing business in Dublin, in particular the interference of greedy politicians seeking money at every turn.

O'Callaghan met Ahern again in May 1998 to discuss the prospect of Government support for the stadium project, which now had an estimated cost of £55 million. Ahern was apparently still prepared to talk to O'Callaghan about the stadium, even though over the years he had publicly, but unsuccessfully, argued for the construction of a new sports stadium, which the media labelled the 'Bertie Bowl', at a site along the M50 motorway at Abbotstown in north county Dublin. The Neilstown venture did not succeed either, and the sixty-one acres there were later sold by O'Callaghan and Deane, at a profit of some £12 million.

While the stadium project was now dead in the water, the construction of Liffey Valley Shopping Centre at Quarryvale was well under way, with Councillor Therese Ridge turning the sod in 1997 and the retail cap lifted on the recommendation of the South Dublin county manager in September 1998, as predicted by O'Callaghan.

Owen O'Callaghan may have been justified in thinking he had jumped the final hurdle in his gigantic efforts to control, and build on, the Quarryvale site as the official opening of Liffey Valley Shopping Centre approached. However, another obstacle to his ambitions was also taking shape, in the form of the Flood Tribunal.

Chapter 9 ～

'I DON'T WANT TO SEE THE SKY OVER DUBLIN AGAIN'

Ray Burke TD was appointed Minister for Foreign Affairs in the Fianna Fáil-Progressive Democrats coalition by the incoming Taoiseach, Bertie Ahern, after the 1997 general election. Questions were raised about his suitability for office because of previous allegations that he had received substantial corrupt payments from business interests. Burke strenuously denied the allegations, details of which I first published in the *Sunday Business Post* in 1996 and 1997.

The allegations were based largely on interviews I carried out with a retired businessman, James Gogarty, a former chairman and director of the Dublin engineering firm Joseph Murphy Structural Engineers, who claimed to have been present in Burke's house in Swords, county Dublin, in 1989 when his employer, Joseph Murphy (junior), and a builder, Michael Bailey, gave a large cash payment to Burke during that year's general election campaign and in relation to the rezoning of land.

For months senior Fianna Fáil sources insisted there were no grounds for the allegations; but as the 1997 election approached there was heightened media interest in the story and a certain nervousness within the party about the potential negative impact on its electoral support.

After voting concluded on the day of the election, I met Bertie Ahern in the Goose Tavern, a pub in Marino, Dublin, when he asked me to explain the allegations concerning Burke. I informed him generally about the claims by Gogarty; he responded by stating that he would 'not have a fucking Michael Lowry' in his Government—a reference to the former Fine Gael minister forced to resign from the outgoing Government. I also advised the man who expected to win the election and become Taoiseach that a visit to James Gogarty's home a few miles away would provide any evidence he might need to assist with his inquiries into the allegations against Burke.

After he appointed Burke to his first Government, Ahern famously said he had climbed every tree in north Dublin in his investigation of the allegations of corruption against his new Minister for Foreign Affairs and found no basis for them.

Burke had served as chairperson of Dublin County Council in the mid-1980s, when allegations of improper payments to councillors by developers and builders regularly surfaced, and had been the subject of media investigations into money he received from the house-builders Brennan and McGowan as far back as 1974. In an emotional Dáil speech in his defence he complained about my investigation into the manner in which he obtained his house in Swords from the same building company, while vigorously denying the Gogarty allegations. Nevertheless, within months of his appointment the allegations of corruption had become an ever-increasing source of embarrassment to his party and the Government, and Burke resigned from the cabinet and the Dáil in October 1997. In the course of a Dáil speech on the controversy, Ahern protested that Burke was a good man who was unfairly 'hounded out of office' by certain journalists.

These allegations, and the widespread belief that there was extensive corruption in the planning process during a time of rapid expansion in the city, led to the setting up of the Tribunal of Inquiry into Certain Planning Matters and Payments. Established by order of the Oireachtas in October 1997 and chaired by a retired High Court judge, Feargus Flood, it quickly became known as the Flood Tribunal.

While the tribunal's legal team was preparing the ground for public hearings into the various matters concerning Ray Burke, it came across a record of the Garda investigation in 1989 into the allegations by Tom Gilmartin about planning corruption and the manner in which he was being blocked from progressing his projects at Bachelor's Walk and Quarryvale. The investigation exonerated those whom Gilmartin had accused of wrongdoing, and claimed that Gilmartin refused to co-operate with the inquiry. In 1990 the Garda inquiry had ended up on the desk of the then Minister for Justice, Ray Burke, and nothing had been heard of it since.

The tribunal lawyers wondered why Gilmartin had refused to co-operate, and sought him out. It was not very difficult to track him down: they found his home telephone number in Luton in a copy of the brochure setting out the details of the proposed Quarryvale scheme that had been prepared for the public launch of the project in 1990.

A barrister for the tribunal, John Gallagher SC, also had contact with Father Liam Murtagh, a priest from his native county Mayo who had worked for many years in Luton and who knew Gilmartin.

In the early spring of 1998 Gilmartin received a phone call from Dublin Castle, where the tribunal of inquiry had its offices. The tribunal team wanted to talk to him. His first impulse was to ignore the request. He did not want to revisit those years in Dublin when his reputation and his livelihood were brought to the edge of destruction. A tribunal lawyer, Pat Hanratty SC, told him he was coming to London with his colleagues, including Judge Flood himself.

Small in stature, Feargus Flood had a reputation as a genial and fair-minded judge but tough when he was required to be. At their first meeting, in the Trust House Forte Hotel at Heathrow Airport, which Gilmartin had reluctantly agreed to attend, the atmosphere was frosty. Flood handed Gilmartin a letter setting out the terms of reference of the tribunal. He formally explained his role to the potential witness: he said he had been appointed by the Oireachtas as sole member of a tribunal to investigate irregularities in the planning process in Dublin. His decision to attend the meeting was to assure the potential witness of the *bona fides* of the tribunal and his own determination to get to the truth of the allegations it had received.

Gilmartin read the letter and began to laugh. When the judge asked what was so funny, Gilmartin replied that he thought he was being told a joke. 'I told the lawyers that I'd heard a lot of Irish jokes over the past forty years in England,' he later recalled. 'Some of them were corny, some offensive, and some of them funny, but this was the funniest one of all. This takes the biscuit.'

Asked why he felt that way, Gilmartin told Flood: 'You were probably appointed a judge by Charles Haughey. Now you hand me a letter saying that you are hired by the same people who caused me all these problems, and that you are to report back to them. That's the funniest thing ever.'

After this brief exchange, the judge left the room, leaving Gilmartin to wonder whether he had departed in anger at his remarks. However, Flood was merely complying with his responsibilities: under the procedures of the tribunal he did not attend interviews with potential witnesses.

The two barristers, John Gallagher and Pat Hanratty, accompanied by the tribunal solicitor Máire Ann Howard, asked Gilmartin why he had failed to co-operate with the Garda investigation into his complaints nine years earlier. They were shocked when he told them about the phone call he had received from a man describing himself as a senior Garda who told him to drop his complaint and 'fuck off back to England.' Asked by John Gallagher, himself a former detective-garda, why he didn't report this extraordinary intervention by an alleged member of the force, or take legal action, Gilmartin replied: 'It would be like going to law with the Devil and the court in Hell.'

Although the lawyers were shocked by the abusive comment made by the unidentified caller, it was some of his other remarks and his wording as reported by Gilmartin that made them sit up and take notice. Gilmartin said the caller mentioned that other people like him had made spurious allegations in the past about respected public figures but that they subsequently emerged from investigations with their reputation unsullied and unscathed. When he used the term 'unscathed', not one in the plain-speaking Sligo man's normal lexicon, Gallagher and Hanratty looked at each other in surprise. This was a term used in the 1990 Garda report, which Gilmartin had never seen and was not even aware existed. It made the tribunal team even more anxious to get Gilmartin to co-operate.

Gilmartin had been advised by his Dublin solicitor, Noel Smyth, to co-operate only if he was granted immunity by the Director of Public Prosecutions. He did not believe he required it, as he had done nothing wrong, but it was requested by the tribunal chairman on his behalf, and given.

At this first meeting Gilmartin told the lawyers that he had long left his experience in Dublin behind him and that his family, and his wife in particular, did not want him to get involved with their investigation now. 'I don't want to see the sky over Dublin again,' he told them.

However, after further probing he agreed to show the two investigators some documents he had brought with him to the meeting. Among them was a list of payments to Shefran Ltd and to Frank Dunlop from Barkhill Ltd, compiled by the accountancy firm Deloitte and Touche. Included among the documents was a request from the accountants to Gilmartin to explain a series of large round-figure sums paid out on foot of invoices raised by Shefran Ltd and Dunlop for work done, ostensibly for Barkhill. Gilmartin suggested that the lawyers might investigate why these payments were made by Barkhill to a company of which he had no knowledge and with which he had had no dealings while in Dublin.

Before they departed, Hanratty and Gallagher asked him again to co-operate with the tribunal, which, they insisted, was serious about its work. Gilmartin was not convinced. But despite his initial reluctance and scepticism, and with the encouragement of his son Thomas, he did meet the tribunal's legal team on a number of further occasions during 1998 at Heathrow Airport and in Luton. On one occasion he was accompanied by his solicitor, Noel Smyth. Smyth had represented the businessman Ben Dunne at the Moriarty Tribunal, which was investigating payments to politicians, including Charles Haughey, and knew something of the pitfalls of the process. He had already warned Gilmartin to secure immunity from any possible prosecution if he was to give any further assistance to the inquiry. He also advised him to meet tribunal lawyers only in the company of a solicitor, advice that Gilmartin did not always follow.

Over several meetings with the tribunal lawyers in the Strathmore Hotel in Luton, Gilmartin provided an outline of his extraordinary story and of his dealings with various council officials, councillors, senior politicians, bankers and businessmen following his return to Ireland to develop his projects in 1986.

Though Gallagher and Hanratty were by now thoroughly familiar with the manner in which the former minister Ray Burke had taken corrupt payments and withheld money intended for Fianna Fáil during the 1989 general election campaign, they were not prepared for the level of alleged corruption unveiled by Gilmartin. His story shocked the lawyers, who were well used to extraordinary tales about political malpractice in Ireland. If even a portion of it was true it was the most dramatic account of corruption that the seasoned barristers had heard.

Over the course of several weeks in the spring and summer of 1998 the lawyers tried to piece together the complex story, a task complicated by the fact that, not surprisingly, they were sceptical about some of Gilmartin's claims, which, if proved, would implicate politicians at the highest level. They were also hampered in following a number of trails by their work load and the time consumed in their preparations for the public hearings into planning corruption, which began in early 1999.

Gilmartin's accounts and recollections of dates and events were not always exact, something that gave people reason to cast doubts on some of his claims; but it is important to point out that he was asked by the tribunal investigators to give them, essentially, every piece of information he had. This included not just his first-hand experiences but also second-hand information that had been passed on to him, hearsay, and phone calls telling him of other corrupt practices. Of course, outside his own direct experience he had no way of knowing if some of the things he had heard about certain politicians or business people were true; but he passed on all this information, describing the manner in which he had obtained it, so it was up to the investigators to pursue it if they thought it was warranted. Over time, however, a degree of trust was built as Gilmartin provided leads that supported his account and that tallied with important aspects of information the lawyers had independently obtained from other sources.

While he was prepared to provide some information to the inquiry, Gilmartin was wary of any deeper engagement, not least because of his scepticism of it ever getting at the truth or making any of the great and powerful he had encountered during his time in Dublin account for their misdeeds.

Inevitably word soon emerged in political circles in Dublin that Gilmartin was meeting representatives of the tribunal to discuss allegations of serious political corruption. Contacted by journalists from several newspapers, he soon learnt that his version of events was being disputed and that he was being portrayed as something of a loose cannon, a man who had a massive chip on his shoulder because of his failure to make a success of his business ventures in Ireland.

I spoke to Tom Gilmartin for the first time from the *Sunday Business Post* offices in late summer 1998 and heard a story of alleged corruption that dwarfed all the other investigations I had been involved in over recent years in its political significance and complexity. I had previously broken the story of the Burke payments and had investigated and reported on a range of other corrupt activities involving politicians, public officials, members of the Garda Síochána and rogue business people, but Gilmartin's litany of complaints, which he related over an hour-long conversation, was stunning if it was true. I had phoned him in Luton after obtaining his number from the businessman Colm Scallon (a brother-in-law of the singer-turned-politician Rosemary 'Dana' Scallon). I had been given Scallon's name by the former Taoiseach Albert Reynolds, who first informed me of the emergence of this potentially important new witness at the Flood Tribunal.

Gilmartin was at first reluctant to engage with me, not least because he felt he had been badly served by the media, including the *Sunday*

Business Post, during his time in Dublin in the early 1990s. I told him I was not familiar with any stories written about him at the time, and as the conversation continued he outlined his experience in the city and the various untrustworthy politicians and business people he encountered, as well as their complicit lackeys in the public service and the media.

After the lengthy phone call we agreed to maintain contact, though he insisted that he was not, and perhaps would never be, prepared to go public with his claims. What struck me was his apparent willingness to discuss in such detail and with such openness his personal and commercial affairs with someone, and that someone a journalist, to whom he had never spoken previously. What was also evident was that his story, if true, was by far the most explosive that I had gathered since joining the newspaper in 1993, notwithstanding the convulsions caused by the corruption revelations concerning the former minister Ray Burke.

In September 1998, and completely out of the blue, Gilmartin claimed that he received a phone call from Pádraig Flynn, speaking from his office in the EU Commission in Brussels. Flynn was agitated, as he had been asked a series of questions by the *Sunday Independent* relating to the alleged payment of £50,000 he had received from Gilmartin in 1989. The paper reported that Flynn denied receiving any such payment. He refused to comment any further, despite persistent calls from across the political spectrum for him to do so. He told Gilmartin that there were suspicions that the donation had not been passed on to the party, as intended, and that the tribunal was investigating the matter. The distressed Flynn said he would fly to London and travel to Harpenden in Hertfordshire, near Luton, to try to sort matters out with Gilmartin directly. He claimed he was being 'hung out to dry' by elements in his own party who did not trust the so-called 'country-and-western brigade', a name given to the group of rural TDs around Albert Reynolds (a former country music and dancehall promoter in the midlands), with which he was associated. Reynolds believed he had been shafted as Taoiseach and party leader in 1994 by Bertie Ahern and his Dublin party faction after less than three years in office. Flynn was suggesting to Gilmartin that people around, and possibly including, Ahern were behind the revelations concerning the £50,000 donation.

What upset Gilmartin about this and other conversations he had during this time was the rumour that the money was a bribe. According to Gilmartin, Flynn first suggested that Gilmartin might tell the tribunal that the donation had been returned. Then he asked Gilmartin to say, if he was asked by the tribunal, that he had given the £50,000 as a personal donation to Flynn to cover his election expenses in 1989. Gilmartin insisted that the money was intended for the party, and added that he would perjure himself for no-one. He advised Flynn that it would be unwise for him to come to visit him in Luton, as the tribunal lawyers were regularly in the area.

After several phone calls from Flynn, Gilmartin told him that he did not intend to make any further public comment and that he was not inclined to give public evidence at the tribunal. As he lived outside the jurisdiction, he could not be compelled to attend public hearings. He also told Flynn he did not consider him to be the most corrupt individual he had come across during his days in Dublin, though he reminded him that he had done little to help him when he was being abused by others.

On 27 September 1998, under the heading 'Developer claims he gave Flynn £50,000 for FF funds,' I published details of Gilmartin's claim in the *Sunday Business Post* and the fact that he had agreed, on legal advice, to co-operate with the tribunal. Over successive weeks, and on the basis of conversations with Gilmartin, extensive details of his claims emerged in the *Sunday Business Post* and *Sunday Independent.*

In early October 1998 it was reported that Gilmartin had agreed to testify to the tribunal in relation to the Flynn cheque, and that he had been offered immunity from prosecution by the inquiry. He provided both newspapers with copies of the queries raised by his company auditors, Deloitte and Touche, regarding Frank Dunlop and Shefran Ltd. He was particularly incensed at Dunlop, whom he blamed for much of the adverse media spin against him over many years in Dublin.

Dunlop agreed to meet me to discuss the claims, and in the Temple Bar Hotel in the city I presented him with copies of the material faxed to me by Gilmartin. For all his experience as a professional spin-doctor and former Fianna Fáil press officer, Dunlop admitted more than I expected at this meeting, which he agreed to allow me record on tape. He confirmed that Shefran Ltd was his company, and that he had been given substantial payments in respect of the Quarryvale project over the years, some of which were based on invoices that did not include a charge for value-added tax. He could not explain why the invoices were VAT-free. The payments to him were made through the offshore company, he stated, in order to hide from Gilmartin his involvement in the Quarryvale project, and he admitted that he had been retained as a lobbyist-cum-fixer in early 1991 by Owen O'Callaghan without Gilmartin's knowledge. He also admitted that he was employed by O'Callaghan to help deliver the necessary council votes to steer the Quarryvale development through the complexities of the planning process and to negotiate other political obstacles.

His admissions in the autumn of 1998 had adverse tax implications for Dunlop, who had clearly not declared his full income over the preceding years to the Revenue Commissioners, including huge sums he received in fees from Owen O'Callaghan. Indeed, he conceded through his accountant to a tax inspector that a Revenue audit in 1994 had 'withered on the vine'.

On 4 October 1998 I reported that Dunlop had admitted that he was paid £500,000 for his assistance with securing rezoning and planning permissions in relation to the Quarryvale development over a period of seven years. It was clear from his admissions that the source of these funds was Owen O'Callaghan, and that payments had been made to elected politicians from those funds. (See appendix 1, paragraph 33.)

Following the publication of these admissions in the *Sunday Business Post* in October 1998, Dunlop phoned me. He was angry, and somewhat colourfully said that if he had a shotgun and I was beside him he would shoot me. He appeared to believe that journalists should not report unpalatable facts concerning him, even when he had provided the information. For years he had used his contacts with several influential political and business journalists in the city to place stories in the media. I did not consider it my job to massage stories for the benefit of any source, PR expert or otherwise, and was confident that Dunlop had volunteered the information we published after being faced with the damning material provided to me by Gilmartin about Shefran Ltd and some of the spin-doctor's other activities.

Two days after the article was published Dunlop was served with an order directing him to attend the tribunal and provide extensive documentary evidence on his financial and business affairs.

———

In return for honouring commitments to Gilmartin about the manner in which we would treat the documents he provided, a relationship of trust between us, so essential to proper journalism, was slowly established and was consolidated after a number of meetings in Luton.

During the autumn of 1998 the *Sunday Business Post* also revealed details of Liam Lawlor's extraordinary consultancy arrangement with Arlington Securities, which had netted him a total of £35,000. At first Lawlor confirmed to me that the payments were consultancy fees, but a week later he claimed they were political donations. He had apparently realised that his earlier admission could attract the unwanted attention of the Revenue Commissioners, to whom the income had not been disclosed.

As Christmas approached there was frenetic activity within the political system, and within Fianna Fáil in particular, as well as among Gilmartin's former business partners, in response to the news that he was talking to the tribunal. Some months earlier, dozens of former and current councillors and TDs had received lengthy questionnaires from the tribunal, seeking information they might have in relation to improper zoning and whether they were in receipt of any payments in respect of planning matters during their political careers.

At the Fianna Fáil ard-fheis in late November 1998 there was intense discussion in the bars and restaurants around the RDS Conference Centre in Ballsbridge. That weekend it emerged that the tribunal had written to several parties in relation to the Gilmartin allegations, and had sought relevant financial records. The recipients of these letters included Allied Irish Banks, Owen O'Callaghan, Riga Ltd, O'Callaghan's solicitor and partner John Deane, and Frank Dunlop and his company, Frank Dunlop and Associates. The letters came after the tribunal barristers Gallagher and Hanratty had obtained a sworn statement from Gilmartin in Luton in late September concerned primarily with his dealings with Pádraig Flynn, Liam Lawlor and Frank Dunlop, as well as his relationship with Owen O'Callaghan.

It was enough to set the cat among the pigeons in Dublin and Cork, where various parties, served by the tribunal with the letters and orders for discovery (i.e. the production of documents), scrambled to prepare their defence. Frank Dunlop immediately panicked and, in early October, urgently sought money from O'Callaghan to help clear his tax liabilities. O'Callaghan agreed to pay Dunlop £300,000, plus VAT of £63,000, which Dunlop, it later emerged, used to cover outstanding tax bills.

By coincidence, the newly completed Liffey Valley Shopping Centre at Quarryvale was due to be officially opened, and the Taoiseach, Bertie

Ahern, had accepted an invitation six months earlier to perform the honours. Word spread around the ard-fheis that Ahern had decided not to attend the opening, given the interest the tribunal had taken in its controversial history.

On the Sunday following the ard-fheis an article suggesting that the tribunal had contacted various parties, including O'Callaghan, Riga Ltd, AIB, Dunlop, Gilmartin and others in relation to Quarryvale appeared in the *Sunday Independent*, which sparked an angry reaction from O'Callaghan. The letters included an order for extensive discovery of financial records from all those contacted. Hot on the heels of the story a delegation of lawyers, led by Michael McDowell for O'Callaghan and Colm Allen for Dunlop, attended a less than friendly encounter with Feargus Flood and his tribunal in Dublin Castle.

In his opening remarks at the two-day private session, on 9 and 10 December 1998, McDowell railed at the inquiry for its alleged leaks of the recent correspondence to his client that had appeared in the *Sunday Independent*, which he said had committed a 'serious criminal offence'. He demanded that criminal and civil action be taken against the paper for hindering the tribunal and to prevent it publishing further confidential information concerning his client. He also argued that the scale of the discovery order issued by the tribunal, seeking information from O'Callaghan and his companies from the time of their incorporation in 1988, was too extensive and that it was not justified by the allegations that some elected councillors in Dublin had taken payments. He wanted to know the nature of the allegations against his client and Dunlop and complained that 'very onerous orders' had been made not only against O'Callaghan but against 'his accountants, his bankers and his PR consultants.' He said that while 'some people have a vested interest in collapsing the scrum,' i.e. bringing down the tribunal, through the leaking of confidential information, his client was not one of them. However, he said, Owen O'Callaghan had suffered 'serious grief, serious damage, and serious injury' to his reputation.

Colm Allen also complained that his client, Frank Dunlop, had been treated unfairly and called for action against the journalist in question and his editor. 'If necessary lock them up,' Allen said. He told the tribunal that he had seen a newspaper photographer outside the building before he entered that morning and that he was concerned that details of the confidential discussion might appear in the following edition of the

Sunday Independent, and that he might be blamed as the source of another leak. 'I have a very uncomfortable feeling, speaking personally, that if something appears in the newspapers on Sunday about the fact that Mr McDowell was screeching to have that newspaper with which he is so intimately connected dragged through the courts, and probably writing an article on page 6 of the same edition, I would be afraid that I would be accused of having done it,' he said.

Unfortunately for the barristers, the information that appeared in the *Sunday Independent* on 22 November was not leaked from the tribunal. 'The story did not come from the tribunal,' its author Jody Corcoran insisted later, although he declined to reveal its source. Indeed, Corcoran said he never received any direct leaks from the tribunal.

Some months later, in July 1999, Michael McDowell was appointed Attorney-General and could no longer represent O'Callaghan at the tribunal.

At another private session with Judge Flood and his legal team some days earlier, Liam Lawlor's senior counsel, Adrian Hardiman, also complained about an order directing his client to attend the tribunal for questioning. Hardiman contended that the tribunal did not have the jurisdiction to make such an order, and also submitted that it was 'manifestly unjust' that a request was made for discovery of all bank accounts and financial transactions on the basis of an allegation against Lawlor that he described as 'bizarre', 'incredible', 'crazy stuff', and 'intrinsically unworthy of belief.' The 'bizarre' allegation was that Lawlor had described himself as a 'representative of the Irish Government' when demanding a share of Arlington Securities' proposed development in Dublin.

Adrian Hardiman was appointed a judge of the Supreme Court in February 2000 and, consequently, ended his position as counsel for Lawlor.

Not surprisingly, Tom Gilmartin was having second thoughts about giving public evidence, particularly in the light of what he was hearing from various sources in Ireland. Among the first suggestions put about by those seeking to damage his credibility was that the payment to Pádraig Flynn was a bribe by Gilmartin in order to get a lucrative tax designation for the planned development at Bachelor's Walk.

Ray MacSharry also made efforts to contact Gilmartin. Through a mutual friend, who contacted Peter Kearns in Cork, a request purporting to come from MacSharry sought to have Gilmartin sign a statement to the effect that they had never met. A note containing this request was faxed to Cork and on to Gilmartin's home in Luton, but Gilmartin would have none of it. He distinctly recalled meeting MacSharry to talk about his business plans on two occasions in 1987, once in his ministerial offices and again in MacSharry's constituency office in Sligo. He declined the request, maintaining his insistence that he was not going to be dragged into the Dublin tribunal and the controversy surrounding it.

Ray MacSharry told the tribunal that a fax message sent to Gilmartin asking that he sign a document stating that he had no dealings with himself was sent 'without my knowledge.' (Tribunal transcript: day 856, question 25.) During his evidence MacSharry also confirmed that he had arranged to obtain Gilmartin's phone number in Luton and had passed it to the then EU commissioner Pádraig Flynn in August 1998. This was at a time when Flynn was panicking over Gilmartin's statements to the tribunal lawyers in relation to the £50,000 given to Flynn and intended for Fianna Fáil and was desperately seeking to contact him in Luton.

Following a brief media and political flurry, the public controversy receded and the news agenda moved on, until, on 15 January 1999, Pádraig Flynn accepted an invitation to appear on the country's most popular television chat show, after which all hell broke loose.

PART 2

The witness

Chapter 10

'A PERSONAL POLITICAL DONATION'

The media flurry surrounding Tom Gilmartin at his home in Luton when the details of his allegations were first published had abated, but not for long, as the self-destructive appearance by Pádraig Flynn on the 'Late Late Show' revived the story and led more journalists to his door seeking interviews or comment.

As the fall-out from Flynn's television appearance continued, Gilmartin made a number of statements that included references to his meetings with the Taoiseach, Bertie Ahern. He claimed he had met Ahern on a number of occasions and, he recalled, was even asked by him during one conversation in June 1989 if he would consider making a contribution to Fianna Fáil. Gilmartin claimed he then informed Ahern that he had already made a donation, to Pádraig Flynn. He said he did not know Flynn or any other politicians particularly well but that he had met Ahern more often than he had met Flynn. He also said that Ahern had assisted him with the purchase of land from Dublin City Council in 1989 and had sent his friend and then city councillor Joe Burke to meet him in connection with this. He said that Burke had also asked him to make a financial contribution at a later meeting in Dublin.

In his first public response to questions about his knowledge of Gilmartin, Ahern sought to distance himself when he told the Dáil he had met him no more than once, he believed, in 1988. Gilmartin insisted that he had met Ahern on four occasions, including once at the Taoiseach's former Department of Labour offices in October 1987.

'I have no argument with the man,' Ahern told the Dáil. 'I met him ten years ago. I just remember meeting him once. It's either that or he appeared somewhere else on other occasions and made no impression on me whatsoever. But I have no recollection of meeting Mr Gilmartin on any other occasions. I have checked with my people in departments where I served—Finance and Labour—and two staff [members] who worked with me in 1987 and 1988 are still with me. None of us have any recollection of Mr Gilmartin meeting me.' He also said he had 'no recollection of any telephone conversation with Mr Gilmartin and equally, therefore, I have no recollection of any conversation with him relating to contributions to the party or Mr Flynn.'

Commenting on 24 January 1999, Gilmartin recalled the phone conversation in 1989 when, he said, the then Minister for Labour asked him to make a financial contribution to Fianna Fáil. 'I was stunned. I couldn't believe what I was hearing, because a few months earlier I had given £50,000 to Fianna Fáil. I told him I gave a cheque to Pádraig Flynn. He didn't say anything to that.'

Elaborating on the circumstances surrounding the payment, Gilmartin said he was being told by senior party figures that a donation would help him overcome the obstacles he appeared to be meeting to his business plans. 'It was suggested to me that the best way to ease all the pressure was to make a donation to the party,' Gilmartin told the media. 'That's why I gave the £50,000 cheque to Mr Flynn, who was a Fianna Fáil treasurer. I asked no favours for the money, and none was given. I couldn't have cared less who it was made payable to. All I wanted was to get Fianna Fáil off my back . . . When I refused to cough up more they closed ranks and screwed me big time. Eventually I had to go back to England with my tail between my legs.'

The Taoiseach was now placed firmly and publicly in the frame of the Gilmartin allegations, and it was widely accepted that he could become the subject of investigation by the tribunal, the establishment of which he had proposed to the Oireachtas two years previously. Ahern's priority in his first term as Taoiseach was the stability of his Government, now in its second year in office, especially as the junior coalition party, the Progressive Democrats, had been formed in the mid-1980s largely in response, its leaders claimed, to the growing concerns about the ethical standards of Fianna Fáil and its then leader, Charles Haughey. Mary Harney and her party justified their involvement in coalition by establishing themselves as the moral guardians of the larger party in office. Now a growing scandal involving possibly improper payments to yet another former Fianna Fáil minister had arisen, and Harney was already making noises concerning her continuing participation in the Government.

Back in Brussels, Pádraig Flynn was of little or no help to his party leader at home. Deflecting persistent questions about his role in the affair, he said he was refusing to comment until he came before the Flood Tribunal. It was reported that he refused to respond to the calls from Ahern and senior Fianna Fáil ministers asking him to 'clarify' his position in relation to the alleged payment and said he had every intention of completing his term as EU commissioner, which was due to expire later in the year. 'I'm not making any comment, because one comment just leads to a repetition of the question. And I have made the point that any matters that are proper to the tribunal should be dealt with by the tribunal. If it is proper for me to go there then I will be most happy to oblige.'

Following Gilmartin's claim that he had four meetings with Ahern and spoke to him by telephone on several more occasions during those years, the Taoiseach decided to make a detailed statement in the Dáil about his relationship with the developer. His statement, delivered on Wednesday 27 January 1999, was remarkable for its length, running to eight typed pages.

After some introductory remarks, which included his concern that deputies should 'not undermine the integrity of the tribunal' in 'pursuit of immediate political advantage or otherwise,' Ahern confirmed his personal support for the corruption inquiry. He challenged Gilmartin to make his claims at the tribunal and to face rigorous cross-examination. After promising to fully co-operate with the tribunal, he denied ever asking Gilmartin for a donation to Fianna Fáil at any time. He then confirmed Gilmartin's claim that he had met Joe Burke. 'Former Councillor Joe Burke has confirmed to me that he did meet him but is quite adamant that he did not ask him for or about a contribution to Fianna Fáil, at my behest or otherwise.'

He went on to criticise the intemperate language used by Gilmartin, who was quoted in *The Irish Times* a day previously as stating that, 'even if Bertie Ahern survives this week, he won't survive what I have coming down the line for him.' The comment had been widely repeated on the broadcast media, though Gilmartin later claimed that he had not made the remarks as published. He recalled that he had made some 'off-the-record' remarks to the reporter, including a comment about Ahern. Either way, they provoked an angry response from the Taoiseach in Leinster House. 'I leave it for this house to decide whether this sort of threatening language against a democratically elected Taoiseach is something it would wish to condone or support.'

Ahern insisted that he had not been contacted by the tribunal about any allegations concerning himself made by Gilmartin in his statements to the inquiry team. He then dealt directly with his recollections of meeting Gilmartin during the late 1980s and corrected his early statement in which he claimed to have met Gilmartin on only one occasion. He went on to confirm that his diary and other records showed that he had met Gilmartin in his office over Fagan's pub in Drumcondra on 10 October 1988 and said he was 'accompanied by a local person at that meeting.' The 'local person' was later named as Tim Collins, a member of the trust that purchased St Luke's, a former doctor's surgery at 161 Lower Drumcondra Road, across the road from Fagan's pub, which Ahern used as his constituency office and occasional residence since it was purchased in the late 1980s. Collins was associated with Frank Dunlop in relation to the rezoning of lands at Lissenhall, Cloghran and Kinsealy, county Dublin, that were also the subject of a tribunal investigation.

Having consulted his departmental diaries, Ahern revealed that he also met Gilmartin on 13 October 1988 in his office at the Department of Labour in Mespil Road, and had a further meeting with him on 28 September 1989. He said he had no specific memory of the meetings but was certain that he never discussed the issue of political donations with Gilmartin during their conversations. 'As I have pointed out before, I am quite certain that I would not have solicited a donation for Fianna Fáil from Mr Gilmartin, and I have no recollections of any reference made by him to an alleged £50,000 given to the party treasurer, Mr Pádraig Flynn, in June 1989.'

He also said that he had no record or recollection of the meeting in Leinster House in 1989 during which Gilmartin claimed to have met Charles Haughey and a number of Government ministers, including himself. 'I would have to report to the house that the then Taoiseach's diary contains no record of such a meeting, nor is it recalled by any official likely to have been in a position to know, nor has any record of it, if one existed, so far been found. This does not, of course, absolutely prove that no meeting took place, but we have no corroboration of it. I would also point out that post-1987 the then Taoiseach, Mr Haughey, would not have held meetings involving several people on official business in Leinster House. He would have held them in his own office in Government Buildings.'

Ahern revealed that the general secretary of Fianna Fáil, Martin Mackin, had written to Pádraig Flynn to inquire whether he, or anyone on his behalf, had received £50,000 from Gilmartin. In the letter, dated 6 October 1998, Mackin also asked whether the money, if given, was passed on to Fianna Fáil and, if so, to whom. The letter also inquired whether a receipt had been issued by Fianna Fáil. Almost four months later no reply had been received, and Ahern told the Dáil: 'If I understand them correctly, both Mr Flynn and Mr Gilmartin have denied that any political contribution was made for favours. They have further asserted that no such favours were given or received. It leaves unresolved the question of whether the political contribution allegedly made to Minister Flynn was intended for the national party or for Mr Flynn's own use . . .'

Notwithstanding the detail and length of the statement, the Taoiseach did not fully calm the nerves of his coalition partners, though he had apparently done enough to maintain the Government's stability. While the PD leader, Mary Harney, was said to be upset and disturbed about the claims in relation to Flynn, and privately expressed concern about what else might come out in relation to a number of corruption inquiries, the coalition partners made no explicit threat to bring down the Government. However, for the first time since she entered government with Fianna Fáil in 1997, Harney indicated that her party's support was conditional, stating that Ahern and his party had her confidence 'as of now.'

The statement also failed to satisfy Tom Gilmartin, who nevertheless welcomed the fact that the Taoiseach's memory had improved. 'Last Sunday he hardly knew me. By Monday he could remember one meeting, and by Tuesday he recalled three.'

Visitor records confirmed that on five occasions during 1989 Gilmartin visited the Leinster House complex—3 February, 10 May, 23 May, 20 July and 25 October—being signed in four times by Pádraig Flynn. There was no record of a meeting on 1 February with Haughey and his ministers, though Gilmartin insisted that the date was correct and that he had been escorted into Leinster House by Liam Lawlor.

Flynn remained silent, even when the Government put down a motion calling for him to explain the circumstances surrounding the £50,000 payment. Ahern lost one of his own backbenchers when Flynn's daughter, the Mayo TD Beverly Cooper Flynn, refused to support the Government motion against her father and had the party whip removed from her. She was already embroiled in political controversy following an RTE News report that, while working as an official with National Irish Bank before her involvement in politics, she had assisted clients in evading their tax obligations by channelling their funds into an offshore insurance scheme.[f]

Flynn's difficulties were compounded when, along with the entire EU Commission, he resigned from office over an unrelated controversy, and speculation that he would not be reappointed to the post intensified. Indeed one Fianna Fáil TD, Mary Hanafin, said in response to a media question that Flynn 'had landed himself in a situation where he is unreappointable,' as he was no longer politically acceptable to any of the parties.

In late February 1999 Flynn replied to a letter sent to him by the Taoiseach following the Dáil motion, confirming that he had been dealing with the Flood Tribunal and, on legal advice, was not making any further public comment. It emerged for the first time that Flynn had informed the tribunal that the £50,000 he received from Gilmartin was a 'personal political donation'. Oxymoronic as it appears, this became a favoured term used by politicians to describe unexplained financial rewards.

When Ahern finally met Flynn directly in Brussels on 3 March the two men, it was reported, skirted around the 'donation' issue, and Ahern returned to Ireland without achieving any further clarity on the circumstances of the payment or any closure to the damaging affair.

However, the heat went out of the Flynn-Ahern controversy for the time being while attention refocused on the public hearings and other extraordinary developments surrounding the tribunal of inquiry. The most dramatic was the arrest of the former assistant city and county manager George Redmond in February 1999 as he arrived in Dublin Airport on a flight from the Isle of Man with some £300,000 in cash and cheques in his possession. He claimed the money was to assist with his legal fees, though there was speculation that he had sought to hide it in the Isle of Man but that finance houses there had refused to accept the lodgement and he had been forced to return home with his case full of loot. However they had found out about his overseas trip, detectives from the Criminal Assets Bureau were awaiting Redmond's arrival at the airport, where they intercepted him and seized his briefcase.

It emerged that Redmond had moved considerable funds offshore from 1996 and that he had no less than twenty accounts in more than a dozen banks and building societies. In the decade from 1979 to 1989 he had moved £1.2 million through his various accounts while on an annual public service salary of £29,000. For years he insisted that he earned the extra income in return for advice he gave to builders and developers in Dublin, but he later admitted that he had accepted substantial amounts in bribes. It emerged that he had taken money from a range of business interests, some of which was stashed in the bathroom and garage of his house in Castleknock, county Dublin. Among those who 'looked after' Redmond were the builders Brennan and McGowan, Michael Bailey, and the engineering firm Joseph Murphy Structural Engineers, while he enjoyed the benefit of cash he collected from Jim Kennedy's amusement arcade in the city and the use of his purchase card for a Dublin wholesaler.

In the aftermath of Redmond's arrest I was contacted by Brendan Fassnidge, who claimed he had made a substantial cash payment to Redmond in the late 1980s in return for getting access from the new Lucan Road to his car showrooms in Palmerstown. Fassnidge was later a key witness in an unsuccessful criminal prosecution of Redmond. He also claimed he made a similar payment to Liam Lawlor for the same planning favour, but he did not wish to make that public because of his fear of Lawlor. Fassnidge was the man who first led Lawlor to Gilmartin in 1988 following the latter's request for information in the Bank of Ireland in Lucan about the ownership of the Quarryvale lands.

Lawlor made a visit to the High Court in June 1999 in an effort to halt the tribunal's investigation into his labyrinthine financial affairs. It had found that he had accumulated startling sums—more than £4.6 million—in numerous bank accounts at home and abroad since he was first elected a councillor in 1979. Included in these funds was more than £81,000 that Lawlor received from Owen O'Callaghan in relation to Quarryvale between 1991 and 1996.

Unimpressed by his explanations about the origins of this money, and by his reluctance to provide documents in relation to them, the chairman of the tribunal referred Lawlor to the High Court. His obstruction of the tribunal resulted in a three-month prison sentence and a fine of £10,000 for Lawlor—the first Irish politician to be given a prison sentence in connection with an investigation into planning corruption.

In a separate development that had implications for Gilmartin, another serious crisis engulfed the coalition Government when it emerged that a man called Philip Sheedy who had been sentenced in 1996 to four years' imprisonment in connection with the death of a young woman while he was driving in a drunken condition in Tallaght, county Dublin, had been released after serving only one year. He served four months in Mountjoy Prison before being moved to Shelton Abbey, a low-security open prison in county Wicklow, but less than a year later he was released after he was visited by the Taoiseach's friend Joe Burke. Sheedy had worked as an architect for Burke in the latter's construction business.

In May 1999 it emerged that Bertie Ahern had made representations on Sheedy's behalf to the Department of Justice, and the controversy became a full-blown stability crisis for the Government when it was learnt that Mr Justice Hugh O'Flaherty of the Supreme Court, Mr Justice Cyril Kelly of the High Court and a senior court registrar were also involved in the complex machinations that led to Sheedy's early release from prison. Despite murmurs of dissatisfaction from the PDs, the Government survived the second major political crisis of the year, assisted by the arrival of the lengthy Dáil summer recess. The two judges and the registrar were forced to resign, the latter replaced by Susan Ryan, a solicitor who had been acting for Tom Gilmartin in his dealings with the tribunal. Following her promotion and her resignation from Eugene F. Collins and Company, Gilmartin took on a new firm of legal advisers, A. and L. Goodbody.

The first two years of public hearings in the Flood Tribunal in Dublin Castle were centred on the allegations against former minister Ray Burke and his acceptance of large payments from a number of business interests over his many years in politics. The tribunal had discovered hidden offshore accounts where Burke had secreted hundreds of thousands of pounds, the sources of which he could not, or would not, explain. The tribunal had established that substantial payments, totalling well over £100,000, had been made to Burke in 1989 alone from Joseph Murphy Structural Engineers, Michael Bailey (Bovale Developments), Oliver Barry (founder and chief executive of Century Radio), and Robin Rennick (chief executive of a sign-making company, Rennick's, a subsidiary of Tony O'Reilly's Fitzwilton Group).

When this detailed inquiry involving hundreds of witnesses was complete, the tribunal moved on to others implicated in planning corruption in Dublin. From Gilmartin's viewpoint, a seminal moment in the long-running investigation came on 26 April 2000 when Frank Dunlop admitted that he had given a large number of bribes to several members of Dublin County Council in exchange for their votes on planning and rezoning motions. Dunlop had been warned the previous day to come clean about the circumstances surrounding his 'Rathfarnham (AIB 042)' account in the Terenure branch of AIB, through which hundreds of thousands of pounds had passed.

When he returned to give his evidence, a physically diminished and ashen-faced Dunlop provided the tribunal with lists of the names of councillors he had paid and the developers who had provided him with the money for disbursal. By tracking his evidence back to specific votes and decisions made by the councillors in the late 1980s and early 90s the inquiry was able to establish a pattern that appeared to corroborate Dunlop's claims of corruption against some current and many former members of the county council. As the result of his evidence a string of councillors appeared and reappeared in the course of inquiries into a number of land acquisitions and controversial rezonings throughout county Dublin, from Carrickmines, Monkstown and Bray in the south of the county to Swords, Baldoyle, Lissenhall, Kinsealy and Portmarnock in the north. Dunlop named a number of his developer clients and other business people who were aware that he was bribing public representatives but crucially insisted that the man who was by far his most lucrative source of income, the Cork developer Owen O'Callaghan, did not know of any corrupt payments he made in relation to Quarryvale.

In his evidence to the tribunal Dunlop tarred each of the three main political parties with the same brush and indeed made out that it was a Fine Gael politician, the deceased councillor Tom Hand, who demanded the largest sum of money from him—the request for a staggering £250,000. Clearly his intention was to spread the political muck as far and wide as possible, though he made no allegations against politicians at the higher end of the political food-chain. He also sought to pay back some former cronies who had become his enemies, not least the man he named 'Mr Big' in the corruption stakes. It did not take long to work out that this referred to Liam Lawlor, who was forced, in the wake of a party inquiry into Dunlop's revelations, to resign from Fianna Fáil and from his incongruous role (on Ahern's appointment) as vice-chairperson of the Select Committee on Members' Interests of Dáil Éireann (commonly called the Ethics Committee).

Colm McGrath, an independent councillor, was given the nickname 'Mr Insatiable' by Dunlop, as he always came back looking for more, while Senator Don Lydon, Tony Fox, Marion McGennis, Finbarr Hanrahan, G. V. Wright, the late Seán Gilbride and the late Pat Dunne were some of the Fianna Fáil members from the period who were implicated in Dunlop's evidence. Others he named included the scion of the famous Fine Gael dynasty Liam T. Cosgrave, as well as Therese Ridge and Michael Joe Cosgrave of the same party, while the Progressive Democrat member Colm Tyndall also featured.

For Gilmartin, Dunlop's admissions confirmed what he had suspected for many years but could not prove, specifically his role in bribing politicians to ensure that Owen O'Callaghan could leverage control of the Quarryvale development.

A few weeks after Dunlop gave this evidence to the tribunal he had a meeting with the Taoiseach, Bertie Ahern, according to Dunlop's diary, though it remains unclear why the country's most senior politician would engage with a man who had just confessed publicly to widespread corruption. He also urgently met O'Callaghan, who had reason to be concerned that Dunlop would implicate him in the developing scandal. Dunlop received a further £300,000 at this time from O'Callaghan, ostensibly to go towards his spiralling legal costs, after which he continued to maintain that O'Callaghan had not known of his carousel of corrupt payments.

During the same week that Dunlop confessed to serial bribery and corruption of the political system the *Sunday Business Post* published an article concerning an allegation brought to me by a Cork businessman, Denis O'Brien, and implicating two senior Fianna Fáil politicians in corrupt payments in 1989.

Chapter 11 ∿

| THE STARRY O'BRIEN AFFAIR

O ne of the most bizarre episodes in the tribunal's tortuous inquiry into the murky world of political corruption involved a businessman called Denis O'Brien, known in Cork circles as 'Starry'. O'Brien was a former builder who had been described in 1989 as a perjurer and forger in a judgement following a case taken against him by Ulster Bank.

In early 1999 a phone call came through to my desk at the *Sunday Business Post*. A man with a Cork accent asked me if I would meet him urgently. He was walking up the Liffey quays and was on a mobile phone. I arranged to meet him in a riverside café called the Courts. The man, who seemed to be in his early sixties, identified himself as Denis O'Brien and said he was a businessman and property developer. Over coffee he told me he was on his way to the Law Library to meet lawyers in relation to his involvement with a property company, Edenfell Holdings, as he claimed he had been forced out of a planned housing development on a lucrative site at Carrigaline, county Cork, owned by the company.

He claimed that his experience bore a marked similarity to what happened to Tom Gilmartin, and that he wanted to expose alleged improper dealings involving Cork's leading property developer, Owen O'Callaghan, and some of the country's most powerful politicians, including Bertie Ahern. He said he had documents, including copies of cheques made out to the politicians, bank statements and building society lodgement books that could back up his story.

This was an intriguing new development in the unravelling story about planning corruption in the late 1980s and early 90s from a man who claimed to be not only an insider but one who was prepared to do the dirty work on behalf of richer and more powerful players. In the course of his early conversations with me he conceded that he had been implicated in illicit dealings in the past, having been accused by a High Court judge of perjury and forgery. When we parted we arranged to meet again on the next occasion he came to Dublin, and I passed on the information to my editor, Damien Kiberd. We agreed to maintain a tight veil over the story and to see how it unfolded.

In the following weeks O'Brien visited Dublin frequently, ostensibly to meet his lawyers to discuss his continuing legal battle with Anglo-Irish Bank, which was seeking outstanding debts from him totalling several hundred thousand pounds. He supplied me with extensive documents concerning his dispute with the bank, the Revenue Commissioners, accountancy firms and solicitors. Also among his letters was a personal offer of assistance from the former Taoiseach Charles Haughey, written in the mid-1980s.

At the core of O'Brien's story was his sensational claim that he had personally given Bertie Ahern a cheque for £50,000 in September 1989 in the car park of the Burlington Hotel, Dublin, on the night of the all-Ireland football final. He claimed to have given another former senior politician a cheque, also for £50,000, in the Silver Springs Hotel in Cork at a Fianna Fáil party function in late August or September the same year. He claimed he had met this politician some weeks previously at Kruger's pub in Dún Chaoin, county Kerry, before the politician boarded a helicopter to visit Charles Haughey on the island then owned by the Taoiseach, Inis Mhic Aoibhleáin (also known as Inishvickillane) in the Blasket Islands.

He alleged that the money came from Owen O'Callaghan through a branch of a bank in South Mall, Cork, and that the cheques were issued by Irish Nationwide Building Society in Patrick Street. He had copies of a deposit book for the building society that purported to show the lodgement of the funds on which he later drew the two £50,000 cheques. He assured me that he also had copies of the original cheques but that they were being kept by a former teacher of his, a Christian Brother who lived in Ennis, county Clare.

After a number of discussions, including almost daily telephone conversations, we agreed that he should sign an affidavit before a solicitor outlining his allegations; this would provide some form of protection for the newspaper and also the basis for a formal statement that could be given to the planning tribunal. The prominent Dublin solicitor Padraic Ferry agreed to witness an affidavit made out before him by O'Brien. This was passed to the tribunal's legal team, who called O'Brien for an interview in their offices at Dublin Castle within a matter of days.

If there was a plot to implicate the tribunal in what was at best a wild-goose chase and at worst an exercise to destroy its—and my—credibility it was well on course at this point in early 1999. However, it was clear that any attempt to publish the extraordinary story, which contained a variety of extremely colourful elements, would require much more investigation. To compound the difficulty, the tribunal issued the *Sunday Business Post* with an injunction preventing it from publishing any details of statements given to it by O'Brien, or any details of the existence of the injunction itself. It was in effect a gagging order, not only preventing the publication of O'Brien's sensational claims but also the fact that he had brought them to the tribunal and even the existence of the gagging order itself.

However, there was no shortage of news at the time, and the paper did not intend to lock horns with the tribunal over a story that contained rocket fuel and that was also extremely difficult to substantiate. The politicians involved vehemently denied to the *Sunday Business Post* having received any such bribes in 1989, and O'Callaghan also rejected the allegations. In any case, Denis O'Brien was not exactly the most upstanding and respected citizen in the country, and, more to the point, he had failed to deliver on his main promise, which was a copy of the relevant cheques that he claimed were stored in the religious house in county Clare. A visit by me to the elderly Christian Brother in the house yielded no result, while the tribunal lawyers were also finding that the trail went dry every time they looked into the matter. The brother said he had once looked after some documents for O'Brien but did not know anything of their contents and that they had long since been removed by his former pupil. A visit to Kruger's in Dún Chaoin also failed to yield any corroboration of his claims.

Despite the clear lack of progress, O'Brien was either on the phone daily or else seeking a meeting over coffee on the frequent occasions when he visited Dublin to meet his lawyers or to engage in some obscure property deal on behalf of unidentified clients. He constantly raised the possibility of meeting Tom Gilmartin, given what he claimed were the extraordinary similarities in what they had experienced. Unknown to O'Brien, I had already informed Gilmartin about his claims and, agreeing to exercise extreme caution, had decided that under no circumstances would a meeting of Gilmartin with O'Brien be arranged. This was essential, given the risk of contaminating Gilmartin's own evidence and his work with the tribunal. Equally, Gilmartin had been warned by legal sources to 'beware of Greeks bearing gifts,' while the tribunal was also finding it difficult to substantiate O'Brien's claims. John Gallagher SC, following the leads provided by O'Brien, made an equally futile visit with the Cok man to the Christian Brother in Ennis. He and his colleagues, particularly Pat Hanratty, were clearly doubtful of the claims. Gallagher discreetly met O'Brien on a number of occasions; O'Brien gave him the name of the manager of the Mayo football team, John Maughan, as his pseudonym when they spoke on the phone.

However, the tribunal team's scepticism did not prevent them investigating the allegations, and some fifteen months after O'Brien first approached me, in April 2000, a witness was called to give evidence during a public hearing of the tribunal as a direct consequence of O'Brien's claims. On 18 April the chief executive of Irish Nationwide Building Society, Michael Fingleton, was asked to explain why his organisation had failed to comply with an order by the tribunal eight weeks earlier for documents relating to the account opened at one of its Cork branches by Denis O'Brien. 'We haven't got them this morning, we don't know whether we have them or not, we will see what's in the boxes,' Fingleton told Pat Hanratty.

Fingleton, one of the country's most successful businessmen, had single-handedly led INBS to become one of its most profitable lenders. Along the way he had cultivated extensive contacts with influential figures in politics and the media, not least by offering them loans at very attractive rates and on less than rigorous terms.

Fingleton claimed that the documents from the Cork office had been centralised in Dublin, and some had been destroyed in a flood at the building society's offices in Grafton Street some years earlier. Hanratty said that the tribunal was seeking 'the book of cheque counterfoils of the cheques written by the building society on its bank account.' Fingleton replied: 'We don't think we have them . . . We can't find anything like that . . .' He said the documents had been placed in central storage. Asked where that was, he replied: 'Everywhere.'

Warned by Hanratty that he was in breach of a tribunal order, Fingleton said: 'We have done our best to provide those documents.'

The chairman of the tribunal warned him: 'I have to suggest to you, Mr Fingleton, that your attitude to the orders of this tribunal have been cavalier in the extreme.'

'I'm sorry, I can't agree with that,' Fingleton replied.

There was no mention at the public hearing of the background to the discovery order served on the building society.

Faced with tribunal evidence that only the *Sunday Business Post* could explain to the public, the paper was presented with an editorial dilemma. The evidence called was clearly rooted in the O'Brien story, which we had brought to the tribunal. The gagging order that the tribunal had placed on the O'Brien evidence had been lifted some months previously, following a Supreme Court decision in favour of Charles Haughey and his family after an action they brought against the Moriarty Tribunal in relation to the provision of confidential information. The decision in that unrelated case had implications for all gagging orders, including the one imposed by the Flood Tribunal on the *Sunday Business Post*.

While O'Brien was a flawed witness and had not provided, as promised for many months, copies of the actual cheques proving the payments, and while the politicians, O'Callaghan and other parties had strenuously denied his allegations, the tribunal had called evidence that showed that an investigation into his claims was under way. Another factor that influenced the decision to publish was the fear that other media would get in ahead of us and publish elements of the story. Already there was intense speculation in media and political circles about a sensational political story on which the *Sunday Business Post* was sitting.

It was decided to publish the story, though without the names of any of those who allegedly made or received the corrupt payments, including Starry O'Brien himself, O'Callaghan, or Ahern. Under my name and the heading 'New FF bribes probe could lead to election,' the story opened as follows:

'The Flood tribunal is investigating allegations that two senior Fianna Fáil politicians received £50,000 each in 1989 in return for assistance with the development of a major retail project in Dublin. The allegations are of such a serious nature that a general election is inevitable if they were proved. A businessman who claims he paid the politicians on behalf of a leading property developer has told the tribunal of the circumstances surrounding the cheque payments and has confirmed his account in a sworn statement to the *Sunday Business Post*. Both politicians have vehemently denied the allegations.'

I also included details of how, where and when the payments were allegedly made in 1989, and explained the background to the appearance of Michael Fingleton at the tribunal a few days earlier.

When the story was published, on Sunday 23 April, which happened to be Easter Sunday, the proverbial manure hit the fan and the media went into overdrive. The *Sunday Business Post* had by this time an impressive record in breaking corruption stories, and RTE's news programme 'This Week' contacted me to participate in a discussion about the story, clearly the biggest of the year.

While the chattering classes were chattering, the political classes, and particularly the circle advising Bertie Ahern, were preparing a response. I had filed my story from a laptop computer in Cork, and the second line of the story, inserted by a news editor in Dublin, had suggested that if the story was true it would have implications for the survival of the coalition Government. That line narrowed the possible list of recipients of the alleged payments, even though no names were mentioned, as it had to be someone in the present cabinet.

The *Irish Examiner* (formerly the *Cork Examiner*), with a circulation mainly in the south and west, in its first edition on Monday morning published the story that Ahern was the man at the centre of the sensational allegations. By naming him, the paper's editors and lawyers stood the risk of being exposed to a libel or defamation action by the Taoiseach, but they were clearly happy to publish on the strength of assurances received.

Katie Hannon, political correspondent of the *Irish Examiner* in Dublin, felt that Fianna Fáil advisers were 'relaxed' about the naming of Ahern as one of the senior politicians at the centre of the *Sunday Business Post* article. She was preparing an article on the developing story on the Sunday evening for publication the following day. 'I had the feeling that they were relaxed about the naming of Ahern. I think they thought it was helpful and allowed them to deal with it the next day when he was due to participate in the annual Arbour Hill commemoration.'

Ahern and his handlers were well versed in the contents of Starry O'Brien's claims, as I had put questions to him, through his press office, and had spoken to a number of his colleagues implicated in the story several months previously.

Ahern was speaking at the graves of the 1916 martyrs at Arbour Hill that afternoon, where, surrounded by his loyal and outraged troops as well as a posse of print and television reporters, he made an angry denial of the claims. While stating that he had always thought that 'Frank

Connolly was a fairly good journalist,' he said that the paper had got it badly wrong and there was no truth whatsoever in the allegation.

Tim Pat Coogan described the occasion eloquently in his book *Ireland in the Twentieth Century* (2003).

> Apart from the intrinsic unfairness of the allegation which initially exposed Ahern to what he later said was more criticism on the day of the story's breaking than in his previous 25 years in politics, it also had the effect of involving the Taoiseach in what might be taken as a symbolic Irish morality play at the end of the twentieth century. The story broke during April 2000 just before Easter Monday, on which he attended the annual Fianna Fáil commemoration for the Easter Rising, and walked into a barrage of questions from journalists about the accusation. As a result, on the eighty-fourth anniversary of the day the men of 1916 marched into the GPO, the images on television were not of idealistic endeavour extolled but of the men's spiritual successor dealing with charges of corruption.

On the following day I said on RTE radio that I thought Ahern was 'a fairly good politician' but that the story was published in the public interest. The media had a field day, and it was not long before the *Sunday Business Post* was attacked, and myself in particular. Even within the paper senior journalists were questioning how we could have published the story, given O'Brien's previous history, details of which were swiftly and generously supplied to all and sundry by the Fianna Fáil press office and other sources.

The following week the paper responded by confirming the names of all involved, as well as further details of O'Brien's allegations and the tribunal's investigation. Though none of the parties sued the paper, Bertie Ahern sued O'Brien for defamation. Some weeks later the *Sunday Business Post* published a front-page apology to Ahern and O'Callaghan for the error; and life went on.

_____

For Tom Gilmartin, the story had dubious origins from the start, and he remained convinced that, far from Starry O'Brien being a man seeking to make a bit of publicity for himself at everybody else's expense, the whole saga was an attempted sting operation on himself and the tribunal.

Long before the story was published Gilmartin had been warned by his friend Peter Kearns that O'Brien was involved in an effort to discredit him. Gilmartin said he had also received a tip-off from another anonymous caller to the same effect. Kearns lived in Crosshaven, county Cork, close to where O'Brien sometimes stayed in a cottage owned by one of his relatives.

'The O'Brien story was a strange affair,' Gilmartin later told me. 'I was warned by various people, including legal sources, to have nothing to do with this man or his allegations well before the story was published. The story, I believe, was hatched in order to damage my credibility and the tribunal's investigation. You and the *Sunday Business Post* were just used to achieve that end because you were seen as sympathetic to my position.'

He said that one of the reasons he doubted the truth of O'Brien's claim was that Owen O'Callaghan had said on a number of occasions that he personally gave money to Ahern, and did not use any other person to do so.

While the *Sunday Business Post* published an apology to the Taoiseach, the then chief executive, Barbara Nugent, and editor, Damien Kiberd, resisted efforts by Fianna Fáil advisers to include a reference to me in the front-page statement. It seemed there were some people in Ahern's circle who felt it necessary, or at least desirable, that I be made exclusively and personally liable for the article.

Not surprisingly, Starry O'Brien's background featured heavily in the response of other media to the *Sunday Business Post* exclusive. The most self-righteous response, predictably, came from those journalists and newspapers that had spent most of the previous three years waging a war of attrition against the tribunal and its team and any newspaper or media figures that appeared to be sympathetic to their inquiries.

Chapter 12

‘SIN A BHFUIL’

Tom Gilmartin remained in Luton but stayed in contact with the tribunal and other sources in Dublin. His life was now almost totally consumed by his wife's debilitating condition, as he was her full-time carer. His discussions with the tribunal barristers Hanratty and Gallagher by phone continued, and he had several more meetings with them as he prepared a more detailed and comprehensive statement for the tribunal, which he eventually swore in the spring of 2000, with a second draft completed in October that year. Gilmartin and his wife were also discussing the possibility of selling their house in Luton and moving back to Ireland, where Vera would be closer to her extended family, some of whom could assist with her care. The move eventually went ahead, and in February 2001 they returned to county Sligo, from where Tom Gilmartin had emigrated so many years before.

When Gilmartin, with the help of his legal advisers, completed the second draft of his statement in October 2000 it included several references to his dealings with Bertie Ahern, but no explicit mention was made of Owen O'Callaghan's alleged claim to him that he had given Ahern a total of £80,000. This claim entered the public domain only in the autumn of 2002, some eighteen months after it was described in a formal statement submitted by Gilmartin's lawyers to the tribunal.

Gilmartin had told the solicitor Noel Smyth in 1996 that he believed Ahern was 'on O'Callaghan's payroll,' and he told the tribunal lawyers the same thing during their early discussions. He said he had told Hanratty and other tribunal lawyers when he met them in 1998 of Ahern's relationship with O'Callaghan, but the detail of alleged payments was not formally recorded in any statement to the inquiry until May 2001. Only then, for the first time, could the tribunal actually examine Gilmartin's claim that the Taoiseach was implicated in serious allegations of corruption, though it would be some time before the inquiry team would obtain any specific evidence to back up the claim, and it was two years before the tribunal put questions to Ahern. It first needed to get accurate information and records from the other parties involved, including Owen O'Callaghan and Allied Irish Banks. There was also the continuing problem that the tribunal was understaffed and by this stage was dealing with millions of documents that had to be properly recorded and computerised, as well as keeping its public hearings into other controversial rezonings on track.

In July 2001 Liam Lawlor was given a second seven-day prison sentence and a fine of £5,000 for continually refusing to comply with a High Court order obtained against him, but he appealed the conviction and fine to the Supreme Court, delaying his incarceration until early the following year.

During the same month the defamation action brought by Bertie Ahern against Denis 'Starry' O'Brien was heard in the Circuit Court in Dublin. At the hearing O'Brien failed to produce any evidence to support or corroborate the elaborate story he had given to the *Sunday Business Post*. The building society documents were forgeries, and other details of his story were provably false. A solicitor from Cork, the late Cornelius Murphy, who was later appointed a judge of the Circuit Court, claimed that he had been told by O'Brien that he had been fishing off county Wexford on the day of the 1989 football final. For his part, O'Brien insisted privately that he never held a fishing-rod in his life, but he never contested any of the claims made by witnesses called by the Taoiseach's legal team, which was led by Rory Brady (subsequently appointed Attorney-General by Ahern) and included a young barrister and Fianna Fáil supporter, Jim O'Callaghan. The lawyers acting for O'Brien were instructed by their client not to submit any defence, and after hearing evidence from a number of witnesses called by Ahern's counsel the judge ruled that he had been grossly defamed. He awarded him damages of £30,000 and costs against O'Brien. O'Brien did not pay Ahern the £30,000 until he was served with a sheriff's order several years later and reportedly began making monthly payments.

O'Brien was regularly in the High Court over a debt of more than several hundred thousand euro that he owed to Anglo-Irish Bank, which he had refused to honour. He lived in a large detached house in the Cork suburbs (over which the bank had a charge until it was cancelled in 2006), drove an expensive car and made frequent trips each year to a villa in Spain but was apparently reluctant to pay some of his debts. His solicitor, Padraic Ferry, and barrister, Brendan Grehan SC, were also victims in the affair when their client failed to provide any ammunition in support of his case. Indeed he refused to provide a shred of evidence to counter the legal submissions made on Ahern's behalf. They have yet to be paid for their work.

O'Brien's reaction on the steps of the Four Courts after judgement was made against him, when he was photographed with a wide grin on his face, was also peculiar, given the critical comments of the judge concerning his character and the false allegations. 'Sin a bhfuil [That's all],' he told reporters when they asked him to comment on the outcome of the case.

Several months before the publication of the *Sunday Business Post* story a solicitor with the firm Beauchamps, Claire Callanan, acting for Anglo-Irish Bank in its claim against the elusive O'Brien, had sent me a copy of a High Court judgement in the 1989 case brought by Ulster Bank, in which O'Brien was described as a forger of documents and a perjurer, with a view to forewarning me and the newspaper about his flawed pedigree. The caution, and the delay by the paper in publishing O'Brien's allegations, was influenced by this background and the judge's criticism in the Ulster Bank case, but we considered that it was not beyond the bounds of possibility that such a person would be the very type chosen to deliver a corrupt payment or bribe. As it turns out, O'Brien apparently fabricated the entire story from beginning to end, for no obvious or explained purpose.

While the avalanche of media criticism over the O'Brien affair was to be expected, given the decision to make use of a source of such poor pedigree, the motivation for O'Brien's approach to me, his effort to drag Gilmartin into his story and his clear attempt to damage the tribunal have yet to be fully explained. Why would he apparently invent such a cock-and-bull story about his involvement with allegedly corrupt politicians and business people that happened to correspond in some important details to elements of Gilmartin's statement to the tribunal— specifically his claim that O'Callaghan had given a cheque for £50,000 to Ahern at the time of a football match in Dublin in the autumn of 1989?

Gilmartin was also dragged into a defamation controversy when Fianna Fáil's national organiser, Seán Sherwin, brought proceedings against the *Sunday Independent* in the High Court in late November 2001. The paper had published a story in February 1999 that claimed, among other things, that Sherwin had asked Gilmartin for a donation towards the election campaign of his sister-in-law, Catherine Sherwin, a candidate for Fianna Fáil in the Clondalkin area of Dublin in 1991.

Gilmartin's appearance provided an opportunity for those who were, privately and publicly, rubbishing his allegations to assess his abilities in the witness box before the public hearings into the Quarryvale module at the tribunal. While the tribunal team was less than pleased that some of his evidence would be aired in open court before they were ready to convene a public hearing, the outcome did little damage to the inquiry.

Sherwin confirmed that during a meeting in the Fianna Fáil head office in Lower Mount Street in November 1990 Gilmartin had told him of the £50,000 donation he had given to Pádraig Flynn the previous year. Sherwin decided to investigate whether the money had been received and, according to Gilmartin, reported to him that the donation had not made its way into party funds. While Sherwin did not dispute that he had met Gilmartin in Mount Street, he vigorously denied soliciting any money for his sister-in-law, who stood as a candidate for Fianna Fáil some months after their encounter.

Over a number of days in the witness box Gilmartin recounted in detail his experiences in trying to get large-scale development projects going in Dublin and the number of people who asked him for money. During his cross-examination Gilmartin clashed a couple of times with Garret Cooney SC, who was acting for Sherwin and who had previously represented Joseph Murphy Structural Engineers at the tribunal. Cooney, known as a heavyweight barrister who specialised in libel law, had previously exchanged harsh words with the tribunal chairman, Feargus Flood, prompting the judge to walk out on one occasion in 1999.

Gilmartin told Cooney that he would not be inveigled into discussing matters relating to his private statements to the tribunal. He added that if he answered Cooney's questions it might not do his own client, Seán Sherwin, any good. Cooney asked Gilmartin if he was 'threatening' him, to which the witness replied, 'I'm advising you.'

At the end of the libel action the jury decided that Sherwin had not 'wrongly solicited' money from Gilmartin. The jury did not dispute that a contribution was requested, and it awarded a token sum of £250 in damages to Sherwin, who was also landed with significant costs. Gilmartin, who had never claimed that Sherwin 'wrongly solicited' money for his sister-in-law, emerged as a credible witness whose evidence had clearly influenced the amount of the damages awarded by the jury.

After the proceedings, which saved the *Sunday Independent* several hundred thousand pounds in costs, the editor, Aengus Fanning, wrote to Gilmartin to thank him for his assistance in the case and describing him as an 'honourable' person.

———

The following month the Supreme Court made another landmark decision when it upheld the seven-day prison sentence and £5,000 fine imposed on Liam Lawlor by the High Court the previous July. The court ruled that Lawlor had defied an order of the High Court in 2000 to produce documents relating to any accounts held in his name or for his benefit in any financial institution in Ireland or abroad. The High Court order had sought discovery of documents and records from June 1974 to October 2000, a period during which, according to the tribunal's findings, Lawlor operated no less than 110 bank accounts in various countries, from Liechtenstein to the United States. In his judgement Mr Justice Nial Fennelly said that in relation to lands at Coolamber House in Lucan and an Isle of Man company, Navona, through which the property was to be purchased, Lawlor had 'patently defied the order of the Court and, more particularly, had sworn at least one affidavit that is demonstrably so incomplete as to entail deliberate deception.' The court found that Lawlor had deliberately disguised from the tribunal his involvement in the purchase of the Coolamber House lands from the beef baron Larry Goodman.

The five-judge Supreme Court announced its decision on 12 December but agreed to defer the execution of its order until January, in response to Lawlor's request to be allowed visit his son in New York over the Christmas period. The court also awarded costs estimated at £300,000 against Lawlor, who was brought to Mountjoy Prison for the second time in early January 2002. A month later he was handed a third sentence for failing to comply with the High Court order and served another brief spell in Mountjoy.

———

Over the previous four years the tribunal had investigated a large number of matters involving the former minister Ray Burke, including his role as Minister for Communications in the promotion and licensing of the commercial radio station Century Radio in 1987. The tribunal chairman and legal team spent much of 2002 preparing the long-awaited report of their investigation into Burke's activities over his many years in politics, which was finally produced in late September. From the Government's and the Taoiseach's point of view it was fortunate that it was released some months after, and not before, the general election of June 2002, as the political reverberations were significant. In the election Fianna Fáil, with Bertie Ahern as Taoiseach, was returned to power after forging another coalition arrangement with the Progressive Democrats.

In the explosive 150-page second interim report of the Tribunal of Inquiry into Certain Planning Matters and Payments, published in late September 2002, Feargus Flood pulled no punches in his findings against Ray Burke, who, he said, had taken corrupt payments from the businessman Joseph Murphy (junior) and from the builders Michael Bailey, Tom Brennan and Joe McGowan. The latter pair, with whom Burke had a commercial relationship from the early 1970s, had also given Burke his house, Briargate, on the Malahide Road at Swords, county Dublin, at a knock-down price, thus conferring upon him 'a substantial benefit,' the report concluded. Flood found that Burke had also received substantial offshore payments from the builders as well as an improper payment from the principal of Century Radio, Oliver Barry, in 1989. He concluded that fourteen people, including Burke, had obstructed and hindered the tribunal's work, and that the long-time Fianna Fáil adviser P. J. Mara had failed to co-operate with the inquiry. Flood also pointed out that while the tribunal had so far cost €21 million, the Revenue Commissioners and the Criminal Assets Bureau had raised €34½ million as a result of issues uncovered by the inquiry into political corruption.

The political repercussions were immediate. P. J. Mara was forced to resign as director of elections for the Fianna Fáil campaign to ratify the Nice Treaty, which was under way at the time. The report was described as 'profoundly significant' by the Taoiseach, Bertie Ahern. 'It sends out a clear message. Those who acted improperly and illegally while engaged in public life can be assured that their actions will be exposed,' he said. He had made similar remarks when, as Minister for Finance in 1993, he introduced a tax amnesty and said he would be happy to see those caught evading tax being imprisoned. 'It would give me the greatest of pleasure to see non-compliant taxpayers going to jail,' he told RTE in an interview at the time.

Within days of the publication of the tribunal's report, *Ireland on Sunday*, which I had joined earlier that year, published an article by me that stated that a serving Fianna Fáil minister was under investigation by the tribunal in relation to alleged payments of £80,000 he had received from a developer. 'The allegation by Sligo-born property developer, Tom Gilmartin, has been the subject of detailed inquiries by the tribunal over several months,' the story read. '*Ireland on Sunday* can reveal that the senior politician at the centre of the latest probe is alleged to have received a payment of £50,000 in 1989 in return for assistance with a major development in Dublin and a further £30,000 in 1992 in relation to a tax designation on a site, also in the capital. The tribunal has followed the money trail and is expected to call evidence from the politician and others early next year when the public hearings into Gilmartin's sensational claims are opened.' The paper also stated that it was 'almost certain that Mr Ahern himself will be summoned to give evidence to the Flood tribunal.'

The story, published on 29 September 2002, a few days after the publication of the Flood Tribunal's interim report on Ray Burke, provoked an immediate, and hostile, reaction. The following day the Minister for Justice, Michael McDowell, denied the story on RTE radio in an interview with Pat Kenny. I listened to the interview on the car radio as I travelled to work. McDowell, the Progressive Democrat TD for Dublin South-East, who had served as Attorney-General in the final years of the previous Fianna Fáil-PD Government from 1999 to the election in 2002, had been appointed a minister for the first time a few months earlier. His party had been embarrassed by an article I wrote in the *Sunday Business Post* some years earlier when we published copious details about its financial donors, who were identified in documents found in a skip outside its offices in Dublin. McDowell insisted to Kenny that the story was without foundation and went on to claim that it was not the first time that I had concocted a story about bribes to a senior politician—a reference to the Denis 'Starry' O'Brien episode and the Taoiseach's subsequent vindication in the Circuit Court.

I phoned RTE on my mobile phone and joined the minister on air.

As the discussion became more heated I asked him to inform listeners as to which line or paragraph in my report was inaccurate. I also referred, inaccurately, to the Starry O'Brien case as having 'collapsed': it had not collapsed, but O'Brien had failed to lodge any defence in the proceedings and so his false claims were disproved. The minister was repeating his claim that I had got it wrong when I reminded him that he was more informed than most about the background to the story, as only a few years previously, in his capacity as a barrister, he had acted for the businessman at the centre of the corruption allegation described in the *Ireland on Sunday* article, namely Owen O'Callaghan. McDowell referred to this comment as being somewhat 'below the belt', as Kenny sought to calm matters down. The minister then asked me to identify the politician under investigation, which I refused to do, on the grounds that it would expose me and the newspaper to a libel action, a probable result of which he, as an experienced barrister, was well aware. He then offered, on air, to meet me privately 'for a pint' to discuss the issue, an invitation that I said I would not refuse.

Within days the Taoiseach used the opportunity of my careless description of the Starry O'Brien case as having 'collapsed' to remind the public that he had been vindicated in the Circuit Court when it ruled that he had been the victim of completely unsubstantiated and untrue allegations. 'I have never taken a bribe from anyone in my life,' Ahern said. 'I sued Denis "Starry" O'Brien so that my reputation would be vindicated. I won that case, because the allegation that I had received a £50,000 bribe from Denis "Starry" O'Brien was baseless and totally untrue. I succeeded in my Circuit Court action for one reason and one reason only, that is, that I was defamed and lies were told about me. It is wrong for Frank Connolly to say that the case "collapsed", because Denis "Starry" O'Brien "decided not to contest the charge".'

Ahern said that a bank account purporting to show evidence of the payment had never existed, and no cheque or cash was given to him by O'Brien. He said that O'Brien was not even in Dublin on the day of the alleged handing over, and that the judge had said that the allegation was 'utterly, completely and absolutely false and untrue.'

'I have proven my good reputation in court when it was challenged,' Ahern said. 'I think the least I am entitled to is a clear and unequivocal acceptance that I won my case because lies were told about me.'

Ahern was already under pressure, in the wake of the Flood Report, over his decision to appoint Ray Burke to the Government after the 1997 general election when it was widely known, including by the Taoiseach, that he was the subject of serious corruption allegations, details of which I had first revealed in a series of exclusive articles in the *Sunday Business Post* from early 1996.

The other member of the Government to dismiss the *Ireland on Sunday* story was the Minister for Foreign Affairs, Brian Cowen, who said that 'speculation' over the story about an alleged payment of £80,000 to a serving minister was 'without foundation'. Cowen, who had replaced P. J. Mara as Fianna Fáil's director of elections, was asked about the story during the launch of a poster for the Nice referendum campaign. 'I know nothing about it,' he said. 'I don't know anyone else who knows anything about it, and I really don't think it serves the purposes here. The tribunal have issued their report. They deal with the findings and the facts, and if anyone has any evidence of any problems the tribunals are there to deal with it, and they have the powers to deal with it.' He said that Fianna Fáil fully accepted and welcomed the report by Judge Flood and went on to insist that the party knew nothing of the corrupt behaviour of Ray Burke.

———

After resisting repeated requests from Flood for extra staff and resources, the Government formally appointed three lawyers to assist him. Two barristers, Alan Mahon and Mary Faherty, were appointed as members of the tribunal, while a third, Gerald Keys, was named as a reserve member. All three were made judges of the Circuit Court in accordance with their promotion in early 2002. The Government also conceded significant pay increases of up to €800 a day to the tribunal lawyers, some of whom were now being paid at the rate of €2,250 per day.

One of their main challenges was to control the direction of the inquiry, which had been following a path set by Frank Dunlop two years earlier when he admitted to bribing councillors in relation to more than a dozen controversial rezonings in the Dublin region in the late 1980s and 1990s. To the annoyance of those whom he accused of corruption, and their lawyers, there appeared to be a pattern whereby Dunlop deliberately exaggerated the scale of wrongdoing by some former and serving councillors while concealing or playing down the role of others, particularly more senior politicians. Dunlop had faithfully recorded hundreds of meetings and engagements in his diaries over the years, providing an invaluable source of information to the tribunal. However, the infamous Dunlop diaries were also a source of some mystery to the tribunal, as it emerged that he had originally presented a heavily edited version of his records to the inquiry and had then provided a version that included previously hidden entries of meetings and other matters. After the tribunal employed the FBI to re-examine the second version of the diaries provided by Dunlop, using chemical x-ray technology, it emerged that he had erased vital information concerning his encounters with a number of influential figures, including Owen O'Callaghan and Bertie Ahern, together with businessmen and certain executives of Allied Irish Banks.

At one point he was caught in the headlights of his own deceit when a witness emerged to disprove an elaborate proposition put forward by him about his relationship with two councillors, Liam Creaven (Fianna Fáil) and Michael Joe Cosgrave (Fine Gael). The two councillors had sworn that they had not colluded in the preparation of their statements to the tribunal, while Dunlop had said that he had not given illicit payments to either and denied any suggestion that he had helped them prepare their statements before their appearance at the inquiry. Mary Maguire, who had worked as a secretary and typist for Councillor Cosgrave, contacted me and described how she was present when Dunlop arrived at the offices of her employer in Baldoyle, north county Dublin. She explained how his diary was cleared on the days Dunlop visited the office, and how Dunlop appeared to disguise his presence by parking a distance from the office and wearing a golf hat. She said that Councillor Creaven was also present on the day Dunlop attended at Cosgrave's office and that after a lengthy meeting with the two councillors she was asked to type their tribunal statements, which had clearly been prepared with Dunlop. She had the records from the computer she used to confirm that the statements were prepared by her on the same day that Dunlop called, and immediately after he left the office.

The tribunal had already sought an explanation from the two councillors for the extraordinary similarities in their statements, and both men had denied any collusion in their preparation. Dunlop and the two councillors insisted that he had only given them legitimate political donations at election times. Mary Maguire exposed a clear example of Dunlop's willingness to mislead the tribunal and to portray as clean some of the elected representatives with whom he had dealings while damning others as corrupt. Dunlop admitted that he and another councillor, Seán Gilbride, who was central to the Quarryvale investigation, had also hatched a plot to give false evidence to the tribunal. He said they had agreed, improperly, to describe any sums Gilbride received as political donations.

As details of Dunlop's involvement with senior Fianna Fáil figures began to emerge from evidence heard during the hearings, the simmering tension between the tribunal and the Government erupted in extraordinary fashion. An allegation surfaced that Judge Flood had been compromised by a guarantee he allegedly made to a barrister acting for Ray Burke that Burke's legal costs would be paid in full by the tribunal. It was an inaccurate claim that deeply upset Flood. His corruption report—the first edition of which sold an astounding 25,000 copies at an imaginative €1 each—had turned him into a nationally respected figure perceived as courageous enough to face down powerful vested interests.

Burke alleged that the deal had been made verbally between his former senior counsel, Joe Finnegan, and Flood. Within days Finnegan, who had been appointed a judge soon after appearing for Burke at the tribunal, confirmed that he had struck no such deal. Finnegan went on to become President of the High Court and then was appointed to the Supreme Court.

The row, which deeply wounded Flood, a private man with a strong sense of his own integrity, had all the air of an attack on the tribunal itself.

In June 2003 Flood told the Government that he intended to stand down as chairman of the tribunal. His wife and family had been deeply concerned at the effect of the controversy on him and eventually prevailed upon him to retire. During one emotional discussion of the circumstances surrounding his departure he told me that his late father, a bank manager, whom he held in high regard, would have been horrified to hear such an allegation against his son. He spoke highly of the judges appointed to replace him.

Within months of his appointment the new chairman, Alan Mahon, became the subject of another brief controversy when it emerged that he had made a settlement with the Revenue Commissioners in 1992 for outstanding taxes while he was a leading barrister in the midlands, which Mahon had said was the 'result of miscalculation'. Here was the man who had been appointed to investigate high-level tax evasion, among other corrupt activities, caught in the headlines of public scrutiny. The settlement, which was public knowledge, was revived in an article published in the *Phoenix*, and there was the inevitable suspicion that it was a carefully planted snippet of information designed to cause maximum damage to the new tribunal and to its chairman in particular.

Flood and his legal team had already exposed the fissures of corruption in Fianna Fáil and the establishment generally and the party's failure to root it out. It was evident from the facts that had already emerged in the investigation that the political system, and the Garda Síochána, had failed to act on information about corrupt activities by Ray Burke and others when they were first exposed as far back as the 1970s.

In his reaction to Flood's request to resign, Ahern told the Dáil that the inquiry, at its present pace, could continue for another fifteen years and eventually cost some €50 or €60 million. He and the Minister for Justice, Michael McDowell, publicly suggested another form of tribunal or 'commissions of investigation' that could be held in private and avoid the costs incurred by the Flood and Moriarty inquiries. It was the first of many criticisms by the Taoiseach and other senior political figures about the duration and cost of the inquiries, which, along with regular, and negative, media updates on the amounts earned by its legal team, did little to uphold public confidence in the tribunal process. Opposition leaders expressed concern that the plan to introduce legislation to transfer certain modules from the planning tribunal to the proposed new commissions was intended to prevent politically sensitive allegations being aired in public, but their concerns were dismissed. The leader of Fine Gael, Enda Kenny, told the Dáil in June 2003 that any attempt to transfer 'embarrassing modules' from the tribunal would 'seriously undermine public confidence in the inquiry. It would be regrettable if the Government were to use its majority in this house to seek to hide from public view matters that are potentially damaging to particular parties.' Following the expressions of concern the Government, through a spokesperson, confirmed that it had 'no desire that issues concerning Tom Gilmartin, Frank Dunlop and Pádraig Flynn should be held in private.'

On its last sitting day before the lengthy summer recess the Dáil passed a motion appointing Alan Mahon chairman of the tribunal, with Mary Faherty remaining a full member and Gerald Keys moving from a reserve to full member of the inquiry. The Dáil debate allowed opposition parties to ask questions about the delay surrounding the appointment of new members of the tribunal and the reasons behind Feargus Flood's resignation, which took effect on Friday 27 June 2003. The Green Party TD Dan Boyle claimed that the delay in appointing additional members, as requested by Judge Flood several months, even years, previously, was a 'deliberate strategy to delay the Flood Tribunal's investigations and ensure that controversial evidence would not be heard before the 2002 general election.' Whether Boyle's claim was true or not, the delay in reaching the public hearings in the first Quarryvale module meant that Bertie Ahern and other ministers were not called to give evidence until long after they were returned to government in that election.

For Tom Gilmartin, the circumstances surrounding Feargus Flood's dramatic departure from the tribunal did not instil much confidence in its future prospects. He had come to respect the judge for his integrity and his ability to confront some of the powerful interests represented at the inquiry, who did not wish it to succeed in its task of unearthing corruption in the planning system. He was facing the inevitable appearance in front of very hostile inquisitors at the tribunal itself, where his claims would be tested in the full glare of public attention. It was a daunting challenge and one this normally reticent and shy man did not relish. The precision and the power of recall that had helped him to learn the skills of mechanical and structural engineering and to become successful in business in England were not what they used to be, and every opportunity to poke holes in his evidence would be taken by the professional lawyers he was to confront.

At the heart of Gilmartin's allegations were twelve claims, which would be put to the test by the tribunal. These were:

(1) that he was asked for £100,000 by a Fianna Fáil councillor, Finbarr Hanrahan, in Buswells Hotel in early 1989;
(2) that he was asked in 1988 by Liam Lawlor for a payment of £100,000 for himself and another £100,000 for George Redmond;

(3) that he met the former Taoiseach Charles Haughey and members of
     his Government in Leinster House in February 1989, after which he
     was approached by an unidentified man and asked for £5 million;

(4) that he was threatened by a man purporting to be a member of
     the Garda Síochána to stop making allegations against Lawlor,
     Redmond and others to an official Garda inquiry in March 1989
     and told to 'fuck off back to England';

(5) that he gave a donation for Fianna Fáil of £50,000 to Pádraig Flynn
     in the early summer of 1989;

(6) that he was approached by Bertie Ahern's friend and adviser Joe
     Burke for a payment of £500,000 in the late summer of 1990 on
     behalf of Ahern;

(7) that he was brought by Owen O'Callaghan and met men in dark
     glasses, one of whom was a Sinn Féin activist, and that he believed
     they behaved in a threatening manner towards him;

(8) that Owen O'Callaghan told him that he had paid Bertie Ahern
     £50,000 in 1989 in respect of Ahern's assistance in the acquisition
     by Gilmartin of lands owned by Dublin County Council at
     Quarryvale;

(9) that O'Callaghan told him in 1992 or 1993 that he had paid Ahern
     £30,000 in respect of the decision by the then Minister for Finance to
     refuse tax relief designation on the rival Blanchardstown Shopping
     Centre;

(10) that O'Callaghan told him that Ahern had also received a large
     payment in return for the designation of the Golden Island retail
     centre outside Athlone in late 1994;

(11) that senior executives of Allied Irish Banks had colluded with
     O'Callaghan and others to force him from control of his company,
     Barkhill Ltd; and

(12) that substantial sums were taken from his company without his
     knowledge and used by O'Callaghan and Frank Dunlop to make
     corrupt payments to politicians.

These claims, if proved to be true, promised to create a political storm
that would dwarf any tribunal-related scandals yet witnessed in Ireland.

Chapter 13 ～

｜ 'THE INVISIBLE MAN'

When the day of reckoning finally arrived, the public interest in Gilmartin's appearance had almost reached fever pitch, given the amount of advance publicity and the long delay between the first surfacing of his allegations in 1998 and his arrival for the hearings at Dublin Castle in March 2004. The media had come out in force, and Gilmartin was in the glare of the cameras when he arrived with his barristers, Hugh O'Neill sc and Donal O'Donnell sc, assisted by his solicitors Joe Kelly and Máire Conneely from A. and L. Goodbody.

Gilmartin described the circumstances surrounding his first public appearance at the tribunal. 'Before I arrived I was a bit nervous and apprehensive. I didn't like being the centre of media attention. I was very conscious of this, and I would have preferred to go in a back door without being seen. There was a huge media presence, cameras and all that. I felt very nervous and uptight but I was warned not to talk to the media and not to say anything. I tried not to.'

The module entitled 'Arlington/Quarryvale and Related Matters' was, the tribunal counsel John Gallagher said, to be broken into two separate sections, known as Quarryvale 1 and Quarryvale 2, and was expected to last about a year. The first inquiry would examine events relating to the Bachelor's Walk project and the assembly of lands at Quarryvale, while the second would look at the development and zoning of the lands from 1990.

After Gallagher had outlined a broad sketch of Gilmartin's allegations and a chronology of his involvement in Dublin between 1987 and 1990, Liam Lawlor, one of the main targets of Gilmartin's widely aired allegations over previous years, rose to his feet and addressed the gathering from the floor. Lawlor had much to lose, having already been at the receiving end of a battering by tribunal, courts and media during the earlier modules of the inquiry, when extraordinary details of his vast financial affairs had been exposed. His continued hounding of Gilmartin and the repeated demands for money he had made on the developer—outlandish demands that Gilmartin had consistently rejected from a man he considered a political grafter—were to feature prominently in this latest module of the inquiry.

Lawlor immediately set upon Gilmartin in a manner befitting a tough former Dublin hurler. He warned him of the danger of throwing stones from inside the glasshouse. '[He is sitting] in the middle of a glasshouse, and by the time myself and others are finished dealing with Mr Gilmartin's lies I respectfully suggest there won't be too many panes of glass left, and I hope as it splinters it doesn't inflict too many deserved wounds on him . . . We are all out of step except Tom. He left the west of Ireland in proverbial bare feet and trousers in a bad condition. He came back to save the country by driving a coach and four through the 1972 development plan. We were to discard the plan to facilitate Mr Gilmartin's greed.'

Before he took the stand Gilmartin had to listen to a half-hour rant from Lawlor, an obvious attempt to unsettle a witness already nervous about the ordeal he faced. But now it was his turn to speak. When he entered the witness box you could hear a pin drop in the silent and packed hall. Watched closely by his son Thomas, who had been a constant adviser to his father and who was familiar with the complex twists and turns in his story, Gilmartin took the oath. Heavy-set and with a pronounced Sligo accent that had hardly changed since his childhood, Gilmartin was the epitome of the hard-working country man made good.

As John Gallagher brought him through his statements about Bachelor's Walk and the early development of Quarryvale in the late 1980s Gilmartin became visibly relaxed and more comfortable in the surroundings. For the next several weeks he talked his way through his experience of business in Dublin in the late 1980s and onto the national stage, where he was either celebrated as a hero in the battle against corruption or, in the case of those whom he criticised and their media defenders, denounced as a fantasist who distorted the truth.

Gilmartin later recalled his first day in the witness box. 'On the first day I did not know what to expect going into the tribunal. Lawlor opened up about me leaving Sligo with no arse in my trousers and in my bare feet. He accused me of throwing stones even though I lived in a bigger glasshouse than others. I had no feeling of animosity towards Lawlor when he opened up. I actually enjoyed it. There were no barefooted Irish

A young Tom Gilmartin (*Courtesy of the Gilmartin family*)

Home from England: Tom with his parents, Jimmy and Kathleen, and wife, Vera, in Co. Sligo in the early 1960s (*Courtesy of the Gilmartin family*)

Vera and Tom on their wedding day in 1965 (*Courtesy of the Gilmartin family*)

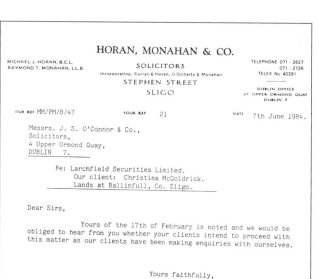

Letter to solicitor J. S. O'Connor in 1984 over land dispute at Lislary (*Courtesy of the Gilmartin family*)

Tom Gilmartin at his desk in Luton
(*Courtesy of the Gilmartin family*)

One of Tom Gilmartin's fleet of trucks at a site in Luton (*Courtesy of the Gilmartin family*)

Tom Gilmartin with the model of the West Park (Quarryvale) development at the launch in the Berkeley Court Hotel, Dublin, July 1990 (© *Irish Times*)

The Quarryvale lands at the junction of the N4 road and M50 motorway in west Dublin (*Courtesy of the Gilmartin family*)

Lawlor 'fees' now donations

Fianna Fail TD reclassifies £3,500 a month payments not listed on register of interests

Liam Lawlor, Fianna Fail TD

Frank Dunlop, PR consultant

By Frank Connolly

Liam Lawlor, the Fianna Fail TD for Dublin West, has claimed that a series of payments he received from builder Tom Gilmartin in the 1980s were political donations and has said that he mistakenly described the same monies as "consultancy fees" to The Sunday Business Post last week.

Lawlor reclassified the payments as political donations after he was told by The Sunday Business Post that the payments from Arlington Securities of £3,500 per month were never listed on the register of interests of Dublin County Council, on which he served at the time.

The Sunday Business Post has separately learned that public relations consultant Frank Dunlop was paid £500,000 in fees for his assistance in acquiring rezoning and planning permissions on the Quarryvale site (owned by developer Owen O'Callaghan and the Duke of Westminster) in west Dublin over the past seven years. Dunlop has confirmed that a part of this sum was used to make political donations, which are fully documented.

Under the Local Government (Planning and Development) Act, 1976 councillors are required to register any business in which they are engaged "which relates to dealing in or developing land".

Lawlor's claim that the payments he received from Gilmartin/Arlington Securities were political contributions would mean he was not obliged to register the payments under the act.

Political donations are not normally taxable, whereas consultancy fees would be treated as income for tax purposes.

A week ago Lawlor told this newspaper that he was employed on a consultancy basis by Arlington, with whom Gilmartin worked on developing a site at Bachelor's Walk in Dublin, and had helped prepare demographic and economic data for the company as well as identifying and approaching property owners along the quays when the site was being assembled.

On Friday last he said that the payments he received from Gilmartin, amounting to £3,500 per month, were normal political contributions.

"I got about two or three contributions or subscriptions from Gilmartin when there was a series of elections in the first half of the 1980's," Lawlor told The Sunday Business Post.

"I did up a report for them and went to England at my own expense. We were talking about the possibility of me taking space in the development for a bowling leisure idea. I advised him but there was no formal consultancy arrangement. There was no requirement on me to register my interest," said Lawlor.

Gilmartin said that he had never personally retained Lawlor as a consultant.

"I would not have that man consulting on a shithouse," said Gilmartin in one of his rare public outbursts.

It is accepted by both men, however, that Lawlor was paid £3,500 per month by Arlington Securities for a period during the 1980s.

Lawlor told said that he believes the arrangement lasted for up to four months.

Dunlop has confirmed that as part of his duties as a lobbyist he has made political contributions to a range of politicians and parties over the years, all of which are documented and available for inspection by the Revenue Commissioners, the Flood or Moriarty tribunals.

Front-page lead story in the *Sunday Business Post*, 4 October 1998 (© *Sunday Business Post*)

Mail on Sunday cover, 29 April 2007 (© *Mail on Sunday*)

Frank Dunlop at a Dublin County Council meeting, October 1982 (© *Derek Speirs*)

Ray Burke and Charles Haughey, February 1987 (© *Derek Speirs*)

Bertie Ahern canvassing, May 1989 (© *Derek Speir*s)

Liam Lawlor canvassing for election, June 1989 (© *Derek Speirs*)

Charles Haughey, Bertie Ahern and (right) P. J. Mara, June 1989 (© *Derek Speirs*)

Charles Haughey and Bertie Ahern at the Fianna Fáil ard-fheis, March 1992 (© *Derek Speirs*)

Brian Cowen, Charles Haughey, Albert Reynolds and Bertie Ahern at the Fianna Fáil ard-fheis, March 1992 (© *Derek Speirs*)

Joe Burke (*front left*) with Ahern supporters at the Burlington Hotel, Dublin, November 1994 (© *Derek Speirs*)

Des Richardson and (*behind*) Fianna Fáil general secretary, Pat Farrell, May 1997 (© *Derek Speirs*)

Ahern and Celia Larkin at the election count, June 1997 (© *Derek Speirs*)

Owen O'Callaghan (© *Photocall Ireland*)

Tribunal judges Gerard Keys, Mary Faherty, Feargus Flood and Alan Mahon (© *Photocall Ireland*)

George Redmond (© *Photocall Ireland*)

Pádraig and Dorothy Flynn
(© *Photocall Ireland*)

Tom Gilmartin and Thomas Gilmartin (junior) (© *Photocall Ireland*)

Mary O'Rourke (© *Photocall Ireland*)

Ray MacSharry (© *Photocall Ireland*)

Noel Smyth (© *Photocall Ireland*)

Edward Dadley and Raymond Mould (© *Photocall Ireland*)

AIB executive David McGrath (© *Photocall Ireland*)

John Deane (© *Photocall Ireland*)

David McKenna (© *Photocall Ireland*)

Eamon Dunphy (© *Photocall Ireland*)

Tribunal lawyers Des O'Neill and Patricia Dillon (© *Collins*)

Michael Wall (© *Photocall Ireland*)

Tom Gilmartin's son Thomas and relatives carry his remains for burial at Urris, Co. Donegal, 26 November 2013. His wife, Vera, follows behind, accompanied by her daughter Anne and sons James and Liam. (© Trevor McBride)

in Luton. Many of them were doing pretty well. It was an insult and a put-down of decent people who did more for this country than Lawlor and his ilk. He was hoping to cast a slur on me and giving fodder to Paul Sreenan [O'Callaghan's counsel] and Co. when they came to cross-question me. He wanted to discredit me, bring me down a peg or two and unnerve me. But he did far from unnerve me. All I did was smile, and actually it steeled me for what was to come.'

In his evidence Gilmartin came across as a straight-talking man with no pretensions to grandeur who seemed to be blessed with an uncanny recollection of detail. In the absence of documents, diaries or records for much of what he wanted to prove, Gilmartin's grasp of detail was perhaps his greatest strength, even if it failed him on some notable occasions. At times, when he insisted on actual dates and times for events fifteen years previously, his memory let him down. He sometimes ignored advice from his legal team not to paint himself into a corner by providing precise times but said it as he thought it was.

With a growing confidence, Gilmartin gave concise answers to John Gallagher's opening examination, though veering off on occasion to place events in context. He explained that he had no intention of building anything in Dublin but had planned to acquire sites at Bachelor's Walk and then bring in investors to develop his vision for a major retail complex that would transform the north inner city. Similarly, in Quarryvale he would strategically assemble the development and then attract the financial institutions and the eventual tenants for the massive retail and business scheme. His motives were simple and derived from his experience of the poverty of young Irish immigrants in England.

He told the tribunal: 'Well, possibly it would have been better for me to give an indication of how this all came about in the first place. In the early 1980s, '85 and all that, there was, you know, hundreds of youngsters, Irish youngsters, in England walking the streets and couldn't get jobs because at that time we had the "winter of discontent" and the strikes, and then . . . Maggie Thatcher took on the unions and there was absolute chaos because of strikes like electricity, which in turn forced me out of the engineering company, because we just couldn't work. And there were lots and lots of young Irish walking the streets of Luton and London, some of them begging on the underground. As a matter of fact the majority of people begging on the underground were Irish.'

He described how he convinced some of his business associates that

Dublin could be a good investment opportunity and that he had access to up to £500 million for suitable developments. It was the sort of money that ministers could have only dreamed about at the time and was the reason why Gilmartin stirred such interest when he arrived in the city. His oral evidence was supported by records of meetings obtained over the previous months and years by the tribunal, including one document confirming the support of the Minister for the Environment, Pádraig Flynn, for the extension of tax designation at Bachelor's Walk. Gilmartin agreed that he and Arlington Securities were anxious to maintain a veil of secrecy over the plans, lest they might alert speculators and other property interests who would inflate the cost of sites in the city. He was described in Arlington documents as the man responsible for the assembly and development of the site at Bachelor's Walk and another scheme to the south of the city, at the former Christian Brothers' house of St Helen's in Booterstown, which never progressed. One Arlington memo recorded: 'Tom Gilmartin to endeavour to assist with both projects including their promotion and implementation both in the street and politically.'

Asked what the political promotion of the projects implied, Gilmartin told the tribunal: 'Well . . . I didn't have a lot of political influence here, but because I was Irish and I came up with the scheme, and that was [the] way they worded it—that was from the Arlington suggestion.' In fact, he said, he had no political contacts in the Dáil or the Seanad and did not know any politicians. He had known of a fellow Sligo man, Ray MacSharry, since he was a young man but had never met him until 1987.

Taken by surprise, John Gallagher asked when this meeting took place, as it was not included in Gilmartin's original statement to the tribunal. Gilmartin described how he visited MacSharry, then Minister for Finance, in his constituency office in Pearse Road, Sligo, while home from Luton on summer holidays during August 1987. As MacSharry had already denied during a private session with the tribunal that he had ever had any dealings with Gilmartin, this early revelation added a certain *frisson* to the already charged proceedings. Gallagher decided to explore the matter further, even though it meant he was deviating from his intended line of questioning.

Gilmartin went on to describe another meeting with MacSharry in December 1987 in the minister's offices in Government Buildings. He described how the minister was not all that interested in his plans at the meeting and indicated that he was planning to leave national politics and go to the European Commission, which he did just over a year later. Claiming that he discussed both the Quarryvale and Bachelor's Walk projects with MacSharry, Gilmartin insisted that the minister said that all road blocks would be removed but that it would be up to others and not him to see that through.

Gilmartin's version of events was supported by a memo made in late 1987, which was submitted to the tribunal by Arlington's Dublin solicitor, Jack Kirwan. It read: 'Tom told me that he had met MacSharry last Thursday and there was a further meeting on Friday with the representatives of the Department of Finance and the Revenue Commissioners.' Kirwan's note appeared to confirm that Gilmartin had met MacSharry on 10 December 1987, contrary to MacSharry's statement. Gilmartin further recalled discussions with the minister on the EEC's restrictive multi-fibre agreement, which was barring some retailers from coming to Ireland, as well as the three-year extension of the tax designation along the quays. 'Given that Mr MacSharry has said there was no such meeting, is there anything that you can recall which may assist in . . . jogging his memory?' Gallagher asked.

Gilmartin's humorous response referred to the number of people who appeared to have forgotten their encounters with him. 'All I know is I was there. And I seemed to have an awful problem with being invisible or some form of ghost that turns up.'

Another man present in MacSharry's constituency office in Sligo on that day in August 1987, Pádraig Leonard, came forward to confirm Gilmartin's account after hearing MacSharry's denial. Ironically, Leonard, an assistant school principal in Grange, county Sligo, where Gilmartin's sister Una lives, declared his intention to inform the tribunal of his presence at the meeting while he was having a cup of tea in the home of one of MacSharry's relatives. He immediately sent off a fax to the tribunal with his detailed recollection of the occasion and later gave credible evidence of the meeting at a public hearing.

Gallagher then asked about Gilmartin's first meeting with Bertie Ahern, which he said took place at Ahern's ministerial offices at the Department of Labour in Mespil Road in October 1987. The appointment had been made by telephone a few days previously, when Gilmartin introduced himself and told the minister that he wanted to discuss his plans for Bachelor's Walk. He described how he met a man in the reception area who described himself as a retired garda. He then went upstairs to brief Ahern on his business plans for Dublin. He said Ahern was supportive and enthusiastic. Gilmartin did not ask for any particular assistance but was there merely to advise the minister on the progress of the Bachelor's Walk development.

Ahern's advisers went to the trouble of contacting former security personnel at the Mespil Road building to verify whether any of them were retired members of the Garda Síochána. They could not trace any former gardaí who worked there; yet it was clear that Gilmartin had no reason to make up a story about an innocuous meeting with a minister or about his conversation with the man in reception.

Gilmartin also recounted his first dealings with Liam Lawlor and described how Lawlor had bullied himself onto the Arlington payroll. He described his meeting with Lawlor in the Dead Man's Inn and how Lawlor had forced the Arlington executives to give him monthly consultancy payments of £3,500. The sheer arrogance of the former Dublin TD, Government backbencher and Fianna Fáil councillor, as described by Gilmartin in the witness box, unleashed a simmering but increasingly vocal response from the public gallery as well as murmurs of disapproval from Lawlor himself. At one point, when the tribunal was examining the lodgement history of the monthly payments, Gilmartin described how one payment was made at Heathrow Airport. 'Mr Lawlor phoned me in Luton and said he wanted to meet me at Heathrow Airport, so he insisted that he had to have the payment. He was on his way to Baghdad, I believe.'

The reference to Baghdad, which was in the news because of the recent American occupation and conflict, provoked a fit of laughter from the audience, forcing the tribunal chairman, Alan Mahon, to intervene and insist: 'This evidence is very serious, and while it is sometimes impossible not to laugh, you should try to restrain the laughter as much as possible.' As the weeks progressed, not only laughter but frequent booing and clapping interrupted the proceedings, leading to the chairman's threat to bar the public and his decision to bring in gardaí to watch over the crowd in the public gallery.

Gilmartin recalled that Lawlor was accompanied on his Iraqi mission, on behalf of Larry Goodman, by the Cork TD Ned O'Keeffe. In his evidence O'Keeffe recalled the Heathrow meeting and in a statement to the tribunal said that Lawlor described Gilmartin as 'a qualified agricultural adviser who had been unable to secure a position of employment in Ireland and had to emigrate.'

While Lawlor's reputation had preceded him, the image conveyed of his graft and deceit shocked even some of those familiar with his activities after several years of tribunal and other revelations. Yet Lawlor betrayed none of the symptoms of someone who had changed his ways or even regretted his errant behaviour; instead he took every opportunity to bully Gilmartin, and the tribunal itself, as he settled in with copious documents to hand to counter this latest attack on his self-inflated reputation.

Asked by John Gallagher what service or talent or qualification Lawlor could bring to Arlington's project, Gilmartin was at a loss to find one. 'Mr Lawlor was a member of parliament, and I was not 100 per cent enlightened as to what the circumstances or how business operated in Dublin, so I saw it probably naïvely. Mr Lawlor was just there to screw money out of us. I couldn't see what possible role he could play in anything to do with the scheme . . . He had no input into the scheme itself. He had no input into the acquisition of properties. He had no input to any negotiations going on with CIE, and . . . the only other possible thing was that he might have some political clout . . .'

Asked by the chairman if the payments were political contributions, Gilmartin replied sternly: 'No. He was employed by Arlington as a consultant and he was paid a consultancy fee, by Arlington.' Gilmartin's insistence that Lawlor was paid a consultancy fee by the British company was to ensure that no-one would ever accuse him of making illicit or indeed any payments to the man he had described as a 'political hustler'.

Gilmartin went on to describe his first meeting with George Redmond, how Lawlor had asked that both he and Redmond be given £100,000 in return for access to a map showing ownership of the lands at Quarryvale, and how Lawlor arrived, again uninvited, at the Trust House Forte Hotel at Dublin Airport to inform Gilmartin that he would need to deal with Owen O'Callaghan, who had control of the Neilstown lands.

He then described his first meeting with O'Callaghan in late 1988. 'The very first thing he told me was that he had been at a do the previous week in the—in a hotel in Cork where there was some major opening. It may have been to do with the launching of the tunnel, the Lee Tunnel, and he mentioned a number of dignitaries that was there, including Mr

MacSharry, Mr Scanlon [of] AIB, Mr Reynolds, etc., and he pointed out to me that the original line of the tunnel, that they—that it was altered to suit the Mahon site [land in the Mahon area of Cork that O'Callaghan owned]. So he also went on to say that I had to have him on board or— and Ambrose Kelly, because of their clout.'

The claim that a crossing of the River Lee was being discussed by senior politicians, bankers and businessmen in Cork several years before construction began, and long before O'Callaghan had purchased the land where it exited at Mahon, proved contentious and difficult, if not impossible, for Gilmartin to prove. This was used by O'Callaghan's legal team in its efforts to destroy Gilmartin's credibility, both at the tribunal and in the courts, even though the proposal for a bridge or tunnel at that site had been under consideration by Cork City Council from the late 1980s.

Gilmartin described how he had also met Bertie Ahern in his office above Fagan's pub in Drumcondra in October 1988, a year after his visit to him at the Department of Labour. In his evidence, Gilmartin described how a man not known to him had appeared in the room during his first chat with the minister. Ahern later confirmed that this was his close associate and land agent, Tim Collins.

Gilmartin's encounter with Finbarr Hanrahan and his demand for £100,000 after Christmas in 1988 were explored in some detail. 'Well, I thought to myself, if this is an example of how this country is run, God help the poor devils that walked the streets of Luton looking for a job. I probably expressed that sentiment to one or two afterwards,' he told the tribunal after explaining the incident.

In his evidence, Finbarr Hanrahan agreed that he had met Gilmartin in the hotel but denied asking him for money. He insisted that it was the developer who first contacted him, seeking his political support for his project, which, he said, he declined to give.

Owen O'Callaghan later dismissed Gilmartin's account of the incident and the date on which the meeting with Hanrahan in Buswells Hotel took place. He told the tribunal that he paid little attention to Gilmartin's complaints and did not take them too seriously. Referring to Gilmartin's reaction to Hanrahan's request for money, O'Callaghan said: 'Here he was trying to bring all these barefoot Irish emigrants back from Luton and [says], "This fucker asked me for £100,000." He said he was going in the following day to tell the ministers.' Gilmartin was incensed at this second reference to 'barefoot Irish emigrants' by O'Callaghan, as he felt it was an insulting expression and one he would never use.

Gilmartin described how he had complained to the city manager, Frank Feely, and assistant city manager, Seán Haughey, when he met them some weeks later and told them about the requests for money made by Lawlor, Hanrahan and others and the role played by their senior council official, George Redmond, in obstructing his business projects. Feely confirmed to the tribunal that he had met Gilmartin but gave a version of the complaints that conflicted with Gilmartin's in a number of respects, including a claim that Gilmartin had told Redmond that 'he would see him all right if the permission went through.' This suggested that Gilmartin had offered a bribe to Redmond, which the former angrily denied.

Feely also recorded that it was Lawlor who demanded the £5 million from Gilmartin in Leinster House in February 1989. He said he had taken rough notes during the discussion, which he had written up as a memo twenty-four hours later and which were initialled by Seán Haughey. Gilmartin had no such written record but was adamant that Feely's notes were inaccurate and claimed that Feely had not taken any notes at the meeting. The tribunal concluded that 'it was satisfied that Mr Gilmartin did not tell Mr Feely and Mr Seán Haughey that he had informed Mr Redmond that he, Mr Gilmartin, would see Mr Redmond all right.' The tribunal also said that it was not satisfied that Feely's handwritten memo was compiled within twenty-four hours of his meeting with Gilmartin.

Gilmartin explained that most of the documents that recorded many of the events from the period had been destroyed at his home in Luton in 1996. Some documents of potentially crucial importance to the corruption investigation were used by one of his sons for a bonfire on Guy Fawkes Night. At the time he had just agreed the settlement negotiated by Noel Smyth with his partners in Barkhill Ltd and never thought he would have any need again for the documents accumulated during his traumatic years in Dublin. It was a decision he now had cause to regret.

| THE MAFIA AND THE MONKS

The highlight of Gilmartin's early evidence to the tribunal was his account of the meeting on 1 February 1989 with the Taoiseach, Charles Haughey, and members of his Government. His description of what followed was the subject of detailed scrutiny as lawyers for Bertie Ahern and others, including Liam Lawlor, made great play of inconsistencies regarding the venue of the alleged meeting and the layout of the various floors in Leinster House. Descriptions of walls, doors, tables and windows were parsed and analysed as various protagonists sought to confuse Gilmartin's memory or disprove his recollection. The stakes were high because the request for £5 million had taken place in the building of the country's parliament, outside a room containing some of the most powerful politicians in the land.

Gilmartin concluded his account of his conversation with Haughey by describing the Taoiseach's final words.

'Just as I said "cheerio" he asked me if Liam was taking good care of me.' On hearing these words the public gallery erupted into laughter. The graphic image of the disgraced former Taoiseach asking whether the thrice-jailed Lawlor was looking after the innocent developer was like something out of a Mario Puzo novel.

Under further examination by John Gallagher, Gilmartin described how he stood while Haughey rested his knuckles on the end of the table as he spoke to him in Leinster House. He had previously spoken to the assistant city manager Seán Haughey, the Taoiseach's brother, about the holiday home in Lislary and recalled a conversation with him when they first met. 'He asked me where I was from, and I said Sligo, and he said, "You're not one of the Gilmartins from Lislary," and I said, "As it happens, I am." And he said to me, "I've just come back from there, and if you think this is a tan, it's bloody rust." He was referring to the wet weather.'

While this humorous exchange may seem peripheral, it helped to put Gilmartin's subsequent exchange with Charles Haughey in clearer perspective. The Haughey brothers had spent some holiday time near the Gilmartins' family farm at Lislary, county Sligo, and both made reference to it at their first meeting with the developer, as a means of confirming mutual recognition as much as making small talk. Charles Haughey, who declined to make a statement to the tribunal confirming the brief exchange with Gilmartin, indicated through friendly media sources that he had a clear recollection of meeting the man. This was perhaps not surprising, given his battle with Gilmartin's sister Chris over her land at Lislary a few years before he met Gilmartin in Leinster House in February 1989.

Asked whether anyone else in the room contributed to the discussion, Gilmartin said: 'No, they just greeted me when I went in, particularly Mr Lenihan. I had met him on a number of occasions, not officially but in the Shelbourne Hotel. He used to come over to my table and chat on a very friendly basis. But other than the greeting, none of them participated in the conversation with Mr Haughey.' As anyone who had observed at close range Haughey's imperious behaviour towards his Government colleagues could attest, the fact that there was little said by the other ministers was not unusual. Haughey had little tolerance of anyone interrupting when he was being statesmanlike.

When Gallagher said that several of those Gilmartin claimed were present denied attending any such meeting, Gilmartin went through the ministers one by one and described where they stood or were seated around the table. Pádraig Flynn introduced him to Haughey, Brennan and Ahern. Both Brennan and Ahern, whom he'd met previously, said, 'Hello, Tom.' At one point Mary O'Rourke briefly joined the group and was introduced to him by Flynn before leaving the room.

As the questioning continued, a man interrupted from the audience to express his less-than-complimentary view of the politicians and their apparent amnesia. After shouting abuse in no particular direction and in colourful language, he was quickly escorted from the hearing by ushers.

Beside Albert Reynolds at the Leinster House meeting was Gerry Collins, Minister for Justice, while along the right-hand side of the table were Bertie Ahern, Minister for Labour, Brian Lenihan (senior), Tánaiste and Minister for Foreign Affairs, and Séamus Brennan, Minister of State at the Department of Industry and Commerce. Standing behind Brennan was a man he did not recognise and to whom he was not introduced. Ahern, Brennan and Lenihan, all of whom he had previously met, greeted him on arrival in the room. Ray Burke then entered through a door in the middle of the room, followed by Haughey. After the brief and informal encounter with these members of the Government he was ushered from the room.

Gilmartin said he believed the encouragement and promise from the most powerful politician in the country to have all 'road blocks' removed, with the apparent silent assent of his Government, was a significant breakthrough. What happened next, as he left the room, helped to shatter any such illusions.

As he entered the lobby area outside the room Gilmartin said he saw Liam Lawlor and another man in conversation to his left. He was then approached from his right by another man, short in stature with 'salt and pepper' hair and wearing a casual jacket. He said that this man told him that he would do well out of his business projects. He gave Gilmartin a piece of paper with a number written on it. It was the number of an account in the Bank of Ireland in the Isle of Man.[8] The man asked him to deposit £5 million in the account.

'I could not believe what I was hearing, and I did not respond to the man until the piece of paper was put into my hand,' he told the tribunal. 'Bearing in mind that I had just left a meeting with Mr Haughey and ministers of the Government, and that Mr Lawlor was waiting outside the room and witnessed this encounter, I assumed that this approach must in some way have been connected to Mr Lawlor and Mr Haughey. So all in all I could come to only one conclusion: that the place was totally corrupt. And I had good reason for it.' He told the unidentified man that 'you make the fucking Mafia look like monks,' whereupon he was threatened that he could be thrown into the Liffey for making such a remark.

Even by the standards of the other demands made on him for money, this encounter outside the room full of Government ministers was outrageous. There was no suggestion that any of the ministers present were aware of what happened only yards from where they briefly met the developer, but the fact that it happened at all in the hallowed corridors of the institution that represents the pinnacle of democracy and the symbol of political independence for generations of Irish people was astounding. Not surprisingly, the claim was greeted with a high degree of scepticism, not least because several of the ministers said that the Leinster House meeting with Haughey never happened.

Gilmartin went on to recount a further meeting with Pádraig Flynn in Leinster House two days later, on 3 February. He said he did not inform Flynn of the dramatic confrontation and demand after his meeting with Haughey and his ministers two days earlier. John Gallagher asked him the reason why. 'Because I didn't know who it was all about,' Gilmartin replied. 'I didn't know who was involved. It was after coming out of a meeting of ministers, or having been introduced to the Taoiseach, and I wasn't quite sure what the overall game [was].'

The tribunal produced a Department of Finance memo that showed that Charles Haughey had convened a meeting of ministers and a number of city and county managers to review the position of urban renewal designated areas on 2 February, a day after his Leinster House meeting with Gilmartin. This shows, at the very least, that a number of ministers, including Haughey and Flynn, and their respective officials, were in deep negotiation about the urban renewal schemes and their possible extension during this period and fits a pattern that could well have placed Gilmartin in Leinster House on 1 February.

Before completing his opening examination Gallagher explored further the subject of political interference and corruption, with results that clearly surprised the members of the tribunal, the assembled reporters and the ever-growing crowd in Dublin Castle, who by now realised that this was the best entertainment in town. Gilmartin outlined his dealings with Pádraig Flynn and how the latter turned his complaints into the suggestion of a substantial donation to the party. The flawed Garda investigation, during which he received the call telling him to 'fuck off back to England,' was described, and his payment of £50,000 to Flynn for Fianna Fáil in the period leading up to the general election in June. Asked whether this payment could have been interpreted as a bribe to Flynn, Gilmartin replied: 'I would not bribe anybody. I felt it despicable that you come into a country that was on its knees, and there's queues down at the American embassy and elsewhere with the kids leaving and walking the streets of London and on the underground begging when they couldn't get a job—absolutely despicable that the people who run this country have no interest whatsoever in those people, other than feathering their own nest.'

The gallery erupted in loud applause. The chairman intervened and told the audience that such behaviour was not appropriate. 'That can be done outside if you wish, but not in here,' he said.

Believing that the judge's comments were aimed at him, an emotional Gilmartin, who for weeks had been reading scarcely veiled allegations that his payment to Flynn was corrupt, fought his corner, turning to the chairman and stating: 'I have been portrayed in the press recently as being corrupt and bribing. I have a right of reply.'

Judge Mahon explained that his comments were aimed at members of the public, and calm was restored as Gilmartin resumed his direct evidence, which would continue over several further weeks.

Before he faced into cross-examination Gilmartin recalled the telephone threats he received at his home in Luton when it first emerged publicly that he was in contact with the tribunal. According to Gilmartin, he was threatened on more than one occasion by a male caller who warned him not to come to Dublin to give evidence. He said that the threatening phone calls began when news of his contact with the tribunal was revealed in the media during the autumn of 1998. He obtained other information concerning alleged threats against him through his friend Peter Kearns, who died in early 2004 without having made, or being invited to make, any statement to the tribunal about certain threats and other matters central to the investigation.

Describing the threatening phone calls he had received, Gilmartin said: 'The first one said that if I turned up in Dublin for me to remember Veronica Guerin, and I knew what was waiting for me. But in very strong language. The second phone call that came, my son answered the phone and he was told in no uncertain terms to tell me if I give evidence to the tribunal or turn up that I wouldn't be coming back. And the third one I got, I picked up the phone and it was much on the same lines. So I responded to that by saying—more or less saying that "if you think that you're going to"—I asked them who they were, but they wouldn't tell me who they were but they said, "Just remember what we are telling you." I said, "You remember one thing, you'll definitely have to make a good job of me . . ."'

The temperature was raised again when Gilmartin's cross-examination began. Conor Maguire SC, representing the Taoiseach, Bertie Ahern, was first to take the floor. 'Bertie's barrister, Conor Maguire . . . set about trying to discredit me. He started by picking on nitty-gritty things in my diary, which was in fact only a notebook about dates and meetings. He was also cross-questioning me a lot on what I was saying about Owen O'Callaghan, and at one point I asked him who he was acting for. "Who are you acting for, Mr O'Callaghan or Mr Ahern?" I said. The judge told me to answer the questions.

'Then he started cross-questioning me and picking up little things about various dates for meetings and whether such-and-such happened on the 1st of February or the 2nd of February 1989 and about the meeting with O'Callaghan on the 28th of December 1988. He was suggesting there was no way there was anybody around at Christmas time, as they were all away on holiday. This one was in Kerry and that one was in Timbuktu. He was trying to discredit me to prove that the meeting didn't take place.'

The atmosphere markedly worsened on one particular day when Gilmartin arrived at Dublin Castle in foul humour and was less than cautious in his replies to Maguire. It made for entertaining exchanges and provoked laughter and applause from the capacity audience but did little for the speedy execution of tribunal business. 'That day he got under my skin. What happened that day is that my son Liam had a serious operation in Luton. Vera at the same time had a bad infection. That was the day before, and here I was in Dublin. Liam was over there on his own, and Vera said to me that I was always tied up in Dublin with one thing or another when I was needed most, I was always at some stupid thing or other. Which was true.

'I was awake a lot of the night and I was in a bad humour when I got up that morning. I was going to pull out of the tribunal altogether. It was going nowhere, and I'm up against it anyway. Thomas spent an hour trying to calm me down. I couldn't calm down, and then I was listening to Maguire trying to nitpick. He was cross-questioning me about gangways in Leinster House and trying to make out the gangway was a bridge and that there was no meeting in Leinster House on February the 1st 1989, as I claimed, with Haughey and Ahern and the rest of the ministers. He said it couldn't have been there and there was no such meeting. He showed Ahern's diary, which had him handing out certificates in Glasnevin, and a photo of Bertie on the 1st of February. I was listening to him and thinking that I had no need for it all. I could have been a billionaire, not a millionaire, and instead of that I wound up a beggar and a fool. This all bore down on me that morning. Thomas was begging me not to do anything rash.'

Maguire first tackled Gilmartin on his claim that Haughey, at the meeting in February 1989, had mentioned that his son, Seán, was or was going to be Lord Mayor of Dublin. He said it could not have happened, as the young Haughey did not become mayor until July 1989. Gilmartin responded: 'Mr Haughey told me that he was becoming Lord Mayor. I wasn't quite sure exactly whether he said he was Lord Mayor or becoming Lord Mayor. But I did call into the Mansion House in August and I met Mr Seán Haughey, then Lord Mayor, at the request of the Taoiseach. I was passing the Mansion House one day and I walked in . . .'

Maguire then disputed Gilmartin's claim that Bertie Ahern was present at the meeting in Leinster House with Haughey. 'What I'm suggesting to Mr Gilmartin is as follows. I'm suggesting to you that the evidence will be that in fact at the time that you're talking about, and from the description that you have given to the tribunal, that Mr Ahern was elsewhere at that time.'

Gilmartin replied: 'I'm not aware—I know he was present at the meeting in the Dáil. He greeted me, first-name terms. He had three meetings before that with me. We were on first-name terms, and the three gentlemen I have outlined were sitting around the table in the Dáil when I was introduced to the then Taoiseach, Mr Charles Haughey, and anyone that says that meeting never . . . is lying . . . Mr Ahern met me in the first one or two days of February in the Dáil with a number of ministers around the table. Now are you telling me that the Government of this country is sitting around the table when I come into a room and to lie to try and cover their tracks? What was wrong with that meeting? Can you explain, Mr Maguire, what was wrong with that meeting when they feel it necessary to lie?'

Maguire pointed to Ahern's diaries for 1 February 1989, which placed him at another function in the early evening, the same time as the Dáil meeting with Haughey and his ministers. According to Ahern's diary he was presenting certificates to students on a course at the National Industrial Fire and Safety Training Centre in Glasnevin at 5 p.m. on 1 February.

Gilmartin: 'Well, it's not entirely Hong Kong, is it?'

Maguire: 'What do you mean by that, now, Mr Gilmartin?'

Gilmartin: 'I'm just saying Glasnevin . . . Leinster House is not a thousand miles away.'

Maguire then went on to ask about Gilmartin's difficulties with the British tax authorities and his bankruptcy in 1992. 'Did the Inland Revenue make you bankrupt?'

Gilmartin: 'The Inland Revenue in England did, on a false claim, supplied by one Mr Frank Dunlop, the Government press secretary and Mr O'Callaghan's sidekick.'

Maguire: 'So, you seem to portray yourself as the victim at every stage in relation to this. The Inland Revenue took proceedings against you and bankrupted you, is that correct?'

Gilmartin: 'That's correct, on false information, and I can prove it. I lost a £20 million pound deal in Milton Keynes, as well as an office block that I had already built and paid for, due to a false claim. And the law in England is, when it comes to an Irishman, you're guilty until proven innocent. I didn't get justice there, and I didn't get justice here.'

Maguire: 'I don't say this lightly, Mr Gilmartin, but you're an embittered man, aren't you?'

Gilmartin: 'No, I'm not a bit embittered. Quite frankly, I look at Mr Redmond there, an old man of eighty, and I do actually feel sorry for him, and I'm sorry that I had any part to play in his downfall. I was never bitter. I always thought if the Lord meant me to have something that I'd have it. If not, well, the only bitterness I have in my life is the way my wife has wound up and what was done to her and done to me by Mr Owen O'Callaghan and his crooked politicians.'

Maguire accused Gilmartin of shifting his ground when asked difficult questions and of being a dishonest witness. 'I want to suggest that your evidence is less than frank—in other words that you're shifty and that you have given dishonest evidence.'

Maguire then raised the matter of a court case in 1978 in Cavan during which a district justice had described Gilmartin as 'shifty and dishonest,' a report that had been uncovered in the local newspapers from the time. But it was a move that turned out to be Maguire's biggest mistake and one that his own client, Bertie Ahern, was to disavow when it was his turn in the witness box.

Maguire: 'It's not the first time that you've been described as shifty?'

Gilmartin: 'I was never shifty. If you want to know a little bit more about me, Mr Maguire, enquire about a lot of the people from your county. There's thousands there will tell you about me, and one thing is sure: they found me reliable.'

Maguire: 'Do you remember Judge Sheehy calling you a shifty witness and saying that you had all the hallmarks of a dishonest witness when you were in court in Cavan over land?'

The cross-examination was interrupted by one of the tribunal barristers, Patricia Dillon SC, who objected to the introduction of previously unannounced evidence. 'I'd like Mr Gilmartin not to comment on that answer. This is the third example, sir, today of Mr Maguire abusing the procedures of this tribunal to spring something on this witness, and it's completely wrong.'

When Gilmartin insisted on explaining what happened in Cavan all those years ago, despite the best efforts of the chairman to assure him that he wasn't obliged to address the matter, the crowd in the public gallery erupted in cheers and applause. Gilmartin ignored the tribunal barrister and continued his account of the Cavan land dispute. 'Yes, in Cavan I bought a piece of land, four acres—I was intending to build a house on [it] because at the time we were thinking of returning. I had a sister-in-law living in the area, and my wife liked the spot. I'll just tell you the story of it so that Mr Maguire doesn't go away with any misapprehension of my character.'

The true story, according to Gilmartin, was that the judge in the case had wrongly sided with a crooked land agent in making a judgement against him—a decision that was subsequently reversed and following which Gilmartin was awarded damages as well as the land.

'I bought the piece of land. A gentleman from next door wanted to— sorry, an agent approached me to see if I'd let the meadow on it, so I did. I told him go ahead—I told him actually I didn't want any money for it, they could have the meadow. So he said, "You can't do that, because they may get a claim to your land." So I charged some minimal figure. Some time later that same agent rung me to see if I'd sell it, and I says No, I was not selling it.

'A few days later I got a contract from a solicitor agreeing to the sale of my land. I refused to go along with it, because I had not sold it and I had stated categorically, and [with] witnesses, that I was not selling that piece of land. But I was sued for specific performance, on the grounds that if an agent proved that he acted for me he could sell my land. He sold the land for a pittance, an absolute pittance, to a cousin of his. So I was sued for specific performance. I went to court. That judge wouldn't hear my evidence or any witness on my behalf. As it happened, I was there sullying the names of decent local people. That's right, I was a shifty person, all right, and he didn't even hear my evidence. He didn't allow me to talk in the box. That is a fact, and I will prove it . . . It was an absolute scandal, typical of this country.'

The gallery again erupted in applause.

'I would like to say one thing on that. I appealed the case, and I brought witnesses who were witness to the fact that I refused to sell the land to the gentleman. On the appeal, the people who—on the other side, the plaintiffs, if you like to call them that—suddenly panicked and offered me more than three times the amount of money, just to see if I'd settle. On the advice of my solicitors I did settle, because they said even if you went into court again it may well not go in your favour; so they wound up paying me more than treble what had been agreed. So that is what that is about: another effort to steal my property.'

Following this explanation the audience erupted in cheers and laughter once more before the day's session was brought to a halt. When proceedings resumed later in the week the judge issued a stern warning to the audience and threatened to restrict public access if order was not preserved. He told the packed gallery that they 'shall not engage in loud laughter, clapping or jeering of counsel or anyone else, even where they might feel strongly about something that is said in evidence.'

———

After his cross-examination by Conor Maguire, Gilmartin was taken down various avenues of inquiry by Paul Sreenan sc (acting for Owen O'Callaghan), whose main aim seemed to be to prove that Gilmartin was a man of straw, with ambitions far above his station and who had willingly signed contracts that were not above reproach. At one point Sreenan disputed Gilmartin's claim that O'Callaghan had used the word 'tap' when asking him whether the former councillor Finbarr Hanrahan had 'tapped' him for money. The 'colour' writers of the national newspapers extracted much juicy copy from exchanges between Sreenan and Gilmartin over the incident after Sreenan informed the audience that there was no way that his client, a former house-builder and prominent developer, would ever use the word 'tap'.

Central to Sreenan's approach was an attempt to disprove Gilmartin's recollection of the meeting on 28 December 1988 after which Councillor Hanrahan allegedly asked him for £100,000 in return for his support for the rezoning and development at Quarryvale.

During cross-examination Gilmartin threw another unexpected can of petrol on the fire when he again alleged that the Lee Tunnel (later named the Jack Lynch Tunnel) was sited at a certain point under the River Lee in order to benefit from Owen O'Callaghan's ownership of land at the tunnel's entrance in Mahon. The allegation that a significant piece of the country's infrastructure could have its site decided so as to benefit one rich property developer drew gasps from the audience but also annoyed Gilmartin's legal team, who cast doubt on the allegation by pointing out that a decision on the route of the tunnel had not been made at the time Gilmartin claimed and, crucially, that O'Callaghan did not acquire the land until several years after the route of the tunnel had been decided.

Gilmartin was also forced to retract a claim that he had informed Mary Harney about his meeting with Haughey and his ministers and about the request for £5 million after his visit to Leinster House in February 1989. He had told the tribunal that he met Harney at a party in Dalkey, county Dublin, which, it turned out, had taken place several months before his encounter with Haughey and his ministers. Gilmartin's opponents seized on this error as an example of his so-called 'fantasies', and this, along with the apparent gaffe in relation to O'Callaghan and the Lee tunnel, was used as a weapon with which to damage his credibility.

But the angriest exchanges with Sreenan concerned the disputed contract made by Gilmartin with Owen O'Callaghan in early 1989. Asked about the arrangement to purchase the lands controlled by O'Callaghan at Neilstown, county Dublin, Gilmartin did not pull his punches.

Gilmartin: 'That's a falsified agreement by your crook of a client.'

Sreenan: 'I know that's what you keep on saying.'

Gilmartin: 'I know, and I will prove it.'

Sreenan: 'Just stick to the facts, if you would, please.'

Gilmartin: 'I am sticking to the facts ... That's not the agreement I signed.'

Sreenan: 'If you just stick to the facts, rather than descriptions of my client, and tell me, is it the case that the very first time you have told the tribunal that this is not the agreement you signed was when you gave evidence in the course of this hearing?'

Gilmartin insisted that he had not made the agreement that his former solicitor, Seamus Maguire, had provided to the tribunal and went on to describe O'Callaghan in less than glowing terms. 'Yes, and he is very good: he's well known as the "cuckoo". He's managing to get—take over other people's nests, like he did in Limerick and Tom Diskin's ... in Golden Island in Athlone. They couldn't get zoning. They couldn't get planning. But magically Mr O'Callaghan can achieve it.'

Sreenan: 'I suggest that you're motivated by begrudgery because he succeeded and you failed ... All your criticism now has come about after you were given £8 million with the assistance of Noel Smyth, solicitor, to negotiate on your behalf to ensure you got every penny that you were entitled to, and it's motivated by bitterness because you've seen how successful the Liffey Valley development was without you ...'

Gilmartin: 'No, it was motivated after Mr O'Callaghan defrauded me, and the bank with him, to get control of my company. It was motivated by ... I was not going to allow my money to prop the deal up, because Mr O'Callaghan had no money in it and, as a matter of fact, with the help of the bank had stolen over £1½ million to pay Mr Dunlop and his likes, and the crooked politicians that he bought, and they were numerous.'

———

After Sreenan had spent a number of days seeking to undermine Gilmartin in relation to the contracts he signed with his client it was the turn of Pádraig Flynn's barrister, Bernard Madden SC. Flynn had been present for every day of the hearings, making copious notes and nodding to anyone who would talk to him. The tall figure had apparently lost none of its swagger, despite his fall from grace over the previous years, and he went out of his way to greet the man who had contributed to his downfall in as public a manner as possible. Liam Lawlor was similarly the personification of politeness when he spoke personally to Gilmartin, in stark contrast to the personalised and harsh attacks on him when he was in the witness box.

As a result of all the questioning, Gilmartin began to recall details surrounding the £50,000 given to Flynn for Fianna Fáil in 1989 and of the unusual phone calls made to him by Flynn in 1998. During the hearings Flynn's barrister claimed his client had notes of his phone conversations with Gilmartin that proved his claim that the donation was intended for his personal use, and that it was the developer who had initiated the calls.

The tribunal legal team was perplexed about the fact that the cheque for £50,000 that Gilmartin collected in the College Green branch of Bank of Ireland was not issued from that branch. They also wondered why the number of his account at the Blanchardstown branch, and the sorting code, were written in by hand on the cheque. During cross-examination by Flynn's barrister Gilmartin was able to recall a more detailed account of how the cheque was generated within the bank and further substantiated his claim that it was genuinely intended as a donation to Fianna Fáil, despite Flynn's assertion that the payment was intended for his own personal election expenses. Gilmartin explained that he had collected the cheque from the branch in College Green after contacting Paul Sheeran, his manager at the Blanchardstown branch, just before his meeting with the minister, as he had not brought his chequebook with him.

Bemused by the revelations of how his donation to Fianna Fáil had travelled through a number of bank accounts, including some offshore investment vehicles arranged by Flynn's daughter and former financial adviser Beverly Cooper Flynn, Gilmartin felt a level of sympathy for the politician whom he had previously described as 'not the worst of them.'

Chapter 15

'‘AS FAR AS I CAN REMEMBER’'

Public and media attention on the first Quarryvale module of the tribunal reached new heights when Bertie Ahern and his former Government colleague Mary O'Rourke, then Cathaoirleach of the Seanad, took the witness box.

A crucial question for both was their recollection, or lack of it, of the meeting in Leinster House on 1 February 1989 with Haughey and his ministers. Most of those stated by Gilmartin to have been present, including Ray Burke, Pádraig Flynn, Séamus Brennan, Albert Reynolds and Ahern himself, in his statement to the Dáil in 1999, insisted they had no memory of the event.

Mary O'Rourke was called to give her evidence before Ahern and, in a series of replies to questions from the tribunal lawyers, drove a coach and horses through the credibility of her former colleagues. She insisted that she had a clear recollection of meeting Gilmartin, though she was not particularly *au fait* with his business plans. She said she had been present in the room in Government Buildings when the meeting involving various cabinet members took place some time early in 1989. Even more devastatingly for her former colleagues, she had a precise recollection because her mother had died a few months earlier, and when Pádraig Flynn invited her to come over from her office to the meeting he commiserated with her on her loss.

In her statement O'Rourke said that while she could not remember the exact date of the meeting with Gilmartin she thought that February 1989 would be accurate. ‘The meeting was not an arranged meeting as such, at least not arranged to my knowledge . . . It did not seem to me to be a meeting in the fullest sense, in that nobody appeared to be sitting around the table and there did not appear to be an agenda or printed papers of any kind. As far as I can recollect, the following people were in the room: Mr Pádraig Flynn, Mr Ray Burke, Mr Brian Lenihan, Mr Bertie Ahern and the then Taoiseach, Mr Charles Haughey, [and] Mr Thomas Gilmartin. There was much coming and going and milling around the room, so I indeed may have inadvertently left out the names of some of the people who were there and who came and went.'

She described how Pádraig Flynn introduced her as Minister for Education. 'I nodded and Mr Gilmartin nodded and then I turned and left the room.' She said she was not aware of the business of the meeting, only that Flynn had told her that it was about jobs for county Dublin. 'I went back to my office across the corridor to continue my departmental work, but I have never seen or met Mr Thomas Gilmartin since that occasion.'

Her dramatic intervention, which contradicted the evidence of her former Government colleagues, was a significant turning-point in relation to Tom Gilmartin's credibility. Though her description of the venue of their brief encounter differed from Gilmartin's, her recollection of other details served only to reinforce the reliability of her account. Counsel for the tribunal, John Gallagher SC, asked her: 'Now I want you to tell the tribunal where the office, where your ministerial office was in relation to the room where you say this meeting took place.'

O'Rourke: 'Well, as far as my memory—as far as I can remember, Mr Flynn, as I said, knocked on the door and said I'd like you to meet a man . . . who was going to provide thousands of jobs for Dublin. And if I just may say it was a time of huge unemployment in Dublin—15 to 18 per cent and parts of Dublin, pockets of it up to 40 or 50 per cent—so it was quite normal, it would be quite normal to meet people, and still would be if they could give you, if they could provide jobs. I saw nothing untoward and still cannot envisage anything untoward about meeting somebody who was going to provide jobs.

'Now, you have asked me where my room was in reference to the room to which I was brought. In my memory it was across the corridor, and I went into that room and there were the people whom you called out in the letter which I have written, in that room. They were standing up; they were not sitting around or discussing anything. It would seem to me the gathering—and I think I would have referred to it as a gathering—that the gathering had come to an end, it seemed, because there were people coming and going.'

Gallagher: 'Can you say approximately what time elapsed between the time Mr Flynn knocked on your door to ask you to come across to the meeting and the time you actually went across?'

O'Rourke: 'Maybe . . . five and ten seconds. It was very brisk.'

Gallagher: 'I see. You went across immediately after you were asked?'

O'Rourke: 'I was doing my own work. I hadn't a deputation with me. He actually said to me, Mr Flynn did, "This is a man, Mr Gilmartin, who is from your mother's own county." My mother was from county Sligo. My mother had died at the very end of November, and he actually, Mr Flynn, said a kind comment as we crossed, about my mother's demise. That's how it sort of etched in my mind.'

Gallagher: 'I see. Did you say anything to Mr Gilmartin about his county of origin or anything of that nature?'

O'Rourke: 'No, because we didn't speak.'

Mary O'Rourke's mother hailed from Castletown, near Drumcliff, at the foot of Benbulben in county Sligo, and her family was related to the Gilmartins of Lislary through Tom's mother, Kathleen McDermott. Mary O'Rourke's mother's name was Scanlon, and her extended family maintained deep roots in the area. When the six republicans were put to death on the side of the mountain by Free State soldiers in 1922 some of the corpses were carried to the Scanlon farm at the foot of the mountain. Among those who helped carry the bodies down the mountain was Mary O'Rourke's late uncle, Brian. He left the country secretly for Australia after the episode in order to avoid arrest by Free State forces over the help he provided in recovering the bodies, according to Mary O'Rourke, who later told me that this was a story she often heard during her childhood. At the time she gave her tribunal evidence she did not know she was a distant relation of the Gilmartins of Lislary, nor did Tom Gilmartin until Brian Lenihan (junior), Mary O'Rourke's nephew, informed a relation of Gilmartin during a conversation some years later. Just as the atrocity of the Benbulben executions was stitched into the memory of the Gilmartin family, it is also etched into the life history of O'Rourke and the Lenihans.

Under cross-examination by Hugh O'Neill, for Gilmartin, O'Rourke also dismissed the notion that Charles Haughey would not have discussed the forthcoming accession of his son to the Dublin mayoralty during their conversation in Leinster House. Gilmartin had been criticised for suggesting that Haughey would have known in February 1989 who was to become Lord Mayor the following July. O'Rourke said that the identity of the future mayor would have been an open secret at the upper echelons of the party for months in advance, if not a full year. The power-sharing agreement between the political parties on the council meant, she said, that there was normally prior agreement about the affiliation of the next incumbent, while within each party the preferred choice was known well ahead of the election by the city council each summer.

The effect of O'Rourke's testimony was devastating. Though the meeting in Leinster House did not amount to anything of great significance, other than what took place immediately after it, most of the ministers present had vehemently insisted, in statements to the tribunal and in direct evidence, that it had never happened. Of greater import, however, her evidence for the first time elevated Gilmartin's credibility in the eyes of the wider public and focused even greater attention on the hearings in Dublin Castle.

Freda Kelly, the editor of *News West*, a local newspaper in west Dublin at the time of the Quarryvale development, recounted to the tribunal a conversation she had with Mary O'Rourke's brother, Brian Lenihan (senior), who was a TD for Dublin West and a senior figure in Fianna Fáil. She said that Lenihan had informed her that, with other ministers, he had met Tom Gilmartin in Leinster House. She specifically recalled Lenihan telling her that among the ministers present was Séamus Brennan, who consistently denied his attendance to the tribunal.

———

In contrast to Mary O'Rourke's direct style, Bertie Ahern was an expert at disguising his views and his intentions even to the closest of his allies and had a unique ability to make lengthy statements that appeared to have at least two and sometimes a number of interpretations. Coupled with a hesitant and often grammatically challenged formulation and delivery, Ahern over the years had managed to perfect a style that was both evasive and mercurial.

The Taoiseach's appearance at the tribunal on 7 April 2004 was a significant public occasion, and it was evident that he and his legal team, as well as his media advisers and handlers, had thought long and hard about his strategy and tactics. As he arrived in the tribunal building in Dublin Castle for his first appearance at the inquiry Ahern was in no mood for pleasantries with the media scrum gathered outside and entered instead by a side door.

From the outset he engaged in contentious exchanges with counsel for the tribunal, John Gallagher, and later with Gilmartin's senior counsel, Hugh O'Neill, who was concerned to establish why Ahern's barrister had sought to cast doubts on his client's character by having him described as 'shifty'. Ahern insisted that he never suggested that Gilmartin was 'shifty or dishonest', as described in the words of Conor Maguire. He tried to reconcile his previous Dáil statement that he had never attended the meeting of Government ministers with Gilmartin in Leinster House in February 1989 with Mary O'Rourke's recollection that he was definitely present. By recalling the death of her mother, O'Rourke had made it difficult for Ahern, in particular, to disagree with her account. He conceded that O'Rourke's 'attachment' of her mother's death meant that such a meeting with Gilmartin may well have taken place. After several exchanges with counsel for the tribunal he conceded that he may have been present at what he called a 'chit-chat' type of meeting with Gilmartin, though he could not recall it. He had already provided the tribunal with evidence from the Dáil log-book and his own diary about his movements that day, which included his attendance at the award ceremony in Glasnevin at about the time that Gilmartin claimed the meeting took place in Leinster House.

Asked by John Gallagher whether he accepted O'Rourke's recollection of the informal meeting of ministers and Gilmartin, the witness pointed firstly to the discrepancies between the descriptions given by O'Rourke and Gilmartin of the room where the encounter was said to have taken place. 'I have read what Mr Gilmartin's, as you said, very clear view of the meeting was, and what you have just said is Mrs O'Rourke's very clear view of the meeting. There is one slight difficulty: both their views are totally different. So they are very clear views, are entirely different: that's the first point I make . . . If you asked me the question that we are now not talking about a meeting at all, that there could have been a casual chit-chat of a few ministers, as Mary O'Rourke described the other day, where Pádraig Flynn went around into a few offices and pulled a few ministers out to meet, in this case Mr Gilmartin, those kind of issues happen on the hour every day, where somebody brings somebody in to meet somebody. But that's not a meeting in the formal sense, or hardly the informal sense. That, of course, could have happened.'

Gallagher: 'So you accept that an informal meeting could have happened as described by Mr Gilmartin and Mrs O'Rourke, although you do point out that there are differences in their account?'

Ahern: 'The only point, Mr Gallagher, is, I object to the word "meeting", because a meeting in political terms is a meeting. Mr Gilmartin's view is that he remembered precisely where it was: he remembers the doors in, he remembered the doors . . . Mary O'Rourke remembered the doors in, but there is only—if she went out that door she would have fell off the first floor, because there is no door. The fact is, they are entirely different places; and Mr Gilmartin remembered the order people were sitting down; it now—the fact is there are two different places, two different locations. If you asked me is it possible that Mr Gilmartin was brought into Leinster House by somebody, that he was brought over to the ministerial corridor, or somewhere else but more likely the ministerial corridor, I think Mary O'Rourke's view on that would be more right. We wouldn't [sic] in the party room, and somebody caught a few ministers and said hello to somebody and shake hands with somebody or nodded to them, of course, of course, is the answer to that . . . I mean, that could well happen. But I would not—and if you asked me would I remember such an engagement, not a hope. Because I do something like that. And as Mary O'Rourke said the other day, you just call in and you go out. The only thing I probably do is go in and shake hands.'

Ahern also conceded, in contrast to his Dáil statement of January 1999, that his friend Councillor Joe Burke may have spoken to Gilmartin about Quarryvale, and not just about the Bachelor's Walk project. He also said he had asked Burke to contact Gilmartin on foot of the developer's complaints about the delay in the purchase of the council lands. Though he did not recall Gilmartin telling him of the party donation he had given to Flynn, he did remember having a telephone conversation with him at the relevant time in June 1989, a few weeks after the payment was made. He did not recall inviting Gilmartin to a fund-raiser in London, though he accepted that such an event had taken place later that year and that he was present. He insisted that he had not made any request for a donation from Gilmartin and would never do so of anyone, notwithstanding his role as party treasurer.

Gallagher: 'Mr Gilmartin, in his evidence, has said with reference to you, "He asked if I would consider giving a donation."'

Ahern: 'No, I would not ask. It wouldn't matter that I wasn't treasurer or that I was—whatever position. I would not ask anybody, even somebody that I barely knew, like Mr Gilmartin, I would not ask in a telephone call. I am accepting I had a telephone call with him, but I would not ask somebody to give me a donation or my party a donation because I had done something for them, whether I had or I hadn't I wouldn't have ask[ed].'

He may have asked Gilmartin whether he had given a donation to the party, he said, if the issue was raised in the phone conversation, but he did not ask him to give one. He agreed that the payment to Flynn was a 'large donation', even by 1989 standards, though it may not have been the largest.

Reminded of his statement to the Dáil in 1999 in which he said, 'I was shocked that this amount of money could be floating around, because it never floated anywhere that I had been over the years that is inappropriate,' he replied that it was not the sort of money he came across during his years representing the Dublin Central constituency.

After Gallagher had completed his direct examination, Gilmartin's counsel, Hugh O'Neill, got to his feet. He first asked Ahern if he recognised Gilmartin. He then immediately tackled him about the attack on his client's integrity by Conor Maguire. After some tetchy exchanges, Ahern was asked whether he believed Gilmartin was 'shifty', as his barrister had alleged. After evading a direct reply for some time, Ahern was eventually forced to concede that he would not describe Gilmartin as 'shifty'. He also denied being responsible for the trawl that uncovered the local newspaper account of the Cavan court case in May 1978, almost a quarter of a century previously. 'With respect, I am saying that I did not call Mr Gilmartin shifty, and I did not say it was dishonest. I said he changed his position on several times. And that is my answer to your question.'

O'Neill: 'You would appreciate that the questioning that went on, and a very serious allegation made against Mr Gilmartin by your counsel, by Mr Maguire, put very blatantly to Mr Gilmartin that "you are shifty and you have given dishonest evidence"—I want to ask you, and it's a simple answer, Yes or No, do you dissociate yourself from those remarks?'

Ahern: 'I am stating, Mr O'Neill, that I do not and did not and would not say that Mr Gilmartin was shifty or dishonest. I have stated that he did move his evidence around considerable times, but I did not use those words.'

O'Neill went on to deal with the issue of the £50,000 donation to Flynn and his party's response to it. 'I am just asking your attitude in terms of the practice and morality of the Fianna Fáil party as to how you would view the situation where an allegation is made that moneys have been donated, a significant sum of money donated to Fianna Fáil, of £50,000, and there is no record of that within Fianna Fáil. I would have thought that that was a matter of critical importance and significance that would have been investigated thoroughly. Would you expect that to have taken place?'

Ahern: 'Mr O'Neill, I can tell you what would happen now. In my watch, if we were aware that a contribution was given now, that Fianna Fáil was not given, regardless of what the sum was, we would investigate it.'

On the advice of his son Thomas, Gilmartin had instructed his lawyers to deal with the Maguire approach and the Cavan incident before they questioned Ahern on other matters. Thomas also suggested asking Ahern why he appointed Liam Lawlor to the Ethics Committee of Dáil Éireann. The strategy appeared to have worked, in that it forced Ahern onto the defensive at an early stage of the cross-examination.

When he emerged after several hours of intensive examination Ahern was upbeat and said he welcomed the opportunity to give his side of the story. 'I have to say I've been waiting since January 1999 to get this opportunity,' he told waiting reporters. 'I said in the Dáil on the 27th of January 1999 that I would go to the tribunal, that I would fully comply with the tribunal, and I would put up with whatever cross-examination. I've done that for 5 hours and 25 minutes. That's the way it should be, and needless to say I enjoyed putting my story, because it was a long time to wait and do that.'

While some commentators sympathetic to Ahern claimed he walked away unscathed from the five-hour grilling by lawyers for Gilmartin and the tribunal, and despite the 'best foot forward' and smiling-face approach to the cameras after the gruelling interrogation, it was recognised by experienced tribunal-watchers that Ahern was distinctly uncomfortable with the experience, even though no allegations of wrongdoing or inappropriate behaviour were put to him during the day.

It was also noticed that there appeared to be an effort by his handlers to ensure that numbers of Ahern supporters were drafted in from his constituency and occupied most of the seats normally taken by the regular daily audience that had warmed to Tom Gilmartin in the previous weeks. When they returned from the lunch break to hear Ahern's evidence, many of those who had attended daily found themselves locked out of the large hearing room because of lack of space, with many seats taken by what was evidently an organised assembly from Ahern's local organisation.

Chapter 16

‘A SHOCKING LIE’

After Tom Gilmartin's and Bertie Ahern's evidence was taken, the tribunal continued to question other central figures in the Quarryvale controversy, including some of the other ministers present at the Leinster House meeting as well as Owen O'Callaghan, Liam Lawlor and George Redmond.

Séamus Brennan made a brief appearance to claim that he did not attend the meeting in February 1989. The former Taoiseach Albert Reynolds also made a brief appearance to say that he did not recall being present but said that if Gilmartin insisted he had been, and could prove it, he would accept that. Ray Burke said he had no recollection of the meeting.

Liam Lawlor, who represented himself, conducted a cross-examination of Gilmartin that went on for several weeks and was marked by some extraordinarily deprecatory remarks about the witness. Both in direct evidence and in cross-examination Lawlor and Redmond made a series of claims that did not match Gilmartin's recollection of events. Lawlor in particular spent weeks delving selectively into correspondence in order to put certain constructions on the material that were damaging to Gilmartin but that when read in full held a different meaning. At one point he accused Gilmartin of 'lying under oath.'

Owen O'Callaghan made a brief appearance, as the tribunal at this stage was dealing only with the period from 1988 to 1990, before O'Callaghan joined the board of Barkhill Ltd. He told the tribunal that Gilmartin had exaggerated and lied about various things and that he (O'Callaghan) did not report allegations made by his former partner about bribery and corruption on the part of various politicians as he did not wish to spread scandal and rumour. He said he knew nothing about planning corruption in Dublin in the 1980s and 90s and had few dealings with politicians. When counsel for the tribunal, John Gallagher, asked O'Callaghan if Gilmartin had informed him about his meeting with Charles Haughey and his ministers in February 1989 and the subsequent demand for £5 million, O'Callaghan said he knew nothing about it and was amazed when he read of it in the newspapers. He did accept that Gilmartin told him about the alleged request for a huge sum by Councillor Hanrahan in Buswells Hotel in 1989, but he had not paid much heed to the story, or reported it to the Gardaí, because he didn't believe it.

Under cross-examination by Liam Lawlor, O'Callaghan said it was a 'shocking lie' for Gilmartin to suggest that that there was something amiss with the contract they agreed over his sale of the lands at Balgaddy and Neilstown. He accepted that the Quarryvale site was far superior to the one he controlled, which had been nominated for town-centre designation under the Dublin Development Plan, but said he would have proceeded with it if the zoning had not been changed to the better site. He denied that his application for planning permission on the Balgaddy-Neilstown site was merely a 'stunt', as Gilmartin had claimed, and said it was 'completely untrue' that he, in a conspiracy with Allied Irish Banks, had defrauded Gilmartin.

O'Callaghan went further in his criticism of Gilmartin when he described him as 'spiteful, vindictive and ungrateful.' He said it was outrageous for Gilmartin to describe him as a 'crook, a gangster and a cuckoo' who stole other people's business projects. In a further exploration of avian metaphors he agreed with Lawlor that Gilmartin was a 'magpie' and a 'scavenger'.

O'Callaghan said that he went into business with Gilmartin at the suggestion of the banks, and that while he himself had a business employing some four or five hundred people his partner in the Quarryvale project 'was going around on his own with just a briefcase.' Gilmartin had owed him £1½ million, and he told the tribunal: 'If Tom had paid us the money we wouldn't be here today.' He said that Gilmartin's claim to have introduced the Duke of Westminster, who took a 50 per cent stake in Liffey Valley Shopping Centre and effectually made the Quarryvale project a viable and indeed hugely lucrative development, was 'false'. He said that Gilmartin was foolish to try to build a 1½ million square foot development at Quarryvale. (Gilmartin's original plans had envisaged only a 500,000 square foot retail scheme.) 'Anyone with any knowledge of planning would not have attempted what he attempted. It was extremely foolish, and the size was way too big for Dublin,' O'Callaghan insisted.

On the same day that O'Callaghan was giving his evidence at Dublin Castle the members of South Dublin County Council agreed to a major expansion in the size of Liffey Valley Shopping Centre and rejected a Green Party motion, by a majority of two to one, to defer the rezoning of the centre until after the planning tribunal had reported, as it had agreed two years previously. On the advice of the council management and planners the elected members granted town-centre status to Quarryvale, which would allow it to expand significantly.

———

As Dublin Castle continued to hear hours, days and weeks of conflicting evidence, a tribunal ghost of the past appeared in the form of Ray Burke, who was facing a lengthy prison sentence after he pleaded guilty in the Circuit Criminal Court to tax offences. In mid-July 2004 he admitted in court that he had furnished incorrect information in 1993 to the Revenue Commissioners during the Government's tax amnesty, introduced by his former colleague Bertie Ahern, by failing to declare income of £151,980. He also admitted to providing incorrect information to the inspector of taxes on or after 15 December 2003 by failing to declare income of £24,038. It also emerged in the court that Burke had made a settlement of €600,000 with the Criminal Assets Bureau. In 2005 he was given a six-month prison sentence for the tax offences. The Garda investigation had begun after the Flood Tribunal found he had received illicit payments of almost £250,000 and had acquired his house in Swords from the builders Brennan and McGowan for far below its market value, thus conferring a 'substantial benefit' on him.

———

Owen O'Callaghan's first appearance at the tribunal on 7 July 2004 was followed in quick succession by George Redmond and Pádraig Flynn, both of whom also disagreed with almost everything Tom Gilmartin had said about them. A day after Ray Burke's court appearance Redmond admitted at the tribunal that he had accepted massive payments from business interests during his thirty years with Dublin City Council and that he had hidden them in accounts in Belfast, England and Spain using an Irish version of his name. Consistent with his reputation for miserliness, he told the tribunal that he never did anything with the money he accumulated. The payments, he told the tribunal, were in return for the expert advice he provided for people, though he agreed that the vast sums of money funnelled to him were related to decisions he made as a senior council planner.

He denied Gilmartin's claim that Liam Lawlor had asked Gilmartin for £100,000 on his behalf, and denied providing the developer with a map showing landowners in Quarryvale, though he did agree that they met in 1988. He also accepted that he had told John Corcoran, the principal of Green Property, about the planned sale of council lands at Quarryvale to Gilmartin in 1989. He accepted that he told Corcoran about the price of £40,000 an acre tendered by Gilmartin for the seventy acres he needed to develop his scheme and that Corcoran, armed with this inside information, had proceeded to put in a rival, and higher, bid. Gilmartin was forced ultimately to pay the council £70,000 an acre for the land.

————

As the summer and the end of the legal term approached, the excitement and controversy that had surrounded the appearances of the Taoiseach and serving and former ministers at the planning tribunal subsided while the tribunal turned its attention to other matters.

Tom Gilmartin also found that he had more important issues to deal with when his doctors discovered that a previously detected heart condition had seriously deteriorated and recommended immediate surgery. On 28 July 2004 he underwent a quadruple bypass operation, and he was advised that he could not attend any further public hearings until he had made a full recovery. Other than some minor complications that were resolved in the following months, Gilmartin, an otherwise strong and healthy man, made a full recovery and was given the all-clear six months later, a month before he was expected to resume his oral evidence.

His appearance was further delayed, however, following a Supreme Court judgement delivered by Mr Justice Adrian Hardiman on 9 March

2005. The court ruled that the Mahon Tribunal was wrong to refuse Owen O'Callaghan access to statements made by Gilmartin privately to the inquiry, and that the tribunal had breached O'Callaghan's constitutional rights by depriving him of material that could have been of use in his cross-examination of Gilmartin at public hearings. The ruling upheld an earlier High Court decision in favour of O'Callaghan, who had argued that the tribunal had breached his constitutional right to fair procedures by refusing him access to the various statements made by Gilmartin. Mr Justice Hardiman said that Gilmartin had made grave and sometimes dramatic allegations against O'Callaghan during his tribunal evidence in March 2004, which were not in the statement circulated before the hearings to O'Callaghan and others. When O'Callaghan sought the details of earlier versions of Gilmartin's statements, the tribunal had refused, on grounds of confidentiality.

The ruling had an immediate impact on the tribunal, which was forced to further postpone the start of the Quarryvale 2 hearings until it had complied with the court rulings and circulated the relevant documents to O'Callaghan and other parties.

At the end of May 2005 counsel for O'Callaghan argued in the High Court that fifty-four documents provided to him by the tribunal on foot of the Supreme Court decision were redacted or edited. His counsel, Paul Sreenan SC, said that his client was entitled to see the documents in unedited form. He also claimed that Gilmartin was being treated more favourably than his client, who had provided no less than 35,000 documents to the inquiry since 1998. The court heard a claim that, in private sessions, Gilmartin had made 'preposterous and spurious allegations' to the tribunal, to the effect that O'Callaghan had made large and improper payments, including offshore payments, to Bertie Ahern and the former Taoiseach Albert Reynolds. The tribunal lawyers argued that the editing was necessary in that it related to material that was outside the terms of reference of the tribunal and not relevant to its inquiries or that intruded on the privacy of other parties.

In late 2004 the tribunal had written to Ahern seeking information about his financial affairs dating back to the mid-1980s. In a letter of October 2004 the tribunal solicitor Susan Gilvarry sought details of all bank and building society accounts held by Ahern, or for his benefit, over a period of many years. She explained that the information was necessary as the tribunal was investigating a claim by Gilmartin that Ahern had received sums of £50,000 and £30,000 from O'Callaghan between 1989 and 1993. In response Ahern's solicitors, Frank Ward and Company, who were also long-time legal advisers to Fianna Fáil, sought to restrict the inquiry to accounts he held between January 1989 and December 1992 and to lodgements of more than £30,000. This request was made many months before the tribunal discovered that Ahern had no bank accounts in his own name during this period other than his joint account with his estranged wife, which he did not operate. Correspondence continued for over a year, during which the tribunal continued to seek information from Ahern through discovery and production orders.

Again the outcome was less than a happy one for the tribunal, which was ordered in late July to disclose the material that had been edited out but only on condition that it was used solely for the purpose of the cross-examination of Gilmartin and to test the credibility of his evidence. The decision was something of a legal setback for the tribunal and further delayed the resumption of the Quarryvale module. Because the tribunal was forced to release previously withheld or deleted information, an increasing circle of people were now in possession of confidential material. As a result of the court ruling there was less control over the circulation of sometimes extremely confidential information provided to the tribunal, which was now restricted in the exercise of its discretion over what material it should release and to whom. This was particularly relevant when it came to the more politically sensitive aspects of the tribunal's inquiries, such as those relating to Bertie Ahern.

As the Supreme Court upheld the earlier High Court decision in relation to O'Callaghan's request for previously withheld or deleted material in the possession of the tribunal, further details of Gilmartin's claims and allegations were circulated to the relevant witnesses. These included his claim that an official of Bank of Ireland in Jersey had contacted him some years previously to tell him that Bertie Ahern and other prominent Irish politicians had hidden £15 million in the offshore bank. Gilmartin said he did not know the identity of the anonymous caller, who put down the phone in the middle of the conversation, but when he redialled the number that had come up on his phone monitor it was answered by a receptionist at the Jersey bank.

Ahern also learnt of a series of other allegations passed on to the tribunal by Gilmartin, including a claim that he and others had availed of other offshore sites to hide money, including England, Liechtenstein, and the Dutch Antilles. In the course of correspondence between Susan Gilvarry for the tribunal and Liam Guidera of Frank Ward and Company, Ahern's solicitors, the latter vehemently denied the claims and suggested that they merely further illustrated Gilmartin's lack of credibility. In the early stages of the correspondence the Taoiseach's solicitors reminded the tribunal that he had been vindicated in the Circuit Court over similar allegations by Denis 'Starry' O'Brien that he had received improper payments from O'Callaghan.

The exchanges continued during 2005, and a further discovery order was served on Ahern by the tribunal, seeking all his financial and banking records by 30 November. An intense and at times angry private correspondence continued between Ahern and the tribunal, particularly following the order by the High Court in late July that the tribunal make more material available to O'Callaghan than it previously thought was necessary under the terms of the earlier Supreme Court decision.

———

It was an event outside the immediate workings and concerns of the tribunal, however, that caused the greatest shock during 2005 when Liam Lawlor died in a tragic car accident in Moscow. The controversial politician was killed along with businessman Ruslan Suliamanov, the driver of the car in which he was travelling in the early hours of Saturday 22 October. He was accompanied by a 29-year-old Ukrainian legal assistant and interpreter, Julia Kushnir, who survived the accident and who was wrongly described as a prostitute in some of the wildly inaccurate early coverage of the accident.

As the true story unfolded, it emerged that Lawlor had travelled from Prague for some business meetings with unidentified Russian contacts and that the car crashed on its journey from the airport to the city centre, where he was booked into one of Moscow's more expensive hotels. Sources close to Lawlor's family have since confirmed that he was in Moscow in relation to property dealings in Prague, capital of the Czech Republic. Some of his dealings in the region were the subject of investigation during the earlier stages of the tribunal inquiry. That Lawlor would have been involved with business dealings in Moscow came as no great surprise; but the sudden nature and circumstances surrounding his death nevertheless sent a shock wave through the political establishment, not least in the pubs, bars and cafés of Killarney, where the Fianna Fáil ard-fheis was taking place that weekend. The Taoiseach offered his condolences to Lawlor's wife and his four children, one of whom, Niall, travelled to Moscow to identify his father's body and to bring it home for burial.

After Lawlor's death the tribunal continued to investigate his role in a number of controversial rezonings, particularly Quarryvale, and had yet to report on his dealings with Jim Kennedy, a businessman and arcade owner, and John Caldwell, a solicitor, as well as Dunlop and Redmond. Lawlor's wife and son remained on the tribunal's witness list for several more years, as the latter's role in providing his father with assistance and advice in relation to the planned stadium on the site originally proposed for the town centre at Neilstown and Balgaddy was an aspect of the wider Quarryvale 2 module. Hazel Lawlor took legal proceedings to stop the tribunal investigating her and her late husband's affairs, while Niall Lawlor declined to return from the United States when invited to attend at Dublin Castle. Julia Kushnir was later awarded an estimated £500,000 from a number of British and Irish newspapers over their description of her as a prostitute. Because of Lawlor's untimely death, the tribunal was unable to examine in greater detail his role in the Quarryvale saga.

Lawlor was a flamboyant character who was unique among Fianna Fáil TDs in the 1970s and 80s, when he used a chauffeur-driven Mercedes car, financed by his ability to marry his political life with his business interests.[h] He was connected to the 'beef baron' Larry Goodman during this period and on one occasion in the late 1980s travelled to Iraq to negotiate a deal on the sale of live cattle to the country with representatives of its then ruler, Saddam Hussein. During this and other trips abroad Lawlor often introduced himself as a representative of the Irish Government, even when he was on private business and though he had not been appointed by the Taoiseach or any minister to act on their behalf.

His purported familiarity with every blade of grass in west Dublin and his ability make friends and influence people, from local councillors to millionaire property developers, assisted Lawlor with his accumulation of vast sums of money, held over two decades in hundreds of Irish and offshore banks and finance houses. Among those he befriended were the auctioneer and slot-machine millionaire Jim Kennedy and, of course, the former assistant city and county manager George Redmond.

Lawlor fell out of favour with a number of those with whom he co-operated during his decades in politics, including the former Taoisigh Charles Haughey and Albert Reynolds, though Bertie Ahern controversially appointed him to the Ethics Committee of Dáil Éireann, even while he was under scrutiny for some of his business activities, and continued to meet him after the tribunal had uncovered his global network of hidden bank accounts.

Lawlor's legal and other battles with the tribunal, which led to his incarceration on three occasions, are now the stuff of history. He was once famously exposed for destroying potentially valuable evidence when he set fire to bundles of documents in the garden of his mansion in Lucan at a time when he was under an order for the discovery of relevant material concerning his finances and business affairs. He also fell out with successive legal representatives during the years of the tribunal between 1998 and his unexpected death in 2005.

Lawlor was by far the most investigated individual, featuring in a number of modules of the tribunal in public hearings between 2002 and 2008 and giving evidence over twenty-one days. The tribunal was provided with explanations for only 53 per cent of the lodgements greater than £1,000, totalling some £1.4 million, that were identified in bank accounts controlled by or for the benefit of Lawlor in the period 1991–97. In 2001 a list of 'political contributions, donations and consultancy fees' supplied by Lawlor to the tribunal for the years 1973–2000 revealed a total of £1,521,500, including payments from such luminaries of Irish business as Green Property Company (1970s and 80s), Monarch Properties (1970s, 80s and 90s), Michael Quinn (1970s, 80s and 90s), Davy Stockbrokers (1980s and 90s), National Toll Roads (1990s), Ganley International (1990s) and the Jones Group (1990s) and of course Arlington Securities, Frank Dunlop and Associates and O'Callaghan Properties in the 1990s. (See appendix 1, paragraph 34.)

Lawlor's 'brass neck' was recalled by the businessman Declan Ganley, who said he first encountered him when he gate-crashed the Ganley tent at the Galway Races. When it emerged that the uninvited visitor was a Fianna Fáil TD he was invited to Ganley's home the following day for a function. Lawlor told Ganley he was a member of the Trilateral Commission, the secretive global network of politicians, bankers and business people. On foot of his apparent political influence Ganley invited him to work with his company, Anglo Adriatic Investment, which had interests in Albania. On one occasion they met members of the Albanian government. He said that Lawlor had travelled on a number of occasions to Albania, at the behest of Ganley International Ltd, to lobby the Albanian government to close certain 'pyramid' schemes that threatened the company's interests. On the company's behalf Lawlor had introduced international delegations to the Industrial Development Authority, Aer Rianta and ESB International. Ganley believed his company had made total payments in the region of £25,000 to £30,000 to Lawlor for his services and expenses and said he had not been aware of the politician's use of his company's headed notepaper for false invoicing.

Other donors discovered that Lawlor used some exotic locations to disguise the sources of his considerable income. In the mid-1990s Séamus Ross of Menolly Homes Ltd paid Lawlor £20,000 following efforts made by him to persuade the postal authorities to extend a postal district to include lands south of Lucan on which Ross was constructing houses in order to enhance their desirability and sale value. The payment was made in July 1996 on foot of an invoice provided to him by Lawlor in the name of Baltic Timber Products Ltd, with a London address, a company with which Lawlor had no known connection. The description on the invoice referred to a quantity of 'Latvian sawn softwood.' Ross never purchased timber from Baltic Timber Products Ltd, and had never heard of the company, he later claimed.

Ambrose Kelly, who was involved with O'Callaghan and Lawlor in the Quarryvale and Neilstown stadium projects, also employed him as a consultant on property investments in Prague, and they continued working together on eastern European projects until Lawlor's unexpected death.

Notwithstanding his aggressive cross-examination of Gilmartin and his constant interruptions when the latter was seeking to answer his questions at the tribunal, Lawlor was always affable and polite when they met between sessions. Always dressed for the occasion, he was seen by friends and adversaries alike as an incorrigible but likeable rogue, though for others whom he crossed, such as Gilmartin, and those who did not deliver on his insatiable demands he was seen as a dangerous enemy who could make life very difficult. As evidenced by his role in the Quarryvale and other planning controversies, he was a major influence in the determination of zoning decisions by Dublin County Council, influencing votes across the political divide in return for substantial payments from dozens of wealthy landowners and developers. During his years assisting on the Quarryvale development he was simultaneously on the payroll of the developer John Corcoran of Green Property, whose Blanchardstown Shopping Centre was commercially threatened by O'Callaghan's planned Liffey Valley centre. Such apparent conflicts of interest seemingly never caused the larger-than-life politician any lack of sleep. His death following the car crash in Moscow thwarted the tribunal's lengthy investigation into his financial affairs and, in particular, deprived it of one of its most important witnesses and sources of information during the Quarryvale module.

From his first encounter with Lawlor in the Dead Man's Inn in Palmerstown in 1988, Tom Gilmartin regularly witnessed at first hand the extraordinary graft and destructive ability of the former hurler. Gilmartin was also among the more prominent victims of Lawlor's avarice, though his malign influence on the development of Dublin's outer suburbs meant that the lives of many thousands of citizens were damaged by his corrupt activities over three decades. His status also ensured that senior members of the Garda Síochána declined to interview him, despite the serious allegations made to them by Gilmartin and others in 1989 concerning his abuse of office and of the planning process. The tribunal concluded that the failure to interview Lawlor was probably due to his position as a public representative. It was, perhaps, no surprise that Frank Dunlop described Lawlor as 'Mr Big' among the corrupt politicians on Dublin County Council. (See appendix 1, paragraph 35.)

Chapter 17

'LOANS FROM FRIENDS AND GIFTS FROM STRANGERS'

The Quarryvale 2 module finally opened in late November 2005 following years of delay partly, but not solely, caused by the various legal challenges by Owen O'Callaghan and others to the tribunal's methods of work.

On 29 November counsel for the tribunal, Patricia Dillon SC, opened the last major module of the inquiry with a lengthy two-day statement covering the issues that would inform the public hearings. In her opening statement she outlined an allegation that Bertie Ahern had received payments totalling £80,000 from O'Callaghan, including £30,000 in relation to a tax designation matter. She did not identify the circumstances surrounding the first alleged payment of £50,000; instead her comments referred only to the discussions among the board members of Barkhill Ltd in 1993 about a possible designation for the rival Blanchardstown development under the urban renewal incentive scheme.

The tribunal, in the course of its release of other private statements made by Tom Gilmartin, had informed the Taoiseach some six months previously that Gilmartin had also mentioned that he believed Ahern had received a substantial payment from O'Callaghan in relation to the tax designation of the Golden Island retail development outside Athlone in 1994.

Gilmartin had told the tribunal of the conversation with O'Callaghan and others in relation to Blanchardstown Shopping Centre, the nearest competitor to Quarryvale, which was then under construction. Dillon described the Barkhill board meeting, attended by Gilmartin, his then solicitor Seamus Maguire, O'Callaghan, John Deane and a number of senior officials from the head office of Allied Irish Banks some time in late 1992 or 1993, at which Gilmartin had raised the problem of tax designation in relation to the Blanchardstown development, owned by Green Property. O'Callaghan claimed after a phone call that he had got it 'from the horse's mouth' that Blanchardstown would not get tax designation. Asked to identify the 'horse's mouth' in question, O'Callaghan named the Minister for Finance, Bertie Ahern.

A memo based on a conversation between O'Callaghan and the head of corporate banking at Allied Irish Banks, Michael O'Farrell, also outlined how O'Callaghan appeared satisfied that, through his political connections, Blanchardstown would not be given tax designation, despite the efforts of prominent local politicians. The contemporaneous memos by O'Farrell reflected O'Callaghan's confidence that his political soundings were accurate and his view that Quarryvale had a head start over the rival development in attracting anchor tenants, such as the British retailer Marks and Spencer, and would not need tax designation as long as the Blanchardstown scheme did not enjoy it.

The detailed statement also introduced several new participants into the Quarryvale mix, as well as repeating some previously aired claims. Dillon disclosed that Frank Dunlop had received more than £1.8 million from O'Callaghan in relation to Quarryvale, mainly in what were described as consultancy fees, and a further £360,000 towards the legal costs incurred by Dunlop from his dealings with the tribunal. It was also revealed that O'Callaghan had paid almost £105,000 to members of Dublin County Council, including a total of £36,000 to Liam Lawlor. The details of his generous donation of £100,000 to Fianna Fáil during 1994 were also described, while his earlier contributions to the party's leading representative in Cork, Mícheál Martin, and two other TDs, Batt O'Keeffe and G. V. Wright, were also revealed.

The response from the Taoiseach to the latest claim that he was instrumental in blocking the tax designation of Blanchardstown was fast and furious. Through his spokesperson, Mandy Johnson, he repeated that he had never received any money from Owen O'Callaghan directly or through intermediaries. Once again his vindication in the 'Starry' O'Brien case was cited. 'It is a fact which was established by the Circuit Court in legal proceedings which the Taoiseach was required to take to clear his good name in response to allegations made by Mr Denis "Starry" O'Brien,' Johnson stated. The Taoiseach 'has lately become aware that Mr Tom Gilmartin made very similar allegations to those disproved in court. Like Mr O'Brien, Mr Gilmartin has alleged that the Taoiseach received a large amount of money from Mr O'Callaghan. Like

Mr O'Brien, Mr Gilmartin made these allegations in the period 1998–2000. Like Mr O'Brien, Mr Gilmartin's allegations are utterly false.'

Johnson's comments were made on the same day that the order for discovery made by the tribunal seeking details of Ahern's financial records and bank accounts expired. The public were not to know for many more months that such an order had been made on the Taoiseach.

O'Callaghan's response was equally robust, and his lawyers immediately turned to the High Court for relief, succeeding in forcing the tribunal to postpone the public hearings that were due to resume that day, Friday 2 December 2005, with testimony from Frank Dunlop. Three days earlier O'Callaghan's lawyers had secured leave to take proceedings against the tribunal to stop the Quarryvale 2 hearings. Citing the previously withheld or edited material released earlier in the year, O'Callaghan argued that the tribunal had ignored what he called 'glaring' and 'significant' inconsistencies between Gilmartin's private statements and his public evidence before the inquiry. Paul Gallagher SC and Paul Sreenan SC claimed, on O'Callaghan's behalf, that the tribunal was biased against him and that it had sought to protect Gilmartin by failing to disclose material that might have undermined the credibility of the inquiry's star witness.

The High Court granted an injunction restraining the tribunal from continuing the hearings until after the judicial review proceedings were heard the following January. After seven years of preparation, and at a cost now exceeding £50 million, the tribunal was facing a further, possibly terminal delay as it headed into 2006.

The public statements of Ahern and O'Callaghan centred on the credibility of Gilmartin, who was now openly accused of being a fantasist following the release of the previously withheld transcripts of his private interviews with the tribunal lawyers and others since the mid-1990s. In those discussions he had repeated hearsay allegations made to him by a variety of named and unnamed sources. Most of the serious allegations relating to Ahern, Reynolds, Flynn and others stemmed, he said, from his direct conversations with his former business partner Owen O'Callaghan; other allegations came from telephone calls, some anonymous, to him or to friends and through which, he said, some extraordinary claims were relayed, including one he passed to the tribunal in September 2002 that Ahern and others held more than £15 million in offshore accounts in places including Jersey, Liechtenstein and the Dutch Antilles. When this claim surfaced in the early summer of 2005 it was ridiculed, not least because of the popular perception of Bertie Ahern as a 'common man' who had little interest in money, who enjoyed a modest life and whose only relaxation was football and a pint of Bass in his favourite haunts in north Dublin. Certainly there was nothing similar to the life-style of his predecessor and mentor Charles Haughey, with the horses, the yacht, the island off county Kerry and, of course, the expensive Charvet shirts from Paris. The view that Ahern held hidden financial assets offshore, possibly into the millions, did not fit with the persona he had created for himself; and when the notion of hidden funds came up the most common questions posed by his political opponents as well as his allies were 'Where does he keep it? Where does he spend it?'

O'Callaghan's High Court action, which opened in March 2006, was to have a lasting effect on the operation of the tribunal, in more ways than one. O'Callaghan's legal team argued that the allegations against their client, many of them hearsay, were false and outrageous, and they called for a halt to the tribunal's most politically sensitive investigation, the Quarryvale 2 module. In the process they sought to inflict as much damage as possible on Gilmartin's credibility. At a hearing of O'Callaghan's application to halt the inquiry the High Court heard further details of what his counsel, Paul Gallagher, said were the 'entirely untrue' allegations made against him. Gallagher also claimed that the tribunal was biased against his client and had wrongly granted immunity from prosecution to Gilmartin as an inducement to him to give evidence.

These serious claims were, not surprisingly, rejected by the tribunal, and over the following ten days details of the so-called spurious claims made by Gilmartin were unveiled. The public learnt little of the proceedings in the Four Courts, as there was minimum coverage in the mainstream media. When Mr Justice Thomas Smyth delivered his reserved judgement six months later it was not the result that O'Callaghan, or presumably Ahern, had hoped for. Smyth rejected the claims of bias made against the tribunal and said he was satisfied that the inquiry had disclosed all relevant documents to O'Callaghan, who now had the opportunity to make a full cross-examination of Gilmartin at the public hearings of the Quarryvale 2 module. If Gilmartin had made statements in private that were 'glaringly and significantly inconsistent' with those he made in evidence, these could be tested in cross-examination.

O'Callaghan was now facing legal costs of more than £2 million as the result of his unsuccessful challenge to the tribunal, but he was determined to continue his action through an appeal against the Smyth judgement to the Supreme Court.

Gilmartin could only watch the events playing out in the courts from a distance, as he was not a party to the actions taken by O'Callaghan and his associates against the tribunal. He believed he was being castigated during the proceedings, where he could not defend himself, in particular against the serious claim that he was manufacturing outrageous allegations almost daily. He complained that his name was being 'dragged through the mud' in the High Court and that he was being accused of 'lying and making up stories.'

'Anything I said to the tribunal was based on what O'Callaghan told me, or what I heard from others,' Gilmartin complained to me. 'I knew nothing of Ahern's finances, for example, and had only told the tribunal that O'Callaghan said he gave him money for various reasons. Over the years different people, including the anonymous caller from the bank in Jersey, told me different things, and I informed the tribunal about them as I had promised to do, no matter how incredible they seemed. Some things that did seem incredible turned out to be true, others were never proven. But to then get attacked and vilified in court because I repeated details in confidence to a tribunal was not one bit fair, especially as I was not there to defend myself.'

———

While the battle in the legal arena effectually stymied the tribunal's investigation into Quarryvale, significant and politically explosive details of its private inquiries erupted into the public domain with a sensational report by *The Irish Times* public affairs correspondent, Colm Keena, in late September 2006. Keena revealed that a number of people, including the businessman David McKenna, had been contacted by the tribunal about payments they had claimed to have made to Bertie Ahern in December 1993. The payments, totalling between £50,000 and £100,000, had ostensibly been made to help Ahern pay legal bills he had incurred at about that time. The report said that a solicitor, the late Gerry Brennan, may have had a role in the collecting of money for the then Minister for Finance. It went on to state that Brennan had been a former director of Telecom Éireann before his tragic death in 1997. It said that David McKenna, whose company Marlborough Recruitment spectacularly collapsed in 2002, was closely associated with Ahern's friend and former party fund-raiser Des Richardson.

On the day the story was published on the front page of *The Irish Times* the Taoiseach confirmed that the Mahon Tribunal was investigating payments he received in 1993, and that he had provided extensive details of his bank accounts over many years since the 1980s. However, in an interview on Clare FM he described the figures mentioned in the story as 'off the wall'.

'A lot of what is on the front of the paper is absolutely correct,' Ahern said. 'I have co-operated throughout the last number of years with them. What is in the paper this morning is some of the information I gave them in confidential session—very confidential, as you can see. And somebody has given it to *The Irish Times*. The source of the leak is absolutely impeccable. The person who gave the leak has obviously seen the full file, there is no doubt about that, except for the figures. The figures are off the wall.'

In later comments to the hungry media pack that followed the Taoiseach on his daily rounds he added: 'What I got personally in my life, to be frank with you, is none of your business. If I got something from somebody as a present or something like that, I can use it.' He referred to previously false allegations made against him and said he had given the tribunal details of his financial affairs, including the payment from McKenna and others in 1993, in the context of its inquiries into an allegation that he had received money from Owen O'Callaghan.

The initial focus of the media inquiries was on Ahern's relationship with David McKenna at a time when the latter had an estimated net worth of £60 million. It was known that Ahern had travelled to Manchester United football games as a guest of McKenna and on his private jet. It was known that McKenna was a regular visitor to the Fianna Fáil fund-raising operation run by Des Richardson each year at the Galway races, most recently a few weeks before *The Irish Times* report. It was known that Ahern had appointed McKenna to the board of Enterprise Ireland, and that Richardson had joined Marlborough Recruitment following the end of his term as party fund-raiser. But Ahern insisted that none of these facts were in any way related to his receipt of money from McKenna in 1993 or to the tribunal's investigation into the payment.

As the opposition parties seized on an opportunity to politically embarrass the Taoiseach eight months or so before the expected general election, Ahern, not for the last time, concentrated on the unjustified nature of the leak and said he was not about to disclose details of his personal financial affairs to anyone. 'I'm not answering what I got for my Holy Communion money, my Confirmation money, what I got for my birthday, what I got for anything else. I'm not into that. I gave all the details of everything to do with my life to the tribunal, but I'm not under investigation for any of these things, including the unjust and unfair leak that's in the papers this morning.'

He carefully dealt with the question as to whether he had paid tax on the payments, stating that he had 'dealt properly' with them. 'I would say nobody, nobody has given as much details and co-operation to the tribunals over several years, and then for somebody just to take one particular issue out of an issue is just unjust. And I gave all the information about my separation case and all the information about my legal fees and how I funded everything, but they're personal matters.'

The timing of the story was significant in a number of respects, not least as Ahern was hoping to become a three-term Taoiseach after the coming election. Unknown to the wider public, it also came at a time when the tribunal was privately seeking answers from him about the source of large sums going into accounts under his control when he was Minister for Finance in the early 1990s. Ahern knew that these details were going to emerge at a tribunal hearing at some time in the not-too-distant future, and that he had to have credible answers. He decided to put into the public domain not only the answers but the questions on which they were based by outlining a bewildering set of financial dealings from the time he resumed 'normal banking' in late 1993 up to December 1995.

Ahern appealed directly to the public about the state of his financial affairs in an interview with the RTE news anchor Brian Dobson on the 'Six-One News'. In a lengthy and emotional interview, made in his office in Drumcondra, Ahern revealed the names of others who had given him money during 1993 and 1994. He said the amounts totalled £50,000, and he described the payments as a 'debt of honour' that he intended to repay. He said that the money was given to him as a result of financial difficulties he encountered following his legal separation from his wife in the autumn of 1993.

The payments, or 'dig-outs', as he famously described them, were made up of three separate amounts, he claimed: £22,500 from eight friends in Dublin in December 1993; £16,500 from four different friends in Dublin in 1994; and £8,000 (sterling) from a group of businessmen in Manchester in 1994. He claimed that the first payment of £22,500, which he received in December 1993, came from eight friends, whom he named as Paddy Reilly, Des Richardson, Pádraic O'Connor, Jim Nugent, David McKenna, Fintan Gunne, Michael Collins and Charlie Chawke. He said the second payment was made in 1994 by four other friends: Joe Burke, Dermot Carew, Barry English and (a different) Paddy Reilly.

In the course of the interview Ahern distinguished between accepting large sums in return for political favours and small contributions from friends. 'The difference of talking about somebody taking millions and somebody taking hundreds of thousands in exchange for contracts and other matters and taking what is relatively small contributions from friends who had a clear understanding they were paid back—I do not equate those. When they gave me that £22,500 I said I would take this as a debt of honour, that I would repay it in full, and that I would pay the interest on it—I know the tax law, I am an accountant—and that I would pay that back in full on another date when I could. I haven't paid the money, because they refused to take it. I think they will now, because they see the difficulty, but I offered them a number of times to repay it.'

He described the donors as 'close friends, people who have been close to me for most of my life. They are not political friends, they are personal friends. They are long-standing friends.'

However, Ahern agreed that he had appointed some of these people to public office, including as remunerated members of state boards, but said he did so not because they gave him money but because they were friends. 'I might have appointed somebody, but I appointed them because they were friends, not because of anything they had given me,' he said in a comment that was to be reproduced many times in the media.

As the interview continued, Ahern referred tearfully to his marital separation, and to the fact that he did not operate any bank accounts for a lengthy period yet had managed to save £50,000 in cash between 1987 and 1993. He also referred to another payment of £8,000 (sterling) he accepted in Manchester in 1994. 'That's what it was, the only other thing, Brian, totally separate and nothing to do with this. But I don't want anyone saying I didn't give the full picture. I did a function in Manchester with a business organisation, nothing to do with politics or whatever. I was talking about the Irish economy, I was explaining about Irish economy matters, and I'd say there was about twenty-five people at that. The organisers of it, I spent about four hours with them, dinner, I did questions and answers, and all the time from 1977 up to current periods I got eight thousand on that, which you know, whether it was a political donation . . . I'd actually done the event a number of times, but I only once got a contribution. So I think at all of the times in my personal accounts, I've gone through them and given my personal accounts, that is the only other payment. It's nothing to do with this but it was a payment that was in my accounts, and I did give that to the tribunal as well.'

Asked about the declaration of money he received from his friends and business people, Ahern said: 'Yeah, and I wouldn't have had a difficulty, quite frankly, declaring it. I've broken no law. I've broken no ethical code. I've broken no tax law. I've always paid my income tax. I paid capital gains tax, but I've never had much in my life to pay, and I paid my gift tax. I never—so I broke no ethical code, and if I had to have returned on these things I wouldn't have had a difficulty. I did point out to my friends a number of times that it was better that I clear these, and you know, they would sometimes laugh it off, but they all accept and have accepted that these are loans to be repaid, and will pay.'

His defiant if somewhat staged performance earned Ahern some time and, more importantly for him, public sympathy, but it also created more than one hostage to fortune as commentators—his political allies and enemies as well as other observers—analysed each and every paragraph for inconsistencies. In the days and weeks that followed there was much to chew on as the media focused, among other issues, on the background of his generous benefactors, who became popularly known as the 'dig-out' men. It emerged that no less than five of the twelve Dublin donors had served on state boards. Des Richardson was a director of Aer Lingus for several years, from November 1997 to November 2002, and was previously a director of FÁS International Consulting as well as of the Health and Safety Authority. David McKenna had served on the board of Enterprise Ireland from March 1999 to March 2001, Joe Burke as chairperson of Dublin Port Authority, and Jim Nugent as a director of the Central Bank of Ireland and of CERT, the state tourism training agency. Pádraic O'Connor, a former managing director of National City Brokers (a company founded by the financier Dermot Desmond), had also served on the board of the state telecommunications company, Eircom, and as non-executive chairman of ACC, the state bank, from 1999 to 2002. Ahern's former solicitor Gerry Brennan, who he said helped organise the 1993 'dig-out', had been appointed to the board of Eircom only a year previously, in November 1992. The commercial history of the other donors made for equally interesting reading. It was not the last time that Ahern's circle of friends came under public, or tribunal, scrutiny.

As time went on, scepticism deepened over Ahern's account of the circumstances in which he claimed to have received large sums before, during and after his time as Minister for Finance. As he sought to draw a line in the sand with his RTE interview, he also unleashed a wave of speculation over decisions he made during his time as Minister for Finance and about his relationship, financial and otherwise, with those who benefited from them. Among those who gained most from tax designations he agreed in 1994 was Owen O'Callaghan.

In the early part of the interview with Brian Dobson, Ahern had sought to quash the various allegations that had emerged in respect of his dealings with O'Callaghan. 'Over the last number of years a number of false allegations, half-truths, lies, were made against me to both the tribunals, and there have been so many of them I won't detail them all, but the main ones [were] that I took a bribe of £50,000 in the car park in the Burlington Hotel from Starry O'Brien, which was meant to come from Owen O'Callaghan in the all-Ireland final day of 1989; the second one was that I took a bribe from Owen O'Callaghan of £30,000 in 1992; that I had bank accounts in the Dutch Antilles, Liechtenstein, Jersey, England; that I had £15 million in an offshore account; that I had received £30,000 and a payment of £50,000 from Owen O'Callaghan to another politician some time in 1994 . . . that I fixed a designation for Golden Island in Athlone for Owen O'Callaghan; that I had a bank account in Mauritius and . . . they produced forged documents to show I had this bank account.

'Now, these allegations were made to both tribunals. So the tribunals rightly, under their terms of reference, and had no option, and naturally I was totally obliged and assisted them to produce evidence that these allegations, and there were others too. So I had to make full discovery of all my records, my bank accounts, my wife's bank accounts, bank accounts I had in my children's names, you know, the Fianna Fáil bank accounts associated with my constituency, so I had to give them all those records.'

The leak of some of the confidential correspondence with the tribunal concerning his finances had forced him to go public, he told Dobson. But by doing so he had taken a serious political gamble, which could not be disguised, despite his attempts to do so, by an aggressive attack on the tribunal, which he hinted was responsible for the leak of the McKenna letter to *The Irish Times*. The tribunal indeed took exception to the leak of what it considered ultra-private correspondence that had been circulated only to McKenna, unlike the wider circulation of documents that go to large numbers of potential witnesses before public hearings. It summoned Colm Keena and his editor, Geraldine Kennedy, to Dublin Castle. Both journalists refused a request to reveal to the tribunal the source of their story and to hand over documents that the paper had obtained, including the tribunal's private correspondence with McKenna. The chairman of the tribunal, Alan Mahon, said that only one original copy of the letter existed, and it was in McKenna's, or his solicitors', possession. The tribunal had not retained a copy of the original, so a logical conclusion, Judge Mahon asserted, could be that McKenna or someone close to him was the source of the leak, unless the journalists could suggest otherwise.

They did not wish to provide any information that could lead to the source. Kennedy admitted to the inquiry that she had destroyed relevant documents after being served with an order for discovery by the tribunal. She said it was in the public interest to publish the story, the contents of which had been verified. She confirmed that *The Irish Times* report was based on an 'unsolicited and anonymous communication' that the newspaper had received.

Colm Keena later described how the letter came into his possession after he received a phone call at *The Irish Times*. 'A short time later I had in my hands a number of documents,' as he puts it in his book *Bertie: Power and Money* (2011). The source of the documents remains a mystery. In his book Keena also noted the chilling effect the 'Starry' O'Brien story and court case had on media coverage relating to Ahern's finances. 'The case had the effect of dampening media interest in any rumours about payments to Ahern out of fear that they might again be sold a pup,' he wrote.

The 'dig-out' story was treated carefully by *The Irish Times* editorial team, with a decision to publish it on the front page but not as the lead story. Other newspapers and media also treated it very cautiously until Ahern gave his interview to RTE News. While many observers, and indeed *The Irish Times* journalists, may have assumed that the information came from a source that was disgruntled with Ahern and believed it was in the public interest to release the confidential documents, the suspicion among others, including the tribunal team, was that the information came from someone much closer to, and sympathetic to, Ahern.

Mahon said that the destruction of documents was something the tribunal had to take very seriously. In a written decision he said he had no choice but to refer the matter to the High Court in order to protect the integrity of the tribunal's work and its confidential correspondence with witnesses.

The tribunal team suspected that the leak was intended to damage its inquiry and in particular its investigation into the Taoiseach's finances, just as it was reaching its most sensitive stage. It was also evident that Ahern was using the opportunity to put his elaborate, if somewhat bizarre, construction on the source of the various substantial lodgements to his accounts between 1992 and 1995 before public hearings into the issues began and, crucially, before the coming general election. Whatever the source, Ahern had used the opportunity to set out his stall for the general public, convoluted as it was, before the outcome of the tribunal's inquiries into his financial affairs.

However, if he had hoped that his RTE appearance would help to quickly kill the story of how he accepted money from business associates in the early 1990s, he was mistaken, as pressure mounted on him to make a comprehensive statement to the Dáil on the matter. In the days after the interview he deflected questions from reporters who followed him as he travelled to various functions around the country; but at one stop, in Ballyjamesduff, county Cavan, he provided a further hostage to fortune when he commented on the 1994 function in Manchester after which he had received £8,000 (sterling). He said that he spoke at the dinner involving about twenty-five Irish emigrant businessmen on his own time and that the money was not taxable, as it was a financial gift given to him outside the state.

'So no official script, not an official function, not in my capacity as minister, paid my own way, spoke at the function,' he told reporters. 'And on one occasion the assembled group, about twenty-five, plus a group who were with me in Ireland, gave me the sum of money that I mentioned. That's all that happened. I checked the ethics of that under the regulations some years ago when I was checking these things and it was found to be in order. And I checked the tax position, because a sum like that from outside the state until 1995 wasn't taxable. I can't remember what I said on the night, but other than that, there's no more to that.' Asked whether he now accepted that it had been wrong to accept money for personal use, he replied, 'No, I don't, and I've checked it with those who arbitrate on these matters, and did several years ago when I put all of these things into the tribunal. If it was after 1995 you would have to declare it, which I would.'

Asked about the identity of those who attended the Manchester function, Ahern declined to name any of them but said they were people he knew, 'some of them from back over the years. Some of them are very well known in Manchester. They're hugely helpful to the Irish community in Manchester. They're part of the community, and I would have regular enough contact with them when I go over for matches.' He also revealed that one of those who travelled with him for the dinner and a Manchester United game during the trip was his close friend Senator Tony Kett.

If Ahern's Government partners in the Progressive Democrats were uncomfortable at the 'dig-out' revelations that emerged in the Dobson interview, they were also becoming increasingly concerned about the drip-feed of information now being provided by the Taoiseach about the Manchester payment. The Tánaiste, Michael McDowell, who only weeks previously had assumed the leadership of the party and who had successfully campaigned during the previous general election on the importance of the PDs' function of keeping a watchful ethical eye over Fianna Fáil, was in a particularly difficult position. He held a crisis meeting with his senior party colleagues, after which he demanded further clarity from Ahern in relation to the Manchester payment. 'I have to say that there are very serious matters of concern which are not completely put at rest by the facts now in the public domain,' he said. Refusing to state that he was considering his position in relation to remaining in the Government, he said that 'accountability and credibility' in relation to the Taoiseach's finances were essential.

As the opposition parties raised the political stakes, with a particular focus on the troubled consciences of McDowell and his party, Ahern prepared to make a statement to the Dáil in an effort to defuse the matter. Commentators dredged up previous statements by Ahern himself on the ethics of accepting payments from business people, including a speech he made in September 1997 at the height of the political scandal surrounding his former colleague Ray Burke. At that time he stated: 'Politics and participation in public life is a career of public service. It is not an avenue of enrichment or life-style enhancement from private donors, even where they only want to help people perform in a particular manner . . . Anyone who abuses their position or knowingly flouts the rules will go. The political fabric of our democracy is precious.'

When first pressed in the Dáil on the issues that arose from his RTE interview, Ahern was evasive on the question as to whether the Revenue Commissioners had accepted that the sums he received in 1993 and 1994 were regarded as loans and therefore not subject to gift tax. He had claimed that his tax advisers had long previously said that the two Dublin 'dig-outs' were loans, repayable at an annual interest of 3 per cent (a much more attractive rate than that available from lending institutions at the time). Questions were also raised about his claim that he had no bank account at the time he was Minister for Finance. In one particularly bruising exchange with the leader of the Labour Party, Pat Rabbitte, Ahern was asked whether he had a bank account outside the jurisdiction. Rabbitte also attacked Ahern for what he described as his 'common-man routine'.

'It is a long time, Taoiseach, since you were a common man. You've been driven around this country since 1987. You never put your hand in your pocket at a forecourt to fill the car with petrol. You're earning more that €250,000 per annum, so there is no point in comparing yourself to the man on Hill 16 who got into a bit of trouble and had a whip-around. Mr Haughey's collection started with a whip-around as well, and it was purely an accident that it came out.'

Rabbitte accused Ahern of setting standards for others that he did not live up to himself. 'Are you telling this house that during the period you were Minister for Finance, responsible for running the country's exchequer, that you had no bank account in this jurisdiction? Did you have a bank account outside the jurisdiction?'

Ahern replied: 'I separated at the beginning of 1987, and it didn't conclude until the end of 1993 in the High Court. Over that period my accounts were in the joint names of my wife and myself. For obvious reasons, I did not use our joint account. I used cheques separately to deal with my issues, and I did not open an account in my own name until afterwards.'

As the political pressure mounted, the Government agreed that the Taoiseach would make a detailed statement to the Dáil on Tuesday 3 October 2006. 'In order to assist the tribunal with the inquiries into some of the lurid allegations made against me,' Ahern stated, 'I gave all my bank and financial records to the tribunals for the years they requested. I produced all of my records going back for a long number of years, which show I have not enriched myself through politics and have not abused public office. I disclosed my financial records to the tribunal, and it is deeply regrettable that these confidential records appeared in a newspaper.'

He then stated that he had repaid, with interest, the loans he had received from his friends. The previous weekend the newspapers reported that his friends had donated the repaid money to the charity Children at Risk, associated with Ahern's estranged wife.

Dealing with the Manchester payment, Ahern recounted his long association with the city and its leading football club. 'As is well known, I have always been a supporter of Manchester United Football Club. Since my youth I have regularly travelled to Manchester. From 1979 to 1996 I would have attended roughly six Man United home games each season. I would travel with friends, sometimes by boat and sometimes by plane. Over the years I have developed a very close affinity with that city and with its people. I have had a long-standing association with the Dublin Association in Manchester, the Manchester-Irish Festival and the Irish World Heritage Centre.'

He identified the organiser of the dinner function as the proprietor of the hotel where it took place, Tim Kilroe, one of the owners of Aer Árann, and gave the name of one of the other Manchester businessmen who were present. 'The dinner was organised by the late Tim Kilroe in the Four Seasons Hotel in Manchester. I had a long personal history with Mr Kilroe, whom I counted as a friend. At the end of the dinner, unsolicited by me, I was presented with cash of the order of £8,000 sterling, made up by individual contributions from an attendance of approximately twenty-five people. Mr Kilroe presented the monies to me, and I presume he had collected them as well. Unfortunately, Mr Kilroe has since died and it is not possible to obtain any list of attendees or contributors at this remove, twelve years later.

'I can confirm that Mr John Kennedy attended the dinner, as he has publicly stated. As I attended various other functions in Manchester over the years, I cannot state with certainty who were the other persons in attendance. I do not want to name someone by mistake and then be accused of misleading the house.'

He said he was accompanied on the trip by Senator Tony Kett, and that he believed the money was raised when his Manchester friends learnt of his personal financial circumstances. He said he had not breached any ethical code and that he had been advised that he had no tax liability arising from the 'private gift'.

Ahern failed to name the rest of his generous Manchester benefactors, though the identity of one person who attended the event did emerge in the immediate aftermath of the Dáil statement. In an interview with the *Irish Times*, Michael Wall, who ran a bus hire company in Manchester, confirmed that he had attended the function, though he declined to say whether he had contributed towards the collection for Ahern. He said he believed that the payment was made in the context of Ahern's marital difficulties. 'If I was him I would have found it awfully embarrassing to refuse to accept it,' Wall said 'Most people there didn't know that he had matrimonial problems at the time. I didn't know he had matrimonial problems.' Questioned about Wall's involvement in the Manchester dinner, Ahern said that Wall was there in his capacity as a bus driver and did not actually partake of the dinner provided.

When it then emerged that Michael Wall had purchased the house used by Ahern in Drumcondra in 1995, the depiction of his role at the Manchester function changed. Ahern had spent many years living in other people's homes or above the Fianna Fáil constituency office in Lower Drumcondra Road since the break-up of his marriage in the late 1980s. In March 1995 a nearby house in a gated estate called Beresford, off Griffith Avenue, was purchased for £138,000, and Ahern moved in six months later. However, the deeds of the house were not put in Ahern's name at the time but in that of Michael Wall.

During the Dáil debate following his speech Pat Rabbitte asked some pertinent questions in relation to the Manchester dinner and to the cash savings of £50,000 that Ahern admitted he had accumulated at the time. '[Do] you believe that businessmen happen along to a posh hotel in Manchester to hear any old Joe Soap lecture on the Irish economy and then have an impromptu whip-around to give him something for himself? . . . In normal life you get gifts from your friends and you take loans from strangers. Yet Mr Ahern says he got loans from friends and gifts from strangers . . . Where was the £50,000 resting, since Mr Ahern did not have a bank account? In a sock in the hot press? But he enjoyed a TD's salary, a minister's salary, and the use of a premises bought for him by friends of Fianna Fáil. How can he be portrayed, in those circumstances, as living in straitened conditions? Why, if there were £50,000 in savings, was it necessary to raise a bank loan? And if there was a bank loan in place, why was it necessary to have a whip-around to replace the bank loan?'

Rabbitte also asked whether the Taoiseach had any other accounts, or any offshore accounts, to which Ahern replied: 'The deputy asked the fair question if I had accounts anywhere else, if I had accounts outside the state or if anyone outside the state opened accounts for me. The answer to that question is no. I had no other accounts whatsoever. I operated for a fairly long period without a bank account and did keep that money in my own possession during that period. I had no other accounts.'

While a series of other questions concerning the different payments remained unanswered, the explanation Ahern had provided to the Dáil was enough to keep the Progressive Democrats in the Government. Though he did not reveal any new information other than the name of the organiser of the event, it was enough to take the political heat off him and, perhaps more importantly, off Michael McDowell and the PDS. On the day after Ahern's speech McDowell, surrounded by his party's twelve TDs and senators, made a statement on the plinth outside Leinster House in which he said that they were of the unanimous view that Bertie Ahern was 'fit to continue as Taoiseach.'

But if the PDS were happy to suspend their disbelief for the sake of political stability, and with an eye to the forthcoming general election, there were plenty of others who continued to probe the credibility of Ahern's explanations. By his own account he had taken the December 1993 dig-out of £22,500 from friends and used it to pay off a bank loan he had taken out from AIB in order to pay the legal fees and other costs arising from his marital separation. Yet he had also said he had saved

£50,000 in cash over the same period. He said that his then solicitor had helped to raise the whip-around, even though he presumably would have been aware of Ahern's financial circumstances, including the £50,000 he held in cash, as Ahern would have to have signed an affidavit of means for the High Court in the context of his separation.

The largest donor to the December 1993 whip-around was Pádraic O'Connor, managing director of NCB Stockbrokers, who gave him a bank draft for £5,000, according to Ahern. (The draft was drawn on an NCB company cheque, it later emerged, which was given to Des Richardson, who claimed he used it to purchase a bank draft for £5,000.) A question arose as to how the NCB payment could be construed as a loan from a friend.

———

As the political fall-out from the controversy abated and the Government settled in for its final months in office, the tribunal continued its inquiries into Ahern's finances in private as it prepared for the resumption of the public hearings into Quarryvale. It was also continuing to put out fires from a number of directions, including an attempt in the High Court by Fitzwilton Ltd to stop any inquiry into the payment of £30,000 in 1989 by a subsidiary of the company to the former minister Ray Burke. A court battle with the *Sunday Business Post* over its publishing of confidential documents in respect of its investigation into a module other than Quarryvale was still under way, and it was preparing the ground for a similar legal offensive against the *Irish Times* over its controversial publication of sensitive tribunal correspondence concerning the Ahern investigation. The tribunal was also conscious of a bill being drafted by the Minister for Justice, Michael McDowell, that would give the Government the power to curb or even halt the tribunals through a vote of the Dáil.

There was an atmosphere of almost open warfare between the Taoiseach's supporters and the inquiry established by the Oireachtas— on Ahern's proposal—some nine years earlier. On one occasion, in another effort to protect its integrity, the tribunal summoned a Fianna Fáil minister of state, Noel Treacy, to explain a claim he had made on Newstalk radio that the identity of someone who was leaking confidential material from the tribunal was well known. If he thought he could make untrue and damaging statements about the tribunal without consequence, he was mistaken. 'I have no evidence to say that I have any knowledge of any person in the tribunal leaking,' a humbled Treacy was forced to admit at a hearing in Dublin Castle in October.

The concerted campaign of criticism from political, media and other sources against the inquiry continued; but the most serious and immediate challenge came from the Supreme Court hearing of Owen O'Callaghan's appeal against that month's High Court decision rejecting his effort to halt the Quarryvale hearings. The judgement, when it was finally delivered on 30 March 2007, came as a relief to the tribunal team, though it also contained a significant sting in its tail when Mr Justice Adrian Hardiman took a different view from the majority of the five-member court. In their judgement the other judges—Susan Denham, Hugh Geoghegan, Nial Fennelly and Joseph Finnegan—upheld the High Court decision and found that the tribunal had not behaved unfairly to Owen O'Callaghan, his partner John Deane, and their companies. They rejected O'Callaghan's claim that the tribunal was biased against him and said that the fact that the tribunal had made errors in not disclosing certain documents was no reason to halt its work. Mrs Justice Susan Denham specifically addressed the issue of the tribunal's alleged unfairness against O'Callaghan and rejected the notion that it had prejudged his credibility unfavourably. Denham and Fennelly also found that O'Callaghan had wrongly sought the intervention of the court in the work of the tribunal and said there had been an inappropriate use of judicial review proceedings involving an extensive use of fact to micro-analyse the decisions of the tribunal.

There could not have been a greater contrast with the opinion of Mr Justice Adrian Hardiman, who dissented strongly from the views of his colleagues. In a lengthy statement he argued that the tribunal had indeed treated O'Callaghan unfairly. If the tribunal was permitted to proceed and to issue findings against O'Callaghan it would represent a 'very marked coarsening of our standards of procedural fairness,' he said. He went further and recited a catalogue of allegations that he said Gilmartin had made against O'Callaghan, including a claim that O'Callaghan and his solicitor, John Deane, had fraudulently altered the written contract they had agreed with Gilmartin in January 1989. He cited inconsistencies in Gilmartin's account in private to the tribunal lawyers and later in public about his encounter with Councillor Hanrahan in Buswells Hotel.

He then pointed to an apparent inconsistency in Gilmartin's accounts of the Leinster House meeting in February 1989 with Charles Haughey and his Government ministers. According to Hardiman, Gilmartin had said to the tribunal barrister Pat Hanratty during a discussion in 1999 that he observed O'Callaghan talking to Albert Reynolds in Leinster House on the occasion of the meeting in February 1989. In fact Gilmartin had consistently said that he saw O'Callaghan talking in a Leinster House alcove to Reynolds in 1991, not in February 1989; and furthermore, whatever basis there was for Hardiman's error, Gilmartin always insisted that he never saw O'Callaghan in Leinster House that day in 1989. Either way, a Supreme Court judge was now citing this mistake as proof of Gilmartin's alleged unreliability.

Hardiman also said that a statement attributed to Pat Hanratty to the effect that the tribunal would 'prove fraud against O'Callaghan and the [AIB] bank' was an invention. Similarly, Gilmartin's claim that O'Callaghan had told him in December 1988 that he had the route of the Lee Tunnel altered to meet lands he owned at Mahon in Cork was, in Hardiman's view, seriously mishandled by tribunal lawyers. He said that the tribunal team sought to stop lawyers for O'Callaghan from cross-examining Gilmartin on the claim after they had pointed out that 'the decision to construct the tunnel was not made until 1991, work did not commence until 1995 and the tunnel did not open until 1999.'

Hardiman also cited Gilmartin's incorrect claim that he had told Mary Harney about his Leinster House meeting with Haughey and the subsequent demand for £5 million at a house party in Dalkey, though it later emerged that the party took place several months before his encounter with the then Taoiseach.

Hardiman also mentioned other allegations made by Gilmartin against O'Callaghan, including a claim that he 'connived at the appointment of an important public servant to a position of significance in his own interest,' and that three well-known persons received bribes from O'Callaghan that were lodged in offshore accounts in various named places. Hardiman misconstrued a comment made by Gilmartin about the political downfall of Hugh Coveney when he referred to a claim 'that the demise of a deceased former office-holder' was brought about indirectly by O'Callaghan, and that a named solicitor and other named parties were instrumental in seeking the resignation of another holder of public office in return for a large money payment. Only the last of these allegations was investigated by the tribunal, when it sought information from Gilmartin's former solicitor, Seamus Maguire, about an alleged meeting in his offices in Blanchardstown when a number of prominent businessmen agreed to pay a large sum of money to the former minister Ray Burke in return for his resignation and quiet departure from politics. Gilmartin said he had seen Burke emerging from Maguire's office in 1998 accompanied by the businessmen. He said the solicitor identified them and the reason for their visit to his offices with Burke. Maguire told the tribunal that no such meeting took place.

The tribunal, according to Hardiman, was fundamentally wrong in the withholding of prior inconsistent statements made to it in private from Owen O'Callaghan, who, the judge said, had been wrongly prejudged by the inquiry. 'I very much regret that I must conclude that Mr O'Callaghan, Mr Deane and their associated parties have not been treated fairly by the Tribunal to date.' Mr Justice Hardiman said he saw no reason why a different set of judges could not hear the Quarryvale 2 module of the inquiry.

Although it was a minority opinion, which did not prevent the tribunal from continuing its work, the effect of Hardiman's dissenting opinion was to harden the views of those hostile to the inquiry from within the political, business, media and legal establishments. It also gave free rein to those who wished to further undermine Tom Gilmartin's credibility and reputation before he returned to give evidence in Quarryvale 2.

Adrian Hardiman, who enjoyed a reputation as a fiercely independent and intelligent jurist, was a joint founder of the Progressive Democrats with Michael McDowell and a fellow law graduate of UCD. He had previously castigated Gilmartin as an attention-seeker in an earlier Supreme Court judgement involving the tribunal's non-disclosure of information.

Gilmartin's reaction to Hardiman's minority view was hardly surprising. 'Firstly, I had never told anyone that I saw Owen O'Callaghan with Albert Reynolds in Leinster House on the day I met Charles Haughey and his ministers in February 1989. I did say that I saw the pair talking in an alcove in Leinster House in September 1991, and I have been consistent all along on that. Whether a tribunal lawyer took his notes wrong or not, I can tell you that I never suggested what Judge Hardiman claimed.

'He accused me of getting it wrong about what I said to Mary Harney, but again I corrected my version of events in evidence in 2004 when I agreed that I could not have told her when I first met her at a party in Dalkey about the meeting with Haughey. But Harney and I both agree that I told her about the skulduggery I encountered when trying to do business in Dublin.

'On the Lee Tunnel I have always said that it was Owen O'Callaghan who told me he had been at a function concerning the planned tunnel in December 1988. He said it, not me. He said it as a means of impressing me about his contacts with senior politicians and bankers. As it turned out, the tunnel, when it finally was built, did end up at lands he owned at Mahon Point, even if he only finally purchased those lands some years after our conversation.

'I have always said that the contract I was given concerning my business arrangement with O'Callaghan was not the one I had agreed to.

'It was also wrong to state that I had claimed that O'Callaghan told me he had something to do with the tragic death of Hugh Coveney. When I used the word "demise" in a statement I was referring to his sudden demotion to junior minister in 1995.

'The other four judges disagreed with his [Hardiman's] opinion on the day and the tribunal continued. But I was not happy at the way I was depicted as some kind of crazy fantasist that made outrageous allegations against people. Some of the allegations which people thought were fantastic were later proven to be true. That did not stop sections of the media and the politicians from attacking my credibility, week in and week out. At some points I wondered, What is the point of it all? Vera is lying in a hospital bed. I'm not getting any younger. The kids were all right, but I was like a fish out of water in a place where I hardly knew a soul. As the time approached for my next appearance in the witness box, the personal attacks got worse, but we decided that I should continue my evidence and get it over with.'

———

The tribunal set an opening date of 30 April 2007 for the resumption of the Quarryvale 2 hearings; but a number of dramatic events prevented it, once again, from meeting its latest deadline. In mid-April I published a story in the *Irish Mail on Sunday* concerning an incident in 1994 when Bertie Ahern was said to have carried a suitcase full of cash to Manchester.

The story, which was also reported in the *Sunday Independent*, was based on what a former Garda driver, Martin Fallon, the minister's temporary driver, told two politicians some years after he drove the then Minister for Finance to Dublin Airport.

Fallon had told the two Fine Gael politicians, Jim Higgins and Enda Kenny, that he had brought Ahern's then partner, Celia Larkin, to the AIB in O'Connell Street, where she collected a briefcase. After he drove her back to Leinster House she asked him to keep the briefcase in the car and to collect Ahern the following day in Drumcondra, as he was travelling to Manchester.

Later that evening Fallon said he drove home and, curious about the contents of the case, opened it, to find it filled with banknotes. He panicked, as he was afraid it could be stolen from the car or his house, and so he parked the car with its contents overnight at Garda headquarters in the Phoenix Park. As instructed, he collected the car the following morning, picked up Ahern and drove him to Dublin Airport, from where Ahern took a flight to Manchester.

When Fallon related the story some years later to the two Fine Gael politicians he had retired from the Garda Síochána and later suffered from ill health. When I contacted his wife she refused to comment on the story or to allow him to make any comment to the media. In later years Fallon moved to the west of Ireland and refused to make any comments on the record about his extraordinary story.

After the story was published on Sunday 15 April 2007 a spokesperson for the Taoiseach said that it was untrue. 'The events described in today's newspapers simply did not take place,' she said. 'Mr Ahern is not aware of these allegations being put before the tribunal.' The tribunal had in fact been informed of the story by Jim Higgins several years previously but had apparently failed to get a verifiable first-hand account from the former garda. Significantly, however, it was the second time that Manchester had arisen in relation to Bertie Ahern's financial arrangements, and it was by no means the last.

As the date for the resumption of the Quarryvale hearings, and the general election, approached, the tension between the country's most powerful politician and the inquiry he first proposed in the wake of Ray Burke's resignation in 1997 continued to simmer. It was soon about to explode.

Chapter 18 ～

| 'PLANET BERTIE'

O
n Sunday 29 April 2007 the country awoke to the unexpected news that a general election had been called. While Bertie Ahern's second five-year term as Taoiseach was coming to an end, the manner in which the election was called for 24 May, less than a month later, was as peculiar as it was unprecedented.

A selected number of journalists from the main news media were contacted by the Taoiseach's press office late on Saturday night and told to be prepared for a call in the early hours of Sunday morning. As dawn broke, the journalists were contacted by the Government press secretary, Mandy Johnson, and told to be at at Áras an Uachtaráin between 7 and 7:30 a.m, because the Taoiseach would be arriving to ask President Mary McAleese to dissolve the Dáil.

Ahern spent less than twenty minutes in the building before departing without giving his customary doorstep interview to the small group of assembled reporters. Not only were the media and the public caught off guard but senior members of Fianna Fáil, including its deputy leader, Brian Cowen, had reportedly not been included in Ahern's decision to announce the election that day. Cowen was particularly incensed, as he had laboured for the previous three years as head of the party's election strategy committee, preparing every detail of the campaign that, by his rigorous planning, had been due to begin two days later with an announcement in the Dáil.

There was a long tradition that outgoing Taoisigh would first tell the Dáil about a decision to go to the country. Ahern said his decision to go to the President just after dawn on Sunday morning was due to the imminent departure of the President on a week-long official visit to the United States. According to Ahern, he had only just learnt of her travel plans, and while he could have asked the Council of State to sign the proclamation of dissolution of Dáil Éireann in her absence, he preferred to have it done, as was usual, by the President.

President McAleese said that she had informed the Government several weeks, if not months, earlier of her planned visit to the United States, which had to be agreed, as were all her official trips, by the Taoiseach and his Government. And while Ahern had not let his ministerial colleagues know of his election plan until the very last minute, he did inform the editor of the *Sunday Independent*, Aengus Fanning, who published an interview he had done three days earlier with the Taoiseach on the day of the dissolution. The *Sunday Independent* was also in a position to reveal the date of the general election on its front page, as clear an indication as any that it had been provided by Ahern with an inside track about his election plans.

In the course of the lengthy interview Ahern gave an indication that his early-morning rush to the Phoenix Park may have been motivated by considerations other than the President's American trip. Among the issues bothering Ahern, he told the paper, was his concern about his coming appearance at the Mahon Tribunal. On the day of his surprise trip to the Áras his lawyers wrote to the tribunal chairman, Alan Mahon, asking him to postpone the planned hearings into the Taoiseach's finances until after the general election.

Previously, under Judge Flood, the tribunal had suspended its public hearings in the two weeks before an election, to ensure that its investigations would not negatively affect individual candidates or parties. The tribunal was due to sit on the day after Ahern announced the poll, and in its opening statement of the resumed Quarryvale 2 hearings it was expected to deal with a number of issues concerning the Taoiseach's personal finances, which it had been investigating for almost three years.

In the weeks leading up to the resumed hearings the tribunal had circulated a substantial amount of documentary evidence relating to Ahern's financial affairs, including details of his bank records and the circumstances surrounding the acquisition of his house in Drumcondra. The documents, which the tribunal was obliged to send to all interested parties as a result of O'Callaghan's successful Supreme Court action, also included transcripts of private interviews given by Ahern, his former partner Celia Larkin and the Manchester bus operator Michael Wall to the tribunal in recent months.

As regards their news value, the documents were, to put it mildly, a media sensation, and when I gained sight of the material in late April, from a source I can still not reveal, I immediately recognised that I was sitting on possibly the biggest political scoop of my career. Timing is always important when it comes to a major news story, and in this instance its arrival could not have been at a more appropriate time for the *Irish Mail on Sunday*, which I had joined some months earlier. Although it was certain to provoke deep hostility from the Government and, in particular, from Ahern and his close supporters, it was information that it was most definitely in the public interest to reveal. Given that the information had been widely circulated, it was almost certain that other media had access to the same material or, if not, that they would obtain it in the very near future. As we were obliged, in the interests of fairness, to contact Ahern and the other people implicated in the story before going to press on the weekend of 29 April, it was necessary to disclose to the Taoiseach and his advisers that we were in possession of fairly sensitive tribunal material.

Although it was not conceded at the time, the decision to call the election was hugely influenced by Ahern's concern over the details to be published in the *Mail on Sunday* that day and the imminent tribunal hearings into his personal finances. In his book *Bertie: Power and Money*, Colm Keena quotes Mícheál Martin as saying later: 'That was a bizarre enough election . . . Most ministers found out about one o'clock in the morning that an election was being called at six. My only observation is that he may have been playing cat and mouse with the *Mail*. Maybe he wanted them to throw everything at him and then he would go to war.'

The issue of alleged leaks from the tribunal had been a recurring one over the years, with those most adversely affected by the publication of their private statements or their financial or other details complaining loudest. The tribunal had a practice of asking every witness who appeared before it and had obtained confidential correspondence whether they had given the information to any third party. Over the ten years of the inquiry not one witness confirmed that they had done so, despite the legion of stories that were generated from circulated tribunal documents. A number of investigations into the source of the various stories, including some carried out by the Gardaí at the request of the tribunal, were unsuccessful. While the tribunal had a responsibility to protect the integrity of its inquiry by seeking to ensure that information was not provided to the media, it also had a legal obligation, as the result of O'Callaghan's successful challenge, to circulate the material.

With so much at stake in the reputation and financial well-being of many parties involved, it was inevitable that the media would become a weapon for those with particular, often conflicting, agendas. On the other hand, newspapers do not refuse ink, and they, along with the broadcasting organisations, had a different set of priorities and concerns from those of the tribunal. In short, there was no question in the *Irish Mail on Sunday* whether the hottest political story in years should be published. The editor, Paul Drury, editor-in-chief, Ted Verity, and myself prepared the most sensational splash and spread since the publishers, Associated Newspapers, set up business in Ireland a few years earlier. To add to the drama, the story was published on the very day that the Taoiseach had decided to call a general election—an unexpected turn of events that had a significant effect on the way it was treated, by the broadcast media in particular. It also exposed deep holes in the credibility of Ahern's 'dig-out' story.

On Sunday 29 April the *Mail* led with the exclusive story of Ahern's money trail and revealed for the first time details of his private admissions to Mahon Tribunal lawyers during his recent interviews with the inquiry team. It wrote: 'Taoiseach Bertie Ahern has made a series of extraordinary admissions to the Mahon Tribunal that could prove fatally damaging. The *Irish Mail on Sunday* can reveal that Mr Ahern gave a lengthy private interview to the tribunal earlier this month. He was questioned both about payments he received in Dublin and Manchester in 1993 and 1994 and about the purchase of his house from businessman, Michael Wall. Mr Ahern—who may call an election as early as today for May 24—told tribunal lawyers:

'1) He received a briefcase containing stg£30,000 in cash from Mr Wall in December 1994, which was to be spent on doing up the house; 2) He himself immediately put a further £50,000 in cash towards refurbishing the house—even though, at the time, Mr Wall was still the owner; 3)

His then girlfriend, Celia Larkin, opened two bank accounts in her own name to lodge the money—but on behalf of Mr Ahern and Mr Wall; 4) At the time, he was desperate to acquire a permanent address, because he thought he was about to become Taoiseach; 5) On several occasions in the mid-1990s he bought large sums in sterling, some of it in order to repay Mr Wall—but never did; 6) He was "amazed" to discover that, in 1996, while he was still Mr Wall's tenant, the businessman made a will leaving the house to Mr Ahern.

'But Mr Ahern's are not the only bombshell revelations to have emerged in extensive tribunal investigations into the Taoiseach's private finances. According to informed legal sources, the tribunal has also discovered that:

'One of the so-called "personal friends" involved in the December 1993 whip-around for Mr Ahern says he has never been close to the Taoiseach. This man, former stockbroker Padraic O'Connor, also insists that he never made a personal contribution to Mr Ahern. Instead, his firm, NCB, made a £5,000 contribution to Mr Ahern's constituency expenses. In return, they received an invoice for consultancy work that was never carried out. Another contributor to the whip-around, then Fianna Fáil fundraiser Des Richardson, paid his £2,500 contribution out of a company account through which Fianna Fáil paid him for his work. Fianna Fáil's cheques were co-signed by Mr Ahern. Several other lodgments of Irish punts to various accounts opened by Mr Ahern and Miss Larkin between 1994 and 1995 matched round figure sterling amounts. One large payment matched an exact round figure dollar amount. Mr Ahern routinely kept large sums in cash both in his safe in his constituency office and his office in the Department of Finance.'

The article went on to describe the extraordinary lodgement by Celia Larkin of an amount equivalent to $45,000 in December 1994 and Ahern's explanation that it was money given to him by Michael Wall in connection with the purchase and renovation of his house in the Beresford estate in Drumcondra. 'He said that, at a meeting with Mr Wall in his constituency office on Saturday, December 3, 1994, he agreed to put a sum of £50,000 towards the refurbishment. Both amounts were lodged in separate accounts opened by Celia Larkin, the Taoiseach's then-girlfriend within days of the meeting. Mr Ahern told the tribunal that he wanted to rent the house at Drumcondra as soon as possible as there was a possibility that he could be made Taoiseach within days due to the sudden disintegration of the Fianna Fáil/Labour Coalition headed by Albert Reynolds. He said he did not want questions asked about his living arrangements. He said that he wanted to be able to inform the Garda authorities as to where his personal security should be located in the event of his being appointed Taoiseach. The tribunal has learned that Ahern stored the money he got from Mr Wall in a safe at his constituency offices at St Lukes in Drumcondra. Ms Larkin lodged the £50,000 promised by Ahern but returned it to him in January 1995. The tribunal has also raised the coincidence that the amount given by Mr Wall and actually lodged by Ms Larkin, £28,772.90 within days of the meeting in December 3, 1994 was the exact equivalent of US $45,000. Ahern denied receiving any payments in dollars. Last night, asked to confirm his own lengthy statement to the tribunal, Mr Wall said: "I don't see why I should. I have nothing further to say." A spokeswoman for the Taoiseach said: "We don't comment on confidential dealings with the tribunals. This has been our consistent position. However, it has always been our policy to co-operate fully with all of the tribunals.'

The article was accompanied by substantial extracts from Ahern's private statements and those of Larkin and Wall, as well as Pádraic O'Connor's denial that he gave a personal donation to Ahern or that he was ever a friend of his.

The *Mail on Sunday* report was met with what could only be described as a stunned media silence. Other than the early bulletin covering the newspaper headlines, the exclusive story of the extraordinary admissions by the most powerful politician in the country concerning his bizarre personal finances when he was Minister for Finance was all but ignored by the state broadcaster, RTE, at least for a day or two.

While the details were absorbed by the public, the political classes and the media, the immediate focus turned to the Mahon Tribunal and its planned resumption of public hearings the following day, when the details published in the *Mail on Sunday* were widely expected to get an airing. Instead the tribunal chairman, Alan Mahon, announced that it was to suspend public hearings until after the general election. Only days earlier the tribunal had successfully defended an attempt by Hazel Lawlor to stop it from resuming its public hearings into Quarryvale and its investigation into her late husband's financial affairs. Now it was facing another delay, though only for a month, and 28 May—four days after the general election—was set for its resumption.

The only place, it seemed, where this sensitive information about the Taoiseach was to be aired was the *Irish Mail on Sunday*, which was prepared to 'publish and be damned.' Otherwise it was a matter of trying to coax some reaction from Ahern himself as he galvanised his troops for the election battle.

It was not long before an opportunity arose to question him about the revelations. At a function in Croke Park early in the election campaign Ahern was asked about the £30,000 in cash given by Wall to Larkin to lodge in December 1994. An angry Ahern replied: 'Any money that Ms Larkin received was towards—was a stamp duty issue and it was towards the refurbishment of the house. So it was entirely appropriate—entirely appropriate.'

The political reaction was muted, though evidence of the turmoil within Fianna Fáil and its Government partners, the Progressive Democrats, was beginning to surface. Michael McDowell was first inclined to dismiss the story, claiming he had been told several weeks previously by Ahern that Michael Wall had put money towards the renovation of the house, which was overseen by Celia Larkin. Ahern continued to deflect queries by claiming he would deal with all the relevant matters at the Mahon Tribunal; but, as the campaign continued, the story just would not go away.

The main opposition leaders, Enda Kenny and Pat Rabbitte, were reluctant at first to get involved in another controversy about the Taoiseach's personal finances, having experienced a negative public reaction to their utterances about Ahern when the controversy first broke the previous autumn. Gradually, more voices called for Ahern to make a full statement on his financial affairs in order to clear up the outstanding questions. John Gormley of the Green Party did not pull his punches and within three days of the *Mail* article said: 'The peculiar nature of Bertie Ahern's financial arrangements demands an effort to clarify matters before the public cast their votes.' He added that the attempt by the Taoiseach to suggest that Wall's huge cash payment was related to a stamp duty payment was not credible. 'Perhaps on Planet Bertie landlords give their tenants £30,000 to pay stamp duty, but in the real world this is difficult to believe.'

A particularly embarrassing incident for Ahern occurred three days into the election campaign, during a canvass in Dublin city centre. Viewers of the evening news watched as the Taoiseach declined to answer a question posed by the journalist Scott Millar of the *Irish Daily Mail* about his alleged friendship with Pádraic O'Connor, who had disputed Ahern's claim that he gave him a personal 'dig-out' in December 1993. Six seconds of televised silence greeted the question from the reporter, who was later described by Ahern as a 'guttersnapper' who was 'not from this country.' He was forced to retract these remarks when Millar told him during another encounter that he was born in the Rotunda Hospital in the heart of Ahern's constituency. He had later spent much of his childhood in Scotland before returning to Dublin, where he attended the O'Connell Schools in the city.

———

As other newspapers began to confirm details of the *Mail on Sunday* story and put questions to Ahern, he was forced to issue further statements, however sparse in content. At the end of the first week of the campaign he denied, through his spokesperson, that he had dealt with any dollar lodgements, or that an amount of more than £24,000 lodged to his account in October 1994 was a conversion of a lodgement of £25,000 sterling.

The first major breach in the united Government ranks came after some of the material, including details published in the *Mail* about Ahern's personal finances, was provided to McDowell by a *Sunday Independent* reporter, Jody Corcoran, whose own paper had declined to publish the extraordinary information it had received confidentially. This, according to Corcoran was due to an undertaking given previously to the tribunal that the newspaper would not publish any story based on tribunal documents. Corcoran said he showed the documents to a colleague of McDowell at the request of the justice minister. After hurried consultations with his party colleagues, McDowell told a press conference that he needed to reflect on the new details he had received concerning the Taoiseach's finances and the purchase of his house.

McDowell had dithered when the first information about Ahern's acceptance of cash from various business people had surfaced some six months earlier, and his credibility was seriously dented. Now he was forced to express his unease at the latest set of revelations but was unclear what action to take. The refusal of the Taoiseach to answer questions from the media only compounded the difficulties for McDowell, who was already fighting for his own and his party's political survival.

In response to questions from the *Irish Times*, which had verified much of the *Mail on Sunday* story through its own sources, a spokesperson for Ahern claimed that tribunal documents had 'been unlawfully leaked to cause mayhem and confusion in the course of the General Election. To respond to these selective leaks is merely to contribute to a carefully orchestrated campaign. The Taoiseach's full position is already known to the tribunal and will not be dealt with on a drip-by-drip basis to drip-by-drip disclosures.'

The claim that documents had been 'illegally' leaked in an 'orchestrated' campaign was echoed by a number of his Government colleagues, even though there was no factual basis for either suggestion. What was evident, however, was that tribunal documents, which had been circulated to a wide number of parties, were being passed on to the media.

As Ahern provided more, and increasingly evasive, answers to questions, most notably those put by the journalist Vincent Browne during a stormy press conference to launch the Fianna Fáil election manifesto, considerable pressure was also being applied on him by senior ministers. On the Sunday after the press conference shambles Brian Cowen, Dermot Ahern and Mícheál Martin met Ahern in their campaign headquarters in the Treasury Building in Dublin Castle after apparently declining his invitation to meet at his Drumcondra office. At the meeting Ahern provided some details of his financial records, including receipts for materials used to furnish the Beresford house, and reportedly pleaded for time to deal with the issues that had arisen and to issue a more considered statement. He also stated that he would not be around as party leader for ever. It was here that a termination of his leadership at a date earlier than he had previously envisaged was first discussed, and the three ministers emerged from the difficult discussions with a clear view that Ahern would make a statement clarifying the issues in question, which would, hopefully, calm nerves and public opinion in the later stages of the election campaign.

Brian Cowen was said to be particularly annoyed at the upset caused by the controversy to his carefully devised electoral strategy and made no attempt to hide his anger. It had not gone unnoticed either that Ahern had briefed the PD leader, Michael McDowell, on details of his personal finances but had not extended the same courtesy to his senior party colleagues. At a subsequent press conference there was no sign of Ahern, who took a far less active role than previously for the remainder of the campaign.

The ministers may also have had their minds focused by a report of mine in the *Mail on Sunday* that morning that further exposed deep holes in the credibility of Ahern's public statements. It showed 'glaring contradictions' between his claim at the press conference that the Wall money was intended for Larkin and for use on the renovation of the Drumcondra house and his direct private evidence to the Mahon Tribunal, in which he said the money was in fact given to him by the Manchester businessman. Over several pages the paper reproduced tranches of the Taoiseach's and Larkin's statements to the tribunal. It also explored Ahern's links to the failed £375 million casino project headed by another Manchester businessman, Norman Turner, and also involving the Dublin jeweller Robert White, a former school friend of Ahern's and a contributor to his annual fund-raising effort. A photograph showed Ahern with Michael Wall and several friends, including Robert White and Des Richardson, during a visit to Manchester in the early 1990s.

If the tensions at the highest levels of Fianna Fáil were palpable, the public disquiet and discomfort among the upper ranks of the Progressive Democrats was equally evident. McDowell, who had been among those publicly most supportive of Ahern, was forced to admit that he had been misled by assurances he had received from the Taoiseach several months earlier, and he called on him to make a comprehensive statement. He stopped just short of pulling the plug on the Government but revealed that it had been an option considered over the previous few days by him and his party colleagues. The implication that the PDs had considered withdrawing from the Government did not go down well with their Fianna Fáil partners.

However, with Ahern denying he was a 'crook' on Sky Television and the leader of the Green Party, Trevor Sargent, calling him a political 'dead man walking' (an expression lifted from an article I wrote in the *Mail*), all Fianna Fáil could do was seek to limit the damage caused by the rolling controversy over their leader's personal finances. Cowen railed about the 'ongoing partial leaking of material, which was given in good faith in order to establish the complete untruth of allegations dealing with entirely separate matters,' but accepted that the Taoiseach would shortly make a statement.

The simmering differences between the Government partners were healed somewhat when Ahern had a 'cordial and friendly chat' with McDowell during a flight to Stormont on the Government jet. In an article in *The Irish Times* on 9 May 2007 Vincent Browne again weighed in but this time on what he described as the 'cynical opportunism' of the PD leader, which, he said, was 'all the more odious by its presentation as principled, wrapped in intellectual and moral conceit.' He pointed out that only a week earlier McDowell had 'no reason to be concerned at all over the revelations of Frank Connolly of two days previously in the *Mail on Sunday*.

'McDowell on Tuesday of last week found nothing at all peculiar about this but on Sunday it had blown up into a major crisis. It isn't remotely believable he found out anything of any consequence in the days between Tuesday and Friday, when the PDs first went into a crisis of conscience over continuance in government with Ahern over and above what Connolly had revealed the previous Sunday.' Not only was Browne's column a stinging rebuke to the PD leader but it was also the first positive recognition in any other mainstream newspaper of the significance of the story published in the *Mail on Sunday* on the day the election was called.

As opinion polls showed that a large majority of voters considered his personal finances an issue on which he had significant questions to answer, the Taoiseach prepared, with his legal team and close advisers, a statement that was published on Sunday 13 May 2007 and that was sufficient to satisfy McDowell. While it provided little information that was new, it confirmed, for the first time, that Ahern had recently made a voluntary settlement with the Revenue Commissioners relating to the payments he received in the early 1990s. Refusing to say how much he had paid after the tax authorities contacted him following his admissions to RTE and the Dáil in the autumn of 2006, Ahern said he thought that he would 'get most of it back.' Opposition leaders pointed out that Ahern had told the Dáil that there were no tax issues outstanding over the loans from his Dublin friends or from the Manchester gift, thus exposing him to allegations of misleading the Dáil.

In the statement, which ran to five thousand words, Ahern used the opportunity to deny the allegations by Tom Gilmartin that he had received money from Owen O'Callaghan and that he described as 'baseless ... They are not credible. They are borne [*sic*] out of spite and malice.'

He claimed that Gilmartin had not told tribunal lawyers of the allegation that he had received £30,000 from O'Callaghan until October 1998, several months after he had first spoken to them, and then only after they queried a transaction in the Barkhill account for the same amount in 1992. He also suggested that the allegation to the tribunal that he was given £50,000 by O'Callaghan in 1989 only surfaced in 1999, with a variation in the detail in 2002. He asserted that I was the original source of the Gilmartin allegation. 'This changing and unreliable story is essentially the same as the story which was written by Mr Frank Connolly in 2000 and which was proved to be a lie in the Circuit Court. The £50,000 payment was allegedly made in 1989—five to six years before the transactions now under inquiry. The £30,000 payment was first alleged to have been made in 1992—two to three years before the payments in my accounts now being looked at by the Mahon tribunal. I received no such money at any time. It is as a result of these allegations that I am now the subject of inquiry by the Mahon tribunal.

'I have been in political life for 30 years and I have held government office for eighteen of those years. The only transactions being examined by the Mahon tribunal cover a period of 24 months immediately following the resolution of my matrimonial difficulties and during a period of great flux in my life. The timing of these transactions needs to be seen in that context. There is no pattern over many years or decades in high office of unexplained financial transactions. My life-style is as simple as it is honest. There was and is no vast wealth and no high life-style.' No detail concerning his finances was provided in the statement but instead a comment alleging that the political motivation behind the recent 'malicious leaks' in the media was to damage him and Fianna Fáil.

The statement then dealt, at considerable length, with the circumstances surrounding the acquisition of the Beresford property and the remarkable will made by Michael Wall in 1996, leaving the house to Ahern. He denied any suggestion that he was the beneficial owner of the house since it was first purchased in March 1995. He attacked those who had caused suffering to his family from the 'tactic of selective disclosure' and apologised for any 'confusion or worry' he had caused. 'I have done nothing wrong and I have wronged no one,' he said.

He did not deal at any point in his lengthy explanation with the specific lodgements to various accounts under his control between 1993 and 1996, or indeed the reasons why large sums of money rested for long periods in his safes rather than in an interest-accruing account, including during much of the period while he was Minister for Finance. But the statement was enough to satisfy the Progressive Democrats and allowed Fianna Fáil and the main opposition parties to concentrate on the other issues concerning the electorate. With all the main parties focusing on other issues, the campaign moved in a fashion more to the liking of party strategists and away from their leader's finances.

In a decisive leaders' debate on RTE's 'Prime Time' programme with Enda Kenny, Ahern again emphatically denied that he had received money from O'Callaghan, saying, 'I did not receive a glass of water from Owen O'Callaghan.' The debate, which observers widely believed helped to swing the electorate back to Ahern and Fianna Fáil, made only brief mention of his financial and housing problems.

Chapter 19 ～

‘I PAID THE PRICE, BOY’

After the vote on 24 May 2007 Bertie Ahern re-emerged as the most likely prospective Taoiseach when Fianna Fáil was returned with 78 seats after obtaining 41.5 per cent of the popular vote. Among the casualties of the election was Michael McDowell, who rather petulantly announced his resignation from political life during the final count at the RDS in Dublin and before he had informed his understandably annoyed party colleagues (who, according to one observer, were 'still lying on the battlefields' after losing six of their eight seats). McDowell left politics with a final comment: 'I love my country and I am deeply ambitious for it, but at this point I have to say, with this outcome at this stage of my career, it makes it very clear that, as far as I am concerned, my period of public life as a public representative is over.'

The Mahon Tribunal resumed public hearings a few days after the election was over, beginning with a dramatic and lengthy opening statement by its lead counsel, Des O'Neill SC, which confirmed the information revealed a month earlier by the *Mail on Sunday* over the Wall payment and the Beresford house purchase but also disclosed further, hugely damaging details of various accounts controlled by Ahern and his close associates. In the two-hour opening statement O'Neill dealt with the four transactions involving Ahern and his partner, Celia Larkin, which, he said, were preceded by sterling or, in one case, dollar exchanges. Explaining why Ahern's finances came within the remit of the tribunal's inquiry into the allegation by Gilmartin that Ahern had received payments totalling £80,000 from O'Callaghan, O'Neill said that the period involved was one during which the Taoiseach had said he had no bank account. 'This period encompassed the entire period in which the alleged payments were said to have been made by Mr Owen O'Callaghan. Mr Ahern says that during this period, from 1987 to 1993, he saved approximately £50,000, which he kept in cash in his ministerial offices and in his constituency office at St Luke's, Drumcondra.'

He went on to refer to transactions by Ahern or Larkin between December 1993 and December 1995, some involving sterling or dollars and totalling more than £175,000, that had not been fully explained or where questions remained over the explanations provided.

Ahern's counsel, Conor Maguire SC, accused the inquiry of bias against his client and of creating a risk of interference in the democratic process by circulating details of private statements before the general election, when it was inevitable that they would be leaked to the media. He also disputed the tribunal's analysis of the lodgements in October and December 1994 and the claim that they were consistent with sterling and dollar transactions.

In response to what he called a 'wide-ranging and unprecedented attack on the tribunal,' its chairman, Alan Mahon, rejected the allegation of bias and defended the decision to circulate material before public hearings. 'To withhold circulation would not have been justified simply because of a risk of unauthorised disclosure. The inference that the tribunal rushed to circulate documentation and to proceed to public hearing other than for the purposes of fulfilling its mandate, and in so doing undermined the democratic process, is a particularly serious allegation to level against the tribunal. The tribunal is an independent body established by the Oireachtas to conduct its inquiries and thereafter report its findings to the Oireachtas, and any such inference is absolutely and categorically rejected.'

With regard to media leaks, Judge Mahon pointed out that it was untrue that the tribunal had failed to take any steps to investigate leaked information and pointed to the proceedings it had taken against the *Irish Times* in that regard. 'These legal hearings are now listed for hearing in the High Court in July. What more can the tribunal do?' He commented that the tribunal was 'not allowed to use physical torture on witnesses to find out if in fact they have disclosed material.' In the light of the serious allegations made by Tom Gilmartin, the judge said the tribunal was obliged to probe the significant lodgements to Ahern's accounts that were not accounted for by his income during those years.

After further exchanges between Maguire and the tribunal bench, Gilmartin was invited to resume his evidence concerning events surrounding the Quarryvale development between 1990 and 1993. This proved to be as sensational as anticipated. Over several days of direct examination Gilmartin described, among other details, how he was approached on a Friday evening in the late summer of 1990 by Joe Burke for £500,000 in return for help given to him by Bertie Ahern. He described to Pat Quinn SC, for the tribunal, how he travelled around north Dublin in Joe Burke's truck looking for the then Minister for Labour and was left waiting outside two pubs as Burke searched in vain for his politician friend.

Gilmartin said it was not a direct demand for £500,000 but—as he had said in an earlier statement to the tribunal—made in a 'typical Donegal fashion, talking in circles. Talking around and around a half a million.' He said the request came after he told Burke that he was frustrated from the delays and obstacles to his plans and that he would 'pay a fucking half a million just to get out of here, if I got my money back.' Gilmartin insisted that he had informed the tribunal about the incident during private interviews in 1998, though the lawyers for the inquiry appeared to have no accurate records of the discussions.

He went on to describe how Liam Lawlor had arrived uninvited to the meeting with his property adviser, Richard Forman, and potential investors in Finnstown House in Lucan in September 1990. 'Quite frankly, if I had a gun that day I would have blown his head off,' Gilmartin said.

He told the tribunal he believed the former Taoiseach Albert Reynolds was drafted in by O'Callaghan to help block Gilmartin's planned acquisition of public lands near Quarryvale in 1990. After he agreed to purchase 180 acres on the Fonthill Road across from the Quarryvale site, Gilmartin incorporated them in the plans for the general scheme, which he launched in the Berkeley Court Hotel in July 1990. He intended to develop them for a hotel and conference centre.

Two months later he was informed by a senior official of Dublin City Council, Michael McLoone, that the lands were no longer available. Gilmartin claimed that the Industrial Development Authority had been instructed to acquire the land for industrial development. Documents obtained by the tribunal, including memos from senior IDA executives, subsequently revealed that Liam Lawlor had been involved in discussions with IDA officials about developing the land. Reynolds and O'Callaghan denied that they were in any way involved in getting the IDA to intervene with a land acquisition. The IDA never developed the site.

In an emotional moment, Gilmartin said that Frank Dunlop and others conspired to have the Inland Revenue in England place an unjustified demand on him for almost £7 million in unpaid taxes plus penalties. He stated that his wife was knocked down in the hallway of their home in Luton after a group of journalists and photographers called to enquire about his alleged tax debts.

On Saturday 9 June the tribunal heard an account of the alleged payments by Owen O'Callaghan to Bertie Ahern, the most politically explosive claims in Gilmartin's list of complaints. Before he set out the circumstances in which he was told by O'Callaghan of the separate payments to Ahern of £50,000 in 1989 and £30,000 in 1992 or 1993 he mentioned that other senior politicians, including Albert Reynolds, Ray MacSharry and the Minister for Enterprise, Mícheál Martin, had also got money from the same source. In relation to Mícheál Martin he was forced to correct his claim that Martin had received a 'six-figure sum' from O'Callaghan, stating that he had intended to say a five-figure sum. Martin confirmed through his lawyers that he had received more than £10,000 in political donations between 1989 and 1993 from O'Callaghan, of which over £3,500 was lodged in his wife's bank account.

I had spoken to Micheál Martin in 2000 about payments he received from O'Callaghan, based on comments the developer had made to Gilmartin some years earlier and which the latter had recounted to me. O'Callaghan told Gilmartin that he had made financial contributions to the Cork Fianna Fáil TD and councillor from the late 1980s and believed he had the potential to be a future party leader. Gilmartin claimed that O'Callaghan referred to Martin as 'an up and coming politician who was being groomed to one day become Taoiseach'.

When I contacted Martin, who was Minister for Education, in the early spring of 2000, he immediately responded and offered to meet with me within days for an early breakfast in Jury's Hotel in Dublin. During the meeting he confirmed that he had received a number of political donations from O'Callaghan, including £1,000 in June 1989, the month of the general election when he was first elected as TD for the Cork South-Central constituency. He was also given a £5,000 political donation by O'Callaghan during local elections in June 1991. In total he had received £6,500 from O'Callaghan, who was a constituent of his and whom he had known for a number of years.

Martin received £5,000 in July 1993 from the developer for a charitable purpose involving the dredging of the Atlantic Pond in Cork and another £200 for a project involving his former school, which the politician supported during his term as Lord Mayor of the city in November 1992.

Both these latter contributions went directly to the bank accounts of the charities.

Following discussions with my editor at the *Sunday Business Post,* we decided to hold off publication of Martin's disclosures on the grounds that there was no evidence that they were anything but legitimate political or charitable donations. When he was asked on RTE radio on 13 June 2000 about the £6,500 he received from O'Callaghan, the minister replied that the donations were 'all above board'. Asked why he had not volunteered the information in the light of the controversy engulfing other politicians at the tribunal and had only confirmed the information publicly when details were published in the media, Martin said that he had informed a journalist from 'a Sunday newspaper' about the donations about 'two months ago' and that he had 'answered straight up'. This remark led to some media criticism of me and the *Business Post* following the decision not to reveal the detail of the donations at that time. It also led to some humorous jibes concerning the minister's apparent view that if his explanations were accepted by us then they should be acceptable to everyone else.

In a statement read to the tribunal in June 2007, Martin stated that £3,550 of the £5,000 he received in June 1991 was lodged in his wife's AIB account in Dublin on 4 July and the balance of £1,500 was cashed and applied for political expenditure. On 18 July a further £2,550 was withdrawn, Martin said, for political expenditure. His wife, Mary Martin, worked in Dublin during the years 1984 to 1991, he told the tribunal.

Gilmartin also raised, for the first time in public evidence, a claim that both Ahern and Reynolds had received money from O'Callaghan in relation to the designation of the retail development at Golden Island, outside Athlone, in 1994. Both politicians denied the claim, which was explored at the tribunal at some length. Gilmartin said O'Callaghan told him he had paid Ahern £50,000 in 1989 to ensure that a rival developer did not acquire a piece of council land needed for the Quarryvale development, the payment being made at a football match.

Gilmartin had claimed over the years that he first assumed that O'Callaghan was referring to the GAA football final in 1989 as the place where the payment was made but subsequently said it was more likely to have been a soccer international between the Republic and Northern Ireland, which was held in Lansdowne Road in October 1989 and for which O'Callaghan had told him he was getting tickets. The distinction was particularly significant in the light of the false claim by Denis 'Starry' O'Brien that he paid Ahern £50,000 after the GAA football final in September 1989. The information concerning the payments came from no-one else but O'Callaghan, Gilmartin insisted. 'I am not alleging that Mr Ahern was paid anything. I was told by Owen O'Callaghan. I have never made the allegation that Mr Ahern received money . . . The only allegation I have made is repeating what Mr O'Callaghan told me.' He also dealt with the alleged £30,000 payment in respect of the non-designation of the Blanchardstown retail centre.

Pat Quinn SC: 'The implication, as I understood it from your evidence on Friday, Mr Gilmartin, was that Mr O'Callaghan had paid £30,000 to Mr Ahern to ensure that there would be no designation on the Green Property site?'

Gilmartin: 'That's correct.'

Gilmartin went on to describe his first meeting in April 1991 with Frank Dunlop, after he had been invited by the bank to attend a meeting 'with politicians' in Leinster House, and the extraordinary incident in the pub in Neilstown in October 1990, where he was confronted by a supposed Sinn Féin representative in the area. Gilmartin said he later recognised the man from photographs as Christy Burke, a long-serving and prominent Sinn Féin councillor in Dublin's inner city. The most distinctive feature of the man he met was that he wore tinted glasses, of a type worn for many years by Burke, and had the same sandy-coloured hair. Christy Burke told the tribunal that he had never met Gilmartin and had never been in any pub in Clondalkin or anywhere else during that period, having given up alcohol a year previously because of a serious addiction. He was not a representative for Clondalkin, and he said that while he had some dealings with Frank Dunlop over the years he had no involvement with Owen O'Callaghan or Quarryvale. Gilmartin said he had recognised Burke from a photograph his son Thomas downloaded from a web site in 2004 and, despite the councillor's adamant denials, insisted that if it was not Burke then it must have been 'an identical twin.'

The tribunal heard evidence from John McCann, who was a Sinn Féin representative in Clondalkin in the early 1990s, who confirmed that he was present with a local community activist, Patrick Jennings, at a meeting with O'Callaghan and Gilmartin. (See appendix 1, paragraph 36.)

Gilmartin also described how he witnessed O'Callaghan falling out of a broom cupboard in a toilet at the head office of Allied Irish Banks in Ballsbridge, Dublin, during a break in a board meeting in the early 1990s. He believed O'Callaghan had been attempting to eavesdrop on a conversation he was having with his solicitor, Seamus Maguire.

Dealing with various anonymous telephone calls he received after it emerged publicly that he was talking to the planning tribunal in 1998, Gilmartin said that one unidentified person told him that Bertie Ahern and Albert Reynolds had up to £15 million hidden in accounts in various places, including Jersey, Liechtenstein and the Netherlands Antilles. He did not know whether the caller was trying to set him up, but he passed the information on to the tribunal lawyers at the time. He stressed again that he could not prove that these claims—some of which were highly improbable—were true but that he was merely repeating what he was told by O'Callaghan and other sources, including anonymous callers. He said he was warned by another caller not to get involved in the allegations made by Denis 'Starry' O'Brien to the *Sunday Business Post* during the same period and said, on advice, that he refused to comment on the matter when approached by me.

He revisited earlier evidence about the phone calls from Pádraig Flynn when news of his engagement with the tribunal entered the public domain in September 1998 and described how he told Flynn that he would 'perjure himself for nobody,' a conversation overheard by his son Thomas. He claimed that details that Flynn had said were in contemporaneous notes he had made of their phone conversations were a fabrication with 'an element of truth in them.' He also recalled an anonymous caller who told him to 'remember Veronica Guerin' before he considered coming to Dublin to give evidence at the tribunal.

He recalled a conversation in which O'Callaghan told him of his efforts to obtain a crucial rezoning for lands at Golden Island, outside Athlone, where he wanted to build a shopping centre. Mary O'Rourke, a local TD and a member of the Government, was opposed to the out-of-town development, which she believed threatened commercial interests in the traditional shopping centre of the town. Frank Dunlop was employed to lobby councillors but declined to call on O'Rourke to try to convince her of the benefits of the O'Callaghan scheme, for fear that she might tell him 'where to go.' A local businessman, Tom Diskin, who owned the land at Golden Island, agreed to visit O'Rourke at her home. In an interview in the *Westmeath Independent*, O'Rourke described how

Diskin had called to her house and while he was there had threatened her, putting his hand on her shoulder. 'When I say "put his hand on my shoulder" it sounds like a very benign gesture, but it was done in a more threatening way than it sounds. But Tom Diskin has since passed away, so I'm not going to go into it any more than that. I shouted for my husband, Enda, at the time, and he came out and told Tom that he'd better leave. We didn't call in the Gardaí but we did report the incident to the Guards afterwards, and in hindsight that was the correct thing to do.'

Gilmartin said he was later told by O'Callaghan that he paid Bertie Ahern in the region of £25,000 to £30,000 in return for tax designation for the Athlone scheme after the developers succeeded in getting the town council to rezone the site for commercial development.

While much of the evidence given by Gilmartin during the Quarryvale 2 hearings was previously unheard, there was little media or public interest in it, as the focus was on the fall-out from the general election and the attempts by Bertie Ahern to form a Government. Eventually he made an arrangement with the Green Party and the survivors of the PD collapse. Trevor Sargent resigned as leader of the Green Party, as he had threatened to do before the election if his colleagues agreed to go into government with Fianna Fáil. At the same time he expressed himself 'absolutely' happy with Ahern's word on his public finances in *The Irish Times* on 18 June 2007. Two Green Party ministers, John Gormley, who took over as party leader, and Éamon Ryan, were appointed to the Government, while Sargent was given a position as minister of state. Mary Harney, the sole PD minister, retained the health portfolio.

Among the nominees Ahern appointed to the Seanad was the *Sunday Independent* columnist Eoghan Harris, who had passionately defended Ahern in relation to his questionable finances during a 'Late Late Show' debate in the middle of the election campaign. Harris replaced the retired senator Maurice Hayes, a long-time director of the Independent News and Media group.

———

Before the tribunal broke for the summer it heard further details from Gilmartin of his conversations with O'Callaghan and the latter's tendency to boast about his influence and wide-ranging contacts. During a discussion about the final vote on rezoning Quarryvale in 1992 he said he was told by O'Callaghan that he was not worried by a proposal to cap the size of the retail development at half the scale envisaged by Gilmartin in his original plans for the scheme, as he believed the restriction would be lifted at some time in the future. (The cap was indeed lifted after Gilmartin was forced out of the project in 1996.) When Paul Sreenan SC rejected the claim that a senior public servant could be compromised in the manner described, the tribunal lawyers produced a memo from within Allied Irish Banks that showed that O'Callaghan had also told his bankers that the cap would eventually be lifted, and that he had a guarantee to that effect from the senior public official. This was another shocking revelation, which appeared unbelievable at first but was corroborated by memos and other records obtained from the bank.

When he was recounting the story of a fund-raiser organised by O'Callaghan in the home of the businessman Niall Welch in Cork in March 1994, Gilmartin mentioned that O'Callaghan had told him that Albert Reynolds was collected by helicopter from O'Callaghan's home in the early hours of the morning and flown to Dublin, from where he departed for the United States. Records uncovered by the tribunal from the Air Corps confirmed that a helicopter had collected Reynolds in Cork in the early morning and that he left by Government jet for the United States later that day. This was a turning point for the tribunal and for those in the media and elsewhere who were more sceptical of Gilmartin's claims, which had been dismissed as fantasy all the way to the Supreme Court.

The tribunal also established that £50,000, made up of cheques, bank drafts and cash, was lodged to the Fianna Fáil bank account in Dublin on 14 March 1994, two days after the dinner in Cork attended by Reynolds and the party fund-raiser Des Richardson. The amount did not tally with the sum of £80,000 that Richardson had said was raised from the local businessmen present, or the figure of £150,000 that Gilmartin said he was told about by O'Callaghan.

Fund-raising and American dollars arose again when Gilmartin claimed to the tribunal that not all the hundreds of thousands of dollars raised in America between 1993 and 1996 at functions organised by Fianna Fáil during the most sensitive and successful years of the Northern peace process made their way back to Ireland. Separately,

Gilmartin told the tribunal that relatives in the United States, whose names he did not publicly disclose, were concerned about the manner in which funds collected by Fianna Fáil on the back of the peace process found their way 'floating to the Bahamas and the Cayman Islands.'

———

In yet another twist, it emerged from Air Corps records that at the end of his visit to the United States in March 1994 Reynolds and his official party travelled to the Bahamas, making what tribunal lawyers described as an 'unscheduled visit' to the town of Freeport on Grand Bahama during the official visit before attending a dinner hosted by the local resident and tax exile Tony O'Reilly at his home on another island. Among the Irish contingent was the Fianna Fáil and Government adviser Martin Mansergh, who denied there was anything 'unscheduled' about any aspect of the Bahamian visit. In a statement on the tribunal evidence Mansergh said: 'At the end of the visit on March 19, which included functions in a number of cities as well as St Patrick's Day celebrations in Washington, the Taoiseach flew from Hartford, Connecticut, to the Bahamas for the first official visit from Ireland, which was neither "informal" nor "unscheduled" and which lasted three days from Saturday till Monday inclusive.

'He was greeted with full military honours, including a multi-gun army salute, by the prime minister of the Bahamas at the airport. Later that Saturday afternoon, officials from both governments, including myself, sat down to explore a number of areas of co-operation.

'That evening, Tony O'Reilly, chairman of Independent Newspapers, hosted a dinner for Albert Reynolds and his delegation, which was attended by half the cabinet of the Bahamas, at his home at Lyford Quay [Lyford Cay, on New Providence Island].'

Gilmartin had never implicated the former Taoiseach in any wrongdoing connected with party fund-raising. Reynolds made it clear that he never dealt directly with money raised for the party at events he attended in the United States or elsewhere. Because of ill health, he was not called to give evidence on this and other matters during the Quarryvale 2 module of the tribunal.

Although he gave a strong performance in the witness box, the proceedings were taking their toll on Gilmartin and were delayed at one point when he contracted a serious chest infection and, on his doctor's instructions, was forced to rest. On his return, at the end of his sixteen days of direct evidence Gilmartin told the tribunal that in December 1995 he instructed his solicitor, Noel Smyth, to negotiate a settlement with Allied Irish Banks and O'Callaghan that resulted in a payment to him of £8.7 million, including damages of £1 million and a claim of £150,000 for political donations made, without his consent, in connection with the project.

As would be expected, the cross-examination that followed by counsel for Owen O'Callaghan concentrated on the more dramatic allegations Gilmartin had made in an effort to portray him as a fantasist and headline-seeker who had told a 'malevolent cocktail of lies,' which, over time, became ever more 'bizarre and ludicrous.' Paul Sreenan SC put it to him: 'Out of your own mouth we had Owen O'Callaghan falling out of broom cupboards . . . [and] going into the bedroom of the Taoiseach at three o'clock in the morning to give him £150,000 in cash.'

Gilmartin: 'Mr Sreenan, all these lies that you are claiming I have told—you know, the outrageous lies, unbelievable, outrageous lies, about Mr Lawlor, about Mr Dunlop, that, you know, the Fianna Fáil press secretary was head of a ring of corrupt organising and paying corrupt politicians—it was outrageous lying, wasn't it, Mr Sreenan? Most of what this tribunal has uncovered down the years was all outrageous lies: Walter Mitty, you know, Myles na gCopaleen, Walter Mitty—isn't that right, Mr Sreenan . . . I suffered for not buying favours and paying five millions here and there demanded off me. I paid the price, boy.'

Sreenan: 'Five millions here and there? You have told us of one five million in Dáil Éireann. Where were the other five millions here and there?'

Gilmartin: 'Various demands made of me, like 20 per cent stakes, etc., etc., by Liam Lawlor and others who wanted 100,000 here and there—councillors.'

Sreenan: 'Yeah? Where were the other five millions here and there that you have come out with so willingly in your evidence?'

Gilmartin: 'There was the five million in the Dáil I was referring to.'

Gilmartin denied he was motivated by bitterness and jealousy and accused Sreenan of splitting hairs. Sreenan focused on the claim by Gilmartin that he had been told by O'Callaghan in 1988 that the route of the Lee Tunnel in Cork had been altered to suit O'Callaghan, even though the tunnel was not approved until 1992, the work began only in 1995 and it was completed in 1999. Counsel pointed out that his client had only acquired the land at Mahon where the tunnel emerged several years after he spoke to Gilmartin about it in late 1988, so the allegation was patently false.

'I have made no allegations. I told you this was all a repeat of what Mr O'Callaghan told me. How could I invent an area in Cork like Mahon I had never heard of? I knew nothing about Cork other than the names of towns I had seen on postcards,' said Gilmartin, who did not move to Cork until 2003, when he moved from Sligo to place his wife in a more suitable nursing home.

There were further clashes with Sreenan over the payment to Pádraig Flynn, which Gilmartin angrily denied was corrupt. He said he would rather 'live under a bush than be corrupt . . . I had in my mind to give the party a donation to see if I could stop some of the corrupt practices that were going on . . . We had an awful lot of interference in the purchase of the land, orchestrated by Mr Lawlor. I had in my mind to give the party a donation to see if I could stop some of the corrupt practices, to get a level playing-field.'

Asked by Sreenan what he gained from the donation, Gilmartin said: 'I got myself bankrupted. I got myself destroyed, because your client had far more clout than me.' He insisted 'for the millionth time' that the cheque was for Fianna Fáil, not for Flynn. 'So you can go on and on till Hell freezes over, Mr Sreenan, trying to associate me with bribery and corruption, but you will not . . . because I did not bribe anyone . . . And it cost me. Boy, did it cost me!'

Asked whether he thought the £50,000 donation to Flynn was illegal, he replied: 'Your client would be in jail for the rest of his life' (i.e. if political donations were illegal).

————

During the summer of 2008 Gilmartin was giving evidence only in the mornings because of his recurring health problems, and the tribunal opened another area of investigation at public hearings in the afternoons. In mid-July it began to call witnesses in relation to Bertie Ahern's personal finances.

Overruling objections by Ahern's legal team that the tribunal had no jurisdiction to enquire into his finances, the chairman, Alan Mahon, stated that Ahern 'is and always was a material witness' in the Quarryvale investigation. He did concede that Ahern should not be cross-examined by counsel for Gilmartin until the latter's cross-examination was completed, but the stage was now set for parallel, and dramatic, evidence to be heard from the two adversaries at the tribunal on the same days.

Judge Mahon also defended the continuing trawl of Ahern's finances and said that similar analyses of the finances of other witnesses, including national politicians, had been conducted by the tribunal over previous years. In his ruling he also pointed out that Ahern's lawyers had declined an invitation to cross-examine Gilmartin before their client gave his evidence.

A succession of bank witnesses who had handled transactions for the Taoiseach, including Philip Murphy, assistant manager at AIB in O'Connell Street, Dublin, in the early 1990s, were called. Murphy told the tribunal that on occasion he would collect money from Ahern at St Luke's in Drumcondra and bring it to the bank. He revealed that he had acted as a type of personal banker for Ahern after they first met in 1986, when Ahern was Lord Mayor of Dublin. He said he helped Ahern negotiate a loan from the bank in December 1993 but that he could not recall handling any foreign-exchange transactions on his behalf. Neither could he recall a visit to the bank by Ahern's partner, Celia Larkin, in December 1994 when, she said, she brought a suitcase full of English banknotes into the branch. He did not recall handling any dollars on behalf of his two clients.

Another AIB witness, Jim McNamara, said that Ahern had contacted him in January 2007 to establish whether three lodgements to his account in 1994 and 1995 were preceded by foreign-exchange transactions. He said Ahern told him he was making the enquiry so that he 'would be aware of the same information that we had submitted to the tribunal.' Des O'Neill, for the tribunal, said it appeared that when Ahern contacted the branch he knew that the lodgements involved sterling cash amounts, even though the bank and the tribunal did not.

Rosemary Murtagh, currency service operations manager with AIB, gave arguably the most damaging evidence in relation to the transaction in December 1994 when Celia Larkin lodged £28,772.90 in the O'Connell Street branch. Under detailed examination by O'Neill, she said it was 'most probable' that the lodgement was a result of a $45,000 transaction.

Michael Wall arrived to give his version of events surrounding the sums he claimed were the source of the same transaction. He described how he took £30,000 (sterling) from his safe in Manchester before he travelled to Dublin by car and ferry and booked into the Ashling Hotel in Parkgate Street. That evening, 2 December 1994, he brought his wife and a few friends to Ahern's annual constituency fund-raiser in Kilmainham for what he described as a 'Christmas treat'. He said he took about £2,000 (sterling) with him to the function and left the suitcase with the remaining £28,000 (sterling) in cash in the wardrobe of the hotel room. The following day he travelled to St Luke's in Drumcondra and met Ahern in his office, with Larkin popping in and out a few times with cups of tea. He placed the cash, largely made up of £20 notes and some £50 notes, on a table. He said that Ahern put the money away, he presumed, in a safe place. The cash 'probably' included some Irish pounds, which, he said, he most probably picked up during his spending at the previous night's function.

Wall said the money he gave Ahern was to be spent on the house on which he had paid a deposit of £3,000 a few days earlier, on 1 December. He said he paid £138,000 for the house and that the sale, handled by his solicitor, Gerry Brennan, was closed in May 1995. None of the three counted the money in St Luke's, no receipt was issued, and there was no particular surprise on Ahern's part in relation to this extraordinary gesture by his Manchester friend. Ahern's reaction when given £30,000 in cash on a Saturday afternoon was 'normal', Wall told the tribunal. He said they agreed that Celia Larkin would bank the money, which he said he had 'made available' to Ahern for building a conservatory in the house he intended to rent to his 'close friend'.

Wall said he wanted to buy a house in Dublin, as he intended opening up a private bus operation in the city and wanted to have somewhere to stay other than hotels. His business plan never materialised after he was the victim of a hit-and-run incident in Manchester the following year, from which his injuries left him in hospital for months. After he recovered he decided to leave the house to Ahern or, in the event of the latter's death, to his daughters Cecilia and Georgina, in a will he made solely for this purpose in June 1996. He told the tribunal that he made the decision while lying on his back for months in hospital after what he described as his 'near-death' experience. He later sold the house to Ahern at a personal loss of more than £28,000 in 1997.

The circumstances surrounding the acquisition of 44 Beresford Avenue became even more confused when Celia Larkin entered the witness box in Dublin Castle. In a statement to the tribunal in June 2006 she had claimed that Michael Wall had lodged the £30,000 with AIB after she opened an account at his request. During a private interview the same month she told the tribunal that she had lodged the money after Wall gave it to her in the office of the solicitor Gerry Brennan. She thought the money 'might' have been in sterling. In July 2007 she told the tribunal that she had collected it, at Bertie Ahern's instruction, from St Luke's and brought it to the bank. In her direct evidence she said she now recalled that she had been in St Luke's when Wall brought in the money on 3 December 1994, the day after the annual Kilmainham fund-raiser. She was reminded that this was the weekend before Ahern expected to become Taoiseach for the first time. She said she had seen the money in cash piled on a table in Ahern's office and had no doubt it was sterling. She said she was told the money was for the renovation of the house as well as to cover stamp duty. She told the tribunal she had identified the Beresford Avenue house as one suitable for Wall to buy and for Ahern to rent, though Ahern never stepped inside the door of the property before he moved in nine months later.

She was asked by Ahern to bring the money to the AIB branch in O'Connell Street on Monday 5 December 1994, as he was going to Brussels on Government business. He told her he would phone the bank and inform the staff that she was bringing in the suitcase full of cash. She did not count the money but brought the black briefcase, one of a number in Ahern's office, to the bank, where she handed it to Phillip Murphy and was given a receipt for £28,772.90. At the bank she also opened an account for Ahern, into which she transferred £50,000 from two other accounts he held. The two sums of £28,000 and £22,000, which he had previously lodged in the other accounts, were also to go towards the renovation and decoration of the house, she said.

A month later, however, in January 1995, Larkin said she was driven to the bank by Ahern, now leader of the opposition, and he waited outside while she collected the £50,000 in cash for him. Asked by Henry Murphy sc for the tribunal why Ahern was withdrawing the money in cash, she said, to loud guffaws from the crowd in Dublin Castle, 'Bertie dealt in cash; I think he felt more comfortable with it.'

She said they returned to St Luke's, where, she thought, Ahern put the money in his safe. She could not recall a further lodgement to her own account of £10,000 (sterling) in June 1995, though she was aware of the transaction from the documents supplied by the bank. The lodgements of the two sums of money for Ahern and Wall in December 1994 were made to two separate accounts on the advice of the solicitor, Gerry Brennan, she said, though there was no document, legal or otherwise, to establish that one amount belonged to Wall, whose estate, Judge Mary Faherty (assisting Judge Mahon) pointed out, would have no claim on the money if he, or Larkin, had died suddenly.

The tribunal had already put the suggestion to witnesses that the so-called 'Wall money' converted precisely to $45,000 on one of the rates applying at AIB that day, though this was not put to Larkin. Neither was it explained what particular car her former partner drove to the bank in January 1995, as he had enjoyed the services of an official driver since 1987 and throughout his subsequent political career and did not have a valid driving licence for many years.

———

During this period Tom Gilmartin was suffering from crippling pain from an unexplained condition and was being looked after by his son Thomas while Vera remained in the care of the Cork nursing home. As a result he was not in a position to follow the convoluted trail of evidence given at the tribunal by Ahern, Larkin, Wall and other witnesses called on their behalf. Not surprisingly, he was less than convinced by the explanations given by Ahern and by his friends on his behalf. 'We were able to keep track of the evidence from the newspapers, and Thomas could download the transcripts from the internet to ensure that we were kept up to date. Like a lot of other people watching, I found it hard to believe a word that came out of his mouth.'

Chapter 20 ～

'YOU MUST BE PRETTY SHORT OF MATERIAL'

During the subsequent examination of Bertie Ahern in September 2007 it emerged for the first time that he had been seeking information from his own bank as far back as December 2004 about a series of five-figure lodgements to his accounts in the early 1990s, just as the tribunal of inquiry was beginning its trawl for information on his financial affairs. Under threat of a court order he eventually provided a financial statement of his affairs through his accountant, Des Peelo, in June 2006. He did not mention any foreign-exchange transactions until a private interview with the tribunal in April 2007, when he accepted that he had been dealing with large sterling sums. Neither did he reveal the extent of Celia Larkin's role in opening new accounts for the unexplained sums he received in late 1994, as he was obliged to do under the tribunal's 2004 order for discovery. He never conceded that the lodgement on 5 December 1994 by Larkin on his behalf stemmed from a $45,000 transaction at the bank: he insisted that it was the result of the sterling given to him by Michael Wall, even though the tribunal could prove that less than £2,000 (sterling) was transacted in the bank on that particular day, while unusually large dollar exchanges had taken place.

Ahern repeated the now widely reported, and challenged, description of the so-called Dublin and Manchester dig-outs and the Wall money, while vigorously contesting the growing evidence that his improbable stories didn't explain satisfactorily what appeared to be substantial lodgements to his accounts preceded by evidently large round-figure sterling and dollar transactions. These lodgements totalled more than £80,000, an enormous sum for the time, almost twice his pre-tax annual salary of £42,000 as Minister for Finance, as the tribunal lawyer Des O'Neill put it to him.

The tribunal had been unsuccessfully seeking information on the bank dealings since early 2005, O'Neill said, and all the lodgements were preceded by foreign-exchange transactions. He pointed out that in their early correspondence with the tribunal Ahern's lawyers sought to restrict the inquiry into his financial affairs to the period 1989–92, at a time when he actually had no bank account, and to lodgements of only £30,000 or more. All the lodgements under scrutiny, according to O'Neill, were less than £30,000, and therefore none of them would have been covered by a tribunal order if the restrictions proposed by Ahern's legal team had been agreed.

Ahern said that the Manchester dinner might have been in either May or September 1994 and that he had been in the city for a Manchester United football game (though he could not recall which particular match he attended). 'That night I stayed the full night, and I did talk quite a lot about the economy, what was going on, and all these people invested in Ireland, they have all an interest in Ireland, they are all successful businessmen who have employed a lot of people in Ireland and employed a lot of Irish people when they emigrated. So they are a considerably important group of people, and I spent the time with them, through respect for that, and on other occasions they would have given me gifts.' He had not counted the money, which he said was in big denominations, probably £50 notes, until he returned to Ireland, and the total was 'about £8,000 sterling.' There were no documents to support the facts or the scale of the 'personal contribution', and he did not think any letter of acknowledgement was sent to Tim Kilroe, the hotelier who organised the function. The tribunal and the public were still at a loss about who was present on the night Ahern met what he described as the 'hot group' in Manchester.

In a further appearance at the tribunal later in September, Ahern failed to adequately convince the tribunal over his claimed withdrawal of £50,000 from AIB in January 1995 and what he claimed was his subsequent purchase of £30,000 (sterling) with the money, which he said he intended to give to Wall after he decided not to proceed with the house rental arrangement. When confronted with the information that there was no bank record of any withdrawal of sterling of this amount in the early months of 1995, the Taoiseach said the purchase could have been made in 'instalments' from some other bank. Pressed by Judge Gerald Keys (assisting Judge Mahon) about whether he had informed the bank in advance that he intended to purchase such a large sterling amount, Ahern said he did not recall doing so but that he may have got someone else to make the transaction. However, none of the staff in his constituency office could recall withdrawing £30,000, and the average sterling amount purchased from the bank on any given day during the period was only £2,000.

He told the tribunal that he was not under the same pressure to acquire a house as he would have been had he become Taoiseach, as he had expected in late 1994. As Taoiseach he would need to be able to disclose his living arrangements and inform the Gardaí about where they should install his security protection. He agreed that neither Larkin nor Wall were informed that he had changed his mind and that he had been viewing other houses to buy, without their knowledge, in early 1995.

At yet another hearing a few days later Ahern was forced to concede that the bank records did not tally with his own narrative of the various sterling transactions, but he insisted that he had never dealt with dollars. He cited the evidence of his banking expert, Paddy Stronge, in relation to the lodgement in December 1994 of £28,772.90. Stronge argued that 'the available evidence, including the documentation, is consistent with the composition of the lodgement being largely made up of sterling, with some additional Irish pounds.' Unfortunately for Ahern, his expert witness was unable to supply any specific or fresh mathematical calculations to support his hypothesis, other than to suggest that for the amount to equate to $45,000, as claimed by the tribunal team, a breach in bank procedures must have occurred, as an inappropriate dollar exchange must have been applied. Stronge was not called to give evidence at a public hearing.

The significance of the dollar theory, and Ahern's determination to deny it, went to the very core of the tribunal's inquiry. If there had been a dollar exchange, the question arose of its source and the motivation behind it. If, as the tribunal openly suggested, the house in Beresford Avenue was purchased with money other than Ahern's but on his behalf, a question arose about its origin. And of course an obvious question was also raised: why, with the perfectly adequate financial resources at his disposal and the not inconsiderable incomes derived from his posts as TD, Minister for Finance and then leader of the opposition, did he not simply buy a house for himself at the time?

———

While Ahern was fending off attacks in Leinster House and in Dublin Castle, his nemesis, Tom Gilmartin, was being cross-examined by Owen O'Callaghan's counsel, Paul Sreenan, during which no quarter was given by either side. At one point the chairman intervened to inform Sreenan that, contrary to what some people believed, Gilmartin had no guarantee that his costs would be met by the tribunal. He had secured, on the advice of his lawyers, immunity from prosecution in return for his co-operation, but costs were assessed at the end of the public hearings, not before them.

Gilmartin spoke again of his conversation with Owen O'Callaghan in relation to the tax designation of Golden Island, which, he said, was only finally delivered by the then Minister for Finance in the dying hours of the Fianna Fáil and Labour Government in late 1994 and for which, he was told, Ahern and Reynolds were paid.

Asked by Sreenan about giving bribes to people, Gilmartin raised the role of his late father in the War of Independence and the sacrifices made by that generation of Irish republicans. 'He didn't fight for his country ... for a shower of shysters to run it,' an agitated Gilmartin told the tribunal.

For his part, when Ahern was asked about the latest allegation that he had received an improper payment in return for the rushed designation of the Golden Island scheme in late 1994 he said it was just another in a multitude of false claims made against him by Gilmartin. 'I think at the last count he's made nineteen allegations against me. I can't comment about the ongoing debate, but the one thing I can say [is] that I don't believe Owen O'Callaghan ever gave me a glass of water in my life, not to mind any money. So whatever else I have to answer, I'll be found totally innocent on that, because I never got anything from Owen O'Callaghan.'

There was further elaboration of the circumstances surrounding the alleged Golden Island payment a few days later when Gilmartin claimed that the Taoiseach had received more than £100,000 from O'Callaghan, including the £50,000 and £30,000 so-called 'Quarryvale' and 'Blanchardstown' payments and a further £25,000 or £30,000 in relation to the Athlone designation. O'Callaghan's counsel accused Gilmartin of making up new allegations almost daily and claimed that the allegation regarding £50,000 was made only after 'the journalist Frank Connolly' had heard of a similar claim by Starry O'Brien in 1999. Gilmartin insisted that his source of information was O'Callaghan, who he claimed had taken more than £1 million from his company to make corrupt payments. He also recounted discussions he had with tribunal lawyers when the O'Brien allegations first surfaced in 1999.

In response to questioning on 25 September 2007 Gilmartin made his position regarding O'Brien perfectly clear. He said he had been warned that the whole O'Brien situation was a set-up, and he stayed 'miles clear' of it. The scam was to put up O'Brien, with a claim that seemed to back up Gilmartin's claims about O'Callaghan, so that when O'Brien's story was proved false, as indeed it was, it would cast doubts on Gilmartin's claims too. Gilmartin said that people tried to 'rope me in to backing up Starry O'Brien's story,' but that O'Brien 'was hired to come up with a cock-and-bull story so as that at the end of the day people would be able to turn around and say, "Oh, it was a pack of lies."'

Gilmartin's refusal to accept almost any proposition put to him under cross-examination by Sreenan, and his continued depiction of his former partner O'Callaghan as a 'crook', provoked a lengthy and angry unsolicited public statement by O'Callaghan in late September 2007. 'I have decided to issue this statement as a result of increasing levels of frustration and despair at what I am being subjected [to] at the hands of Tom Gilmartin who has since 29 May this year, been engaged in a tormented marathon of lies and bitterness under the dubious protection of Tribunal privilege and, more seriously, immunity from prosecution which was issued to him by the DPP on 1 October 1998.'

After setting out a chronology of O'Callaghans dealings with Gilmartin, the statement recounts some of the details of what he described as the 'incredible story of criminality and wrongdoing against me.'

'I am supposed to have been hiding in broom cupboards at AIB Bankcentre during Gilmartin's meetings with the bank. I am supposed to have taken him to meet IRA activists who told him to leave Dublin. I am supposed to have paid a Government Minister to have the line of the Lee Tunnel altered in 1988 to suit a site that I then, apparently owned (I did not, in fact, acquire the site until 9 years later, and in 1988, no decision had been made to build a tunnel). I am supposed to have handed vast swathes of cash to our Taoiseach and a former Taoiseach . . . It is deeply disturbing to me that in a modern civilised democracy, a forum can exist where an individual can peddle such monstrous and clearly obvious lies with impunity and immunity.

'I also freely acknowledge, as I have always done, that I paid Frank Dunlop and his companies professional fees in the total sum of £1.62 million, plus VAT, over a period of ten years, from 1991 to 2001. It is utterly incorrect for the Mahon tribunal to state, as they are now doing, that part of these monies were paid by me to a company controlled by Frank Dunlop so that Frank Dunlop and I could create an "untraceable slush fund" in order to bribe councillors. I have never paid a politician to vote in a particular way at a rezoning motion nor have I ever bribed a politician. I have never authorised anybody to engage in such a payment, or a bribe, on my behalf.'

Under cross-examination by Colm Ó hOisín SC, for Ahern, Gilmartin made reference to O'Callaghan's statement as 'the garbage that your client and his cohort, Mr Owen O'Callaghan, put out last week.'

Ó hOisin followed a similar course as Sreenan in seeking to suggest that the allegation against Ahern involving £50,000 in connection with the Quarryvale lands arose only after I had been approached in early 1999 by Denis O'Brien. Counsel for O'Callaghan and Ahern were seeking to suggest that Gilmartin had fabricated his allegation on the basis of O'Brien's claims to me and implied that we were both parties to a conspiracy against Ahern. Ahern's counsel suggested that Gilmartin told the tribunal about the alleged payment only in November 1999, almost nine months after O'Brien had approached me with his false claims. Gilmartin insisted that he had informed the tribunal and others long before November 1999 of the fact that Ahern was, in his words, 'on O'Callaghan's payroll.'

Ó hOisín continued his robust questioning of Gilmartin. He cited a bank memo from 1994 that recorded that Gimartin's friend Paul Sheeran had described him as 'incoherent and paranoid' and a later bank minute that referred to him as 'difficult and irrational.' He described how Gilmartin had made allegations against a wide range of people, including members of the Government, the Garda Síochána, councillors and judges, in England and Ireland.

Ó hOisín: 'So the position is that your good friend Mr Sheeran, who had known you for obviously many years at that stage, in 1994 is describing you as incoherent and paranoid, and the bank who you are having regular dealings with, from some time back, have said that you have always been difficult and irrational. That's their views at the time, isn't it?'

Gilmartin: 'He was making a comment as he saw it, and I would take no offence whatsoever, because Mr Sheeran didn't believe that it was possible that what I was saying could happen.'

Ó hOisín: 'Did anybody advise you at the time that you should get some sort of medical treatment in relation to this, some sort of psychiatric or psychological counselling in relation to this, if you were suffering from paranoia, incoherence and irrationality?'

Gilmartin: 'Well, I'm here, amn't I?'

Ó hOisín: 'Did anybody advise you?'

Gilmartin: 'Do you think that I need some treatment now?'

Ó hOisín: 'I'm asking you a question.'

Gilmartin: 'I spent ten years—I have spent ten years off and on in this arena, now I have been read[ing] . . . totally, all sorts of titles put on me, out of the Dáil, your client, Mr O'Callaghan, numerous other people, constantly I'm reading about this. Now, I know—you just for yourself, do I need medical treatment, you tell me?'

Ó hOisín: 'I'm not going to answer questions that you put to me, Mr Gilmartin.'

Chairman: 'Mr Gilmartin, the question that was put to you was "Were you advised by anyone at this time to get medical treatment?" That's the question. I mean, if you weren't, just say.'

Gilmartin: 'No, I wasn't advised, because I never needed medical treatment until I had my . . . the bypass operation was the first time that I ever needed any, but psychologically—well, psychologically I never believed that I ever needed any such treatment.'

Ó hOisín: 'Did you ever get any psychological or psychiatric treatment or any sort of treatment in relation to these matters?'

Gilmartin: 'Why would I do that?'

Ó hOisín: 'Sorry, you are asking me a question. I just want you to answer the question. You can answer it one way or the other, Mr Gilmartin.'

Gilmartin: 'But why? Why would I get medical treatment for a condition?'

Ó hOisín: 'Do you understand the question?'

Gilmartin: 'For any condition that didn't exist?'

Chairman: 'Well, then, the answer is no, if you didn't.'

Gilmartin: 'No, the answer is absolutely no, because I never needed any such treatment.'

When Ó hOisín accused him of falsifying his diary entries in relation to the meeting in the Dáil in 1989 with a number of Government ministers, including Ahern, Gilmartin responded by describing Ahern as a liar, 'the biggest conman this country has ever seen,' who 'pales Charlie Haughey into the ha'penny place.' He went on to say that since Ahern met the newspaper-owner Tony O'Reilly before the general election 'all we are reading are the thoughts of Chairman Mao'—a reference to what Gilmartin perceived as the uncritical reportage and commentary in the *Sunday Independent*'s coverage of the Taoiseach over the previous months. It had been widely reported that O'Reilly had a meeting with Ahern some weeks before the election, and the *Sunday Independent* in particular was supportive of him during the subsequent campaign. In Gilmartin's view the paper had shamelessly failed to publish material that had come into its possession regarding Ahern's finances; instead it had launched a series of personal attacks on Gilmartin, who only a few years previously had given it important assistance during the Seán Sherwin libel action. When he contacted the editor, Aengus Fanning, and reminded him of a letter he received from Fanning praising him for his evidence in the Sherwin case, he was given no assurance that the reporters would discontinue their campaign of abuse.

After several months of appearances in the witness box, Gilmartin was finally questioned by lawyers for Allied Irish Banks, Councillor Christy Burke of Sinn Féin, Albert Reynolds, and Ahern's friend Joe Burke, all of whom accused him of making false allegations against their clients. George Redmond carried out his own theatrical cross-examination of Gilmartin, who told Redmond that there was no land deal in Dublin 'that you didn't have a hand in.'

Gilmartin's evidence was finally completed on 24 October 2007, although Judge Mahon did warn him that he might be called back for a brief hearing over the following months.

———

With Gilmartin's evidence now completed, the focus of the tribunal returned to those against whom he had made his wide-ranging allegations and, crucially for him, those others who could provide some corroboration of his story. In this respect the arrival into the proceedings of the broadcaster, sports journalist and former professional soccer-player Eamon Dunphy added an unexpected colour and spice to the proceedings. More importantly, it provided essential credibility to the claims that the political system, local and national, during the 1980s and 90s was infected by corruption.

Dunphy had been involved in an ambitious project to bring the London team Wimbledon FC to Dublin and had approached O'Callaghan in the mid-1990s to discuss the possibility of basing the club at the planned stadium in Neilstown. The two men became friendly, enjoying meals and social occasions in Dublin and London.

Dunphy told the tribunal in a statement, details of which I had published in the *Irish Daily Mail* some weeks before his public appearance in February 2008, that he was informed by O'Callaghan during one of their discussions that he (O'Callaghan) had paid money to Ahern, who, O'Callaghan complained, was slow to deliver on promises he made, even when he was 'looked after.'

'The thing about Bertie is that he takes the money and he doesn't do the business,' Dunphy told tribunal lawyers. 'He [O'Callaghan] told me a story over a meal about Bertie, when Albert had to put a gun to his head to get tax designation [for Golden Island]. And he said he was wary of Bertie, he didn't trust Bertie. Owen O'Callaghan told me that there was panic the night before the Government fell. He had to put a gun to Bertie's head. Money was paid to Bertie Ahern, and Albert had to intervene. The conversation took place in which he explains what the designation was and what Bertie's role in it was, how "Albert had to get the gun out at a quarter to twelve." The story was that an unspecified ... he said that Bertie had been bought, had taken money.'

Dunphy said that O'Callaghan told him that Ahern had been 'taken care of' but that 'he doesn't do the deal.' His understanding was that the tax designation was approved only after Reynolds had forced or persuaded Ahern to deliver on the commitment to O'Callaghan. 'This thing about Bertie recurred a number of times over a couple of years, and his unreliability, but he made no bones about him, saying to me, "You can't rely on Bertie," and on that one occasion he specifically said that he [Ahern] would take money, all right, but he won't deliver.'

Dunphy described how on another occasion O'Callaghan complained that in order to do business it was necessary to bribe politicians. While Dunphy was hazy on the dates and details of his meetings with

O'Callaghan—whom he described as a 'thoroughly decent' man—his evidence tallied with the actual events in 1994 when, as counsel for the tribunal, Des O'Neill, illustrated, Ahern in one of his final acts in government signed a ministerial order on 14 December granting designation to O'Callaghan's site the day before the dissolution of the Dáil.

Dunphy confirmed to the tribunal that his name and telephone number had been supplied by me to the inquiry in February 2007, after which he was invited for a private interview in Dublin Castle. I had passed on his details to the chairman of the tribunal, Alan Mahon, as I believed that Dunphy had information that would be useful to the tribunal and that he had previously been unwilling to disclose publicly. Dunphy had informed me of his private discussions with O'Callaghan about Ahern several years previously but was reluctant to come forward on the strength of what he considered were private and confidential discussions with O'Callaghan. The 'iron entered his soul,' he said, as a result of what he considered was the mistreatment of me by the former Minister for Justice Michael McDowell and Bertie Ahern in connection with my role as executive director of the Centre for Public Inquiry in 2004 and 2005. This agency was set up to examine, through investigative journalism, issues of public importance, including the misuse of state funds, the abuse of official power, and corruption. Financing for the centre was withdrawn by the funders, Atlantic Philanthropies, in December 2005 after McDowell placed serious allegations and the contents of a confidential Garda file concerning me into the Dáil record. Among the allegations made by McDowell was that I had travelled to Colombia using a false passport in 2001. I vigorously denied the allegation.

Dunphy described as 'preposterous' a suggestion by O'Callaghan's counsel that he was somehow inventing the allegations of 'financial inducements' given to Ahern at my instigation. 'If you are suggesting for one minute that I would come to this tribunal and perjure myself and damage the Taoiseach of this country and a businessman for whom I have the highest regard in order to wreak revenge, as you put it, for what was done to Frank Connolly,' Dunphy told Sreenan, 'I don't want to be in any way bad-mannered, but that is outrageous. It is a preposterous allegation to make. And if that is what you are suggesting, well, then, you must be pretty short of material, I have to say.' (See appendix 1, paragraph 37.)

Concluding his cross-examination, Sreenan asked Dunphy whether he would accept a denial by O'Callaghan that he had made any illicit payment to Ahern or anyone else. Dunphy said that he would. He later told me that he regretted that response and should have replied that he would 'take note' of any such denial by O'Callaghan.

If Dunphy's unexpected intervention proved decisive in assisting the tribunal to conclude that O'Callaghan was in the habit—as Tom Gilmartin had long alleged—of boasting about his political influence and the inducements he had to make to Ahern, among others, to get his business done, the evidence of the former banker Johnny Fortune was also significantly corroborative.

Fortune gave evidence that he had met O'Callaghan soon after Gilmartin had attended the meeting in Leinster House with the former Taoiseach Charles Haughey and several members of his Government in February 1989. He recalled an upset Gilmartin describing how he was approached by a man immediately outside the room where the meeting took place and asked by him to deposit a seven-figure sum. While Fortune could not remember all the details of the conversation in his office at the Investment Bank of Ireland, he did recall the 'ashen-faced' Gilmartin mentioning Liam Lawlor in connection with the incident. 'When he spoke to me he was extremely angry and upset,' Fortune told the tribunal. 'He mentioned a seven-figure sum, using quite a number of expletives.'

In his statement to the tribunal Fortune said he contacted the inquiry after discussing his recollection with a friend, Paul Carroll, a partner in A. and L. Goodbody, the firm of solicitors acting for Gilmartin at the tribunal.

For Gilmartin the evidence of Dunphy and Fortune, in particular, was a welcome contrast to what he felt were the unfair attacks on his credibility from a range of other witnesses and served to bolster his confidence that the tribunal would eventually concede that the thrust of his story and claims would be substantiated, while some of his so-called 'outlandish' allegations, including the demand for £5 million in Leinster House in 1989, would be shown to have a basis.

Gilmartin's case was not helped, however, when Seamus Maguire, the solicitor who had acted for him in the late 1980s and had attended Barkhill board meetings on his behalf, gave evidence that undermined his own in several respects. Maguire denied the suggestion that he told

Gilmartin of a meeting in his office in Blanchardstown when agreement was reached by a group of businessmen, including Michael Bailey and Joseph Murphy, to pay the former minister Ray Burke a substantial sum to 'go quietly' from political life after the corruption allegations surrounding him erupted and the tribunal was established in 1997. Nor could Maguire recall the incident in the Allied Irish Banks head office in Ballsbridge when O'Callaghan fell out of the broom cupboard, though he did have a memory of Gilmartin complaining that his rival was eavesdropping on their conversations. Crucially, he rejected a claim that he had been negligent in the drafting of the contract between O'Callaghan and Gilmartin, which, in its final form, was less than commercially favourable to his then client, as Gilmartin had claimed.

Albert Reynolds also disputed Gilmartin's claims in relation to his alleged receipt of £150,000 from Owen O'Callaghan in March 1994 and his subsequent trip to the United States and the Bahamas. Responding to evidence given by the commanding officer of the Air Corps, Brigadier-General Ralph James, who recounted the ten-day trip by Government jet and an unofficial six-hour stopover in Freeport in the Bahamas, Reynolds said he had never handled as much as a 'halfpenny' collected by Fianna Fáil in the United States or Ireland and dismissed as 'utter nonsense' the claim that he had received a sum of £150,000 from O'Callaghan.

But the cumulative effect of Gilmartin's own evidence and that of Mary O'Rourke, Eamon Dunphy, Johnny Fortune, Michael McLoone (former city valuer), Noel Smyth (solicitor) and Freda Kelly (editor of *News West*) was to enhance his credibility as he left Dublin Castle for the last time. He returned to his rented house in Cork with a certain amount of satisfaction that many of his claims had been corroborated, though he was annoyed and angered at what he saw as the continuing efforts by lawyers for O'Callaghan and Ahern, in particular, to cast him as a liar and a fantasist who may even have been suffering from mental delusions.

He had reluctantly agreed that his legal team should not cross-examine some witnesses, including some from Allied Irish Banks, but instead to allow the tribunal lawyers to expose flaws in their evidence. In this respect the torrid exchanges between tribunal counsel and the AIB executives David McGrath, Michael O'Farrell and Mary Basquille revealed information that raised further uncomfortable questions about the bank's treatment of their client, Tom Gilmartin.

David McGrath was in difficulties when it came to his role in the sudden flight to London to meet Gilmartin in December 1992 on the day of the council vote on the rezoning of Quarryvale. He confirmed that he had been alerted to the threat, made by Gilmartin to Basquille, to go to the newspapers over what he claimed was 'blackmail and corruption' involving O'Callaghan and the bank. McGrath said he went to London to ensure that Gilmartin could be persuaded not to do anything that could negatively affect the rezoning vote. However, he said it was Gilmartin, not him, who failed to show up at the meeting at Heathrow Airport. He could not recall the contents of their discussions, and had no written record of them.

Asked about his knowledge of corrupt payments to councillors admitted by Dunlop at the tribunal in 2000, McGrath shocked the judges when he said he had not read the detail of Dunlop's admissions in the tribunal transcripts and therefore was not in a position to comment. Neither could he make any definite statement on the fact that the bank had been informed by O'Callaghan that his company had spent £400,000 on lobbying in respect of Quarryvale by 1993 and was in regular contact with senior politicians in relation to his projects. McGrath again had recollection problems when counsel for the tribunal explained that these expenses were agreed by the bank's Group Credit Committee following McGrath's approval.

Asked whether the information published in *The Irish Times* in July 1993 about illicit payments to councillors for their votes at Dublin County Council, including references to Quarryvale, were raised at the meeting he had later in the month with Owen O'Callaghan, McGrath said that 'banks did not take a significant interest in newspaper articles.'

'AIB must have had a profound interest in the articles in *The Irish Times*, because of their potential to impact on Quarryvale,' Patricia Dillon SC remarked. After all, the bank was owed £14½ million and had a 20 per cent stake in the project. 'We had a profound interest in ensuring that we got our loan repaid,' McGrath replied.

These tetchy exchanges in April 2008 led to new information about the bank's role in the Quarryvale affair coming into the public domain and, more importantly, to Gilmartin's attention. Although he had now formally ended his participation, he and his son Thomas kept a keen interest in the subsequent proceedings and their legal and other ramifications.

By and large, though, the feeling he and Thomas had when leaving the inquiry was one of relief. 'We were glad it was all over,' Gilmartin said later to me, 'as it had taken a lot of our time and energy and had resulted in a lot of media attention, which I did not particularly wish for or enjoy. Many people approached me on the streets in Dublin and Cork to congratulate me on bringing forward my story, and it was clear that there was considerable public support for what the tribunal was trying to do in getting to the truth of the corrupt activities of businessmen and politicians. We had also learnt a lot more of what was going on behind the scenes between O'Callaghan and the bank at a time when I was not able to attend Barkhill board meetings. It only confirmed what I had suspected all along, that there was a concerted effort to shaft me. The tribunal was now getting to the essence of the corruption involved, and that was heartening from my point of view.'

I had come to know Tom Gilmartin and his family through the years of covering his story and never found a trace of the bitterness that was ascribed to him by his adversaries. If anything, he maintained a dry humour when it came to dealing with the various claims made against him and published by some media. He was also somewhat amused when some journalists who had pleaded with him to give them details of his story when it first emerged in 1998 studiously ignored and at times misrepresented him when his various claims began to embroil Bertie Ahern and other powerful interests allied to him.

After he retired to Cork, Gilmartin suffered another medical setback, which included a diagnosis of leukaemia, that severely incapacitated him for several months and diverted his attention from the continuing proceedings at the tribunal in Dublin.

Chapter 21

'OWED AN APOLOGY BY THE STATE'

It was the increasingly incredible explanations of the Taoiseach, Bertie Ahern, that dominated the final weeks and months of the inquiry and ultimately led to Ahern's resignation as head of the Government and leader of Fianna Fáil in April 2008. They followed further revelations that raised deeply troubling questions about the source of the large amounts he had received during his term as Minister for Finance.

In early 2008, working with the editor, Sebastian Hamilton, I revealed in the *Irish Mail on Sunday* that the most powerful politician in the country did not hold a tax clearance certificate and had misled the public about his dealings with the Revenue Commissioners. The denial at the tribunal by the chairman of the Irish Stock Exchange, Pádraic O'Connor, that he had given a personal donation of £5,000 to Ahern in 1993 was another significant blow to the credibility of the elaborate but deeply questionable 'dig-out' story. 'I never had a pint with Mr Ahern. I never went to a football match with him. These are things I would do with my friends,' said O'Connor, who accused Ahern of trying to 'protect his political existence.'

O'Connor's evidence raised even deeper questions about the manner in which Ahern, Richardson and others used funds intended for the party during the period. At the tribunal it also emerged that Celia Larkin had received a loan of £30,000 from a mysterious account named 'B/T' opened by Ahern's friend Tim Collins but that Ahern claimed was a constituency fund. Larkin had used the money to buy a house in which her elderly aunts lived in Phibsborough, Dublin. The loan was suddenly repaid to the constituency organisation after I reported details in the *Mail on Sunday* of the property and the tribunal learnt of the 1993 loan. The tribunal discovered, on foot of banking evidence, that the 'B/T' account was in reality an account opened for the benefit of Bertie Ahern and Tim Collins at the Irish Permanent Building Society in

Drumcondra. Ahern and Collins had insisted that the B/T account was a 'sinking fund' used to maintain St Luke's and preventing it from falling into the Tolka River. (See appendix 1, paragraph 38.)

A further embarrassing blow to Ahern resulted from the evidence of his former secretary Gráinne Carruth, who was forced to admit that she had lodged sterling amounts to another account on his behalf in the building society, having previously denied doing so. Her tearful collapse in the witness box when she told counsel for the tribunal that she was hurt and 'just wanted to go home' deeply angered Ahern's own party colleagues around the country as well as the wider public and was the final straw that triggered Ahern's resignation. Many considered that Ahern had allowed his former secretary to take the hit at the tribunal, while she and her immediate family were also angered that she had been exposed for carrying out his instructions in relation to bank lodgements. Indeed a source close to her later insisted to me that she had only ever dealt with the accounts of Ahern's two daughters at the building society, as she repeatedly insisted in evidence, but had reluctantly admitted to the tribunal that she had 'in all probability' lodged sums to his account in order to get her traumatic public evidence over and done with. Ahern told the tribunal after she completed her evidence that it was probable that his 'then security officer' may have carried the larger amounts, including sterling sums, for lodgement by Carruth in the building society.

On the evening of 1 April 2008 Brian Cowen visited Ahern in his office in Drumcondra for tense discussions on the unfolding political crisis, during which the Taoiseach told his nominated successor in confidence of 'his intention to announce stepping down.' The following day he told tearful Government colleagues that he had decided to quit on 6 May, after thirty-one years in the Dáil and eleven years as Taoiseach.

The shock to the political system was short and sharp. Ahern called an unexpected news conference for mid-morning on Wednesday 2 April 2008. Surrounded by cabinet members, he stood on the steps of Government Buildings to announce that he was resigning as Taoiseach and leader of Fianna Fáil. In an emotional statement he said that the work of government had been distracted by 'my life, my life-style and my finances.' He denied that he had done anything wrong and said he had never put his personal interest ahead of the 'public good'.

After thanking party and Government colleagues and recounting the achievements of his political career, including the Northern peace process, a successful economy, social partnership, stable coalition Governments and party unity, Ahern went on to address the issues that had concentrated his mind in the days and weeks leading to his resignation. 'It is a matter of real concern to me that the important work of Government and party is now being overshadowed by issues relating to me at the Tribunal of Inquiry into Certain Planning Matters and Payments. The constant barrage of commentary on Tribunal-related matters has and I believe will continue to dominate the political agenda at an important point for our country.'

Despite the eloquence of his prepared statement that day, his bitterness towards the tribunal and its role in his political demise was barely disguised. It was evident from his demeanour that his premature departure from office was influenced by the recent damaging tribunal evidence more than any other issue. It was also clear that he announced his resignation only hours before he was expected to explain the sterling transactions to the Dáil. His announcement meant he no longer had to do so.

Notwithstanding the hype and, from some quarters, the adulation surrounding his departure as the longest-serving Taoiseach since Éamon de Valera, many uncomfortable questions remained for Ahern. The political legacy he cherished and his ambitions as a future President of Ireland, as a senior EU player or as a much-sought-after international statesman now depended on his ability to escape the inevitable fall-out from the continuing tribunal investigations. He had yet to deal with matters relating to the acquisition of his house, and of course he had yet to be questioned with any rigour about his dealings and involvement with Owen O'Callaghan and the Quarryvale development.

A constant complaint of Ahern's was that the tribunal's emphasis on his personal finances had nothing to do with the allegation by Tom Gilmartin that he had received large sums from Owen O'Callaghan between 1989 and 1993. It was a supreme irony that the allegations that first surfaced in 1998 and about which he had not yet been formally questioned at the tribunal had ultimately sealed his political fate.

Ahern's subsequent and final appearances at the tribunal were reduced to the level of farce, particularly when he sought, during evidence in early June, to explain some of the sterling lodgements as the proceeds of money he won on the horses. Miriam Lord expressed her incredulity at Ahern's flagging explanations in *The Irish Times* the following day (5 June 2008). 'A thoroughly enjoyable gallop through the fertile fields of thinking, as seen through the fearful eye of a cornered statesman. At least we now know from what side of the family Bertie's novelist daughter draws her talent. It took a long time to get to this point, but there was an inevitability to it. When certain people find it difficult to explain to certain authorities how they came by their money—lack of documentary evidence, lack of witnesses, lack of memory, lack of credibility and such-like—there remains an age-old fall-back position.

'"Where did you get your loot?"

'"Won it on a horse, Guv."

'Yesterday, on Day 868 in Dublin Castle, Bertie finally fell back on De horse, eh, de fence. We saw it coming and laughed. But in reality it was bloody sad.'

The horse defence was the last straw for the tribunal audience, which could not resist yet another raucous outburst at Ahern's latest excuse for the sterling lodgements. He said other funds were given to him by his late mother, and protested that he was surprised and shocked when he discovered, only a year earlier, that Michael Wall had left the Beresford house to him in a 'special' will he made back in 1996. What if Wall had died? he was asked. What would he have done?

'Thankfully, nobody died,' Ahern replied.

When it was put to him that the house was purchased with his own money and that the will only made sense if the house was really his from the outset, he said: 'Except that isn't what happened.' He said that if Wall had died he would not have accepted the free house and he would have been 'honour-bound' to pay the man's widow for it in full.

When he did get around to answering the tribunal's questions about his relationship with Owen O'Callaghan it was evident that Ahern at least had the comfort of knowing that there was no paper trail that linked him directly with any alleged payments from the developer. However, there was an extensive series of meetings, diary entries and communications between him as Minister for Finance and O'Callaghan and Dunlop on a range of sensitive commercial matters that could only raise a potential conflict of interest. He had reluctantly admitted to getting his friend Joe Burke to help Tom Gilmartin with the purchase of the council lands and to his meeting O'Callaghan on at least one occasion to discuss the non-designation of the Blanchardstown centre. He had also conceded to meeting both O'Callaghan and Dunlop in relation to their planned stadium development on a number of occasions. He also agreed that he had approved the tax designation for O'Callaghan's Golden Island development but insisted he never received any payment in return.

All three issues involved multi-million projects that stood to hugely enrich O'Callaghan and his associates and for which political support was crucial at various times. O'Callaghan stood to lose £3 million, for example, if the council lands were not acquired by Gilmartin, who owed him the money in connection with his purchase of the Neilstown lands. He needed to ensure that Blanchardstown did not get designation before Quarryvale or he could lose the anchor tenants that Gilmartin had lined up to invest in what would become the Liffey Valley development. O'Callaghan stood to benefit from the promised massive Government support of up to £5 million a year if the stadium project succeeded; and while he enjoyed the encouragement and support of the Taoiseach, Albert Reynolds, he needed the Minister for Finance on his side.

There was also the extraordinary sequence of events leading up to the lodgement on Ahern's behalf of the equivalent of $45,000 in early December 1995. A few weeks earlier Frank Dunlop had made a hasty trip to New York to meet Bill O'Connor after receiving £70,000 from O'Callaghan. Within days, O'Connor, O'Callaghan and Dunlop met Ahern in Dublin, without department officials being present, to discuss the stadium. Ahern claimed he told the delegation that he did not support their stadium project. (See appendix 1, paragraph 39.)

After their meeting in mid-November, O'Connor wrote to Ahern to congratulate him on his appointment as leader of Fianna Fáil and expressed his hope that they could progress the matter of the stadium in the future. A few days after Ahern received this letter the equivalent in Irish pounds of $45,000 was lodged for him in an AIB account by Celia Larkin. When asked by Des O'Neill whether this sum could have been related to the expectation that he was about to become Taoiseach, Ahern responded: 'Never in my forty years working in the public service, never have I taken a bribe or money from any individual, including any of the people put forward in this, whether it's Chilton O'Connor, Mr Gilmartin, Mr O'Callaghan or anyone else associated with it. I never, ever from any of those individuals, to the best of my recollection, got a cup of coffee, not to mind money.'

Several of the other round-figure lodgements to accounts under Ahern's control followed meetings with O'Callaghan and Dunlop. For example, Dunlop had requested a 'ten-minute meeting' with Ahern to discuss the financial projections for the stadium in August 1994, just before a lodgement of £20,000 was made to Ahern's daughters' account, over which he had control. When asked by Des O'Neill whether the lodgement was connected to this meeting, Ahern replied, 'Certainly not.' Similarly, he had met Dunlop on the day that a £30,000 transaction and lodgement took place in the spring of 1994.

This was the context in which O'Callaghan's, and Dunlop's, various engagements with the two senior politicians were being viewed by the tribunal. Asked about Gilmartin's claim that he was told by O'Callaghan that he had given payments exceeding £100,000 to Ahern, he replied: 'I never received a penny, or a cent in today's money.' Referring to O'Callaghan and Gilmartin, he said he could not help what they said to each other. 'I wish I had never heard of either of them.'

Ahern had at all times played down his relationship with O'Callaghan, even denying that he knew of the Cork fund-raiser that took place in the home of Niall Welch on 11 March 1994—coincidentally the same day that he was in Los Angeles. Ahern said he had little or no knowledge of O'Callaghan's contribution to the party that night, or of details of the Cork dinner. When the tribunal produced a record in his diary of a breakfast meeting with his friend and fund-raiser Des Richardson, and the host of the dinner party, Niall Welch, two days earlier he said he thought it unlikely that they would have discussed the fund-raising event. When O'Neill produced the invoice for £31.15 submitted to Fianna Fáil by Richardson to cover the cost of the hotel breakfast, with a reference to the 'Cork event', Ahern appeared surprised. However, he insisted that he would not change his evidence. He also insisted that there were 'Chinese walls' between Government decisions and the party fund-raising system. 'I understand conspiracy theories but . . . there is as good as ever Chinese walls between what happens in cabinet decisions of every nature and . . . the political party system. The way Fianna Fáil works.'

Similarly, the evidence surrounding the decision by Ahern to sign the lucrative designation for the Golden Island retail scheme was also suggestive of a favour delivered to O'Callaghan, a prominent supporter of the party. Counsel for the tribunal noted that O'Callaghan was in Government Buildings, where he met the outgoing Minister for Finance, in the hours before the statutory order designating Golden Island under the urban renewal incentive scheme was signed. The order was also signed by the Minister for the Environment, Michael Smith, at the behest of his Government colleague's department, Ahern said.

Again Ahern denied that he had received any favour from O'Callaghan in return for this 'eleventh-hour' decision. 'To the day I die, Mr O'Neill, I never got a penny from any of these characters. The only sad thing is that I ever met any of them.'

The lack of a coherent paper trail, however, left the tribunal with no choice but to conclude that, while it did not believe Ahern or the witnesses who supported his explanations for the huge sums sloshing around his various accounts during his period as Minister for Finance, neither could it establish whether O'Callaghan was the source of any of them. (See appendix 1, paragraph 40.)

After his final evidence, Ahern was clearly shaken by the depth of the examination and his inability to explain the mounting body of circumstantial evidence pointing to intensive contacts with Owen O'Callaghan over many years that had not been previously revealed. He repeated that 'I never, in my public life, took a bribe, a backhander or anything else, from anybody . . . I have had to deal with it for eight-and-a-half years, a concerted campaign by a few people about this issue who did everything they could to damage me, but I did my best in front of this tribunal to tell the truth.'

His attempt to put the blame on a few unnamed people for his downfall was echoed by Owen O'Callaghan, who claimed that all Tom Gilmartin's allegations were put into his head by 'one or two journalists' in Dublin. Indeed Ahern and O'Callaghan claimed that Gilmartin had been fed the information concerning alleged payments to Ahern and a range of other matters by one journalist, that is to say, myself. According to them, I had come up with the elaborate story because of my disappointing engagement with 'Starry' O'Brien, whose fictitious tales had been exposed in the courts. This particular conspiracy theory was expounded by both men on different platforms and was given oxygen by Eoghan Harris in the *Sunday Independent* on a number of occasions.

Whatever about anyone else, the tribunal lawyers did not accept the claim that Gilmartin's allegations about O'Callaghan's improper relationship with Ahern were the invention of a couple of journalists, including myself. Long before Gilmartin had ever heard of me he had complained of corrupt payments to councillors. He had known of the payments to Liam Lawlor by O'Callaghan and Dunlop as far back as

1991; O'Callaghan had waved a cheque for £10,000 for Councillor Colm McGrath in Gilmartin's face during the same period; Gilmartin had complained of Dunlop's reputation as a 'bagman' to several people as far back as the early 1990s and to the tribunal team when he met them in early 1998, and had also helped them expose the role of Dunlop's company Shefran in the corruption of the planning system. He had told Noel Smyth that Ahern was 'on O'Callaghan's payroll' in 1996. Most of what he knew of illicit and corrupt dealings he had learnt from O'Callaghan himself many years before he outlined his complaints to me or any other journalists in Dublin.

If Dunlop, as he admitted, was bribing politicians in respect of fifteen separate rezonings at Dublin County Council, counsel for the tribunal asked, how did O'Callaghan, his biggest client, not know about his activities? In the dying days of the tribunal's public hearings O'Callaghan claimed that Gilmartin's early complaints about Dunlop's activities were wild guesses and because 'certain journalists had got to him.' Anyway, he asked, had the politicians not denied that the payments they received were improper?

'Why would Frank Dunlop lie to the tribunal about bribing councillors or politicians?' Judge Keys asked him. 'Can you think of one reason why he would make up that story, destroy his own name, destroy his business, destroy everything he stood for? Why do you think he would come in and lie about that?' O'Callaghan said he did not know.

Asked finally whether he had ever made a corrupt payment to a politician, O'Callaghan replied: 'Never in my life.'

'And it's your position in relation to Mr Gilmartin that he is a fantasist and a liar?'

'Notorious liar, yes.'

Yet Gilmartin was able to provide accurate information about Dunlop, the Shefran payments and the corrupt ring of councillors at his first meeting with the tribunal lawyers in early 1998, counsel for the tribunal pointed out, several months before he brought any of his allegations to the media. 'Notwithstanding, I think, your inability to explain how he was able to point the finger so accurately at Mr Dunlop?' Patricia Dillon asked O'Callaghan.

'Because he had been used by one or two journalists here in town, that's the only reason he was able to do that, and you know who they are.'

In a similar vein, Ahern told a TV3 documentary in November 2009 that he had been 'hounded from office' and was the victim of a vendetta pursued by one particular journalist. It echoed his Dáil statement in defence of Ray Burke, who, according to Ahern, was also 'hounded from office' when he was forced to resign and the tribunal was established in late 1997. In truth, the former Taoiseach deserves much more credit than me for his own misfortune.

Announcing the end of his political career, he told the Dublin Central constituency organisation on 30 December 2010 that he did not intend to stand for re-election. Two months later Fianna Fáil was almost wiped out in a general election that returned a Fine Gael and Labour Party coalition to power.

Among his final media appearances before he retired from politics, Ahern was seen sitting in a cupboard in a television advertisement for Rupert Murdoch's *News of the World* (which was subsequently closed down in the wake of the media hacking scandal in Britain). He has since concentrated on business interests in forestry and in trade with China.

─────

While O'Callaghan may have believed the succession of politicians who denied receiving illicit payments from Frank Dunlop, the Criminal Assets Bureau of the Garda Síochána did not, and within weeks of the end of public hearings Dunlop pleaded guilty in the District Court to criminal charges in respect of the corrupt rezoning of lands at Carrickmines, county Dublin. He was sentenced to two years in prison with six months suspended and ordered to pay a fine of £30,000. Dunlop—who once claimed during his evidence that the Flood Tribunal, set up in 1997, was regarded in political circles at the time as something of a joke, 'a PR exercise,' and was 'populated by Muppets'—spent more than a year in prison as a direct result of its investigation.

As the astonishing revelations from the biggest corruption inquiry in the country's history continued to reverberate after public hearings finished in late 2008, Grosvenor Estates sought to sell its 50 per cent share, valued at more than €300 million, in Liffey Valley Shopping Centre in a depressed financial market.

For Tom Gilmartin, living in a rented house in Cork and caring for his wife, the conviction of Dunlop and the prospect of further punitive financial and legal action against various parties identified as corrupt was small consolation. He had done the state a service by exposing some of the corruption in public life that he had witnessed and endured as he tried to do business in Dublin. In return he got little reward except abuse and criticism from those pillars of Irish life whose low standards he had so courageously revealed. He awaited the findings of the tribunal with interest, although he remained unconvinced that it would get to the bottom of the corruption racket he believed had thoroughly infected Irish political and business life during the 1980s and 90s. He had watched with wry amusement the improbable accounts constructed by Ahern, in particular, about his finances, as well the efforts of O'Callaghan, Deane and some of his former bankers to escape any blame for the inappropriate business practices that marked the entire Quarryvale saga.

However, he had more on his plate and might never have lived to see the report at all following a further and sudden deterioration in his health in April 2010. For several months medical consultants could not diagnose the debilitating condition that immobilised him and left him suffering in great pain. His children Thomas and Anne looked after him during the summer months as doctors tried to establish why he had physically weakened to such a degree. Following a collapse in November he was given the last rites at Cork University Hospital before a consultant discovered that he was dangerously anaemic and required the urgent and heavy infusion of antibiotics to treat a serious lung infection. 'I was literally on my deathbed . . . It took them months to find out what was wrong with me. I had a serious blood problem, and my kidney was seriously damaged, which further delayed my recovery. My main concern was for Vera and how she would survive if I didn't pull through. It puts everything in perspective, and I suppose made me wonder what life was all about. The last thing I was thinking about was corrupt politicians and tribunals.'

When the comprehensive report of more than three thousand pages was finally published in March 2012 it was widely recognised that Gilmartin, and those few people who had supported or corroborated many of his claims, had been vindicated. The report was delayed for several months following an appeal by Owen O'Callaghan and his partners to the High Court against the refusal of the tribunal to circulate the findings of the inquiry before its publication. After this was rejected they appealed the decision to the Supreme Court, which upheld the lower court's decision in November 2010. This brought to four hundred the number of legal challenges to the tribunal, the estimated cost of which was now approaching €250 million.

Despite his best efforts to halt it, the final report made serious and adverse findings against Owen O'Callaghan and against Frank Dunlop, Liam Lawlor and senior politicians, including Bertie Ahern, Albert Reynolds, Pádraig Flynn and others. It concluded that O'Callaghan had personally made or authorised corrupt payments totalling almost £120,000 to politicians in relation to Quarryvale. It did not accept that he was 'unaware' of the corrupt activities of Frank Dunlop, who made payments of up to £170,000 on behalf of developers, including O'Callaghan. Lawlor, it said, 'conducted a personal business in the course of which he corruptly sold his expertise, knowledge and influence as a councillor and as a TD for personal financial reward.' His 'demands for payments, and acceptance of money in these circumstances were entirely inappropriate and were corrupt.'

The report stated that corruption 'affected every level of Irish political life,' and 'those with power to stop it were frequently implicated in it.' It concluded that Pádraig Flynn had corruptly solicited and accepted for his own use the donation in 1989 by Gilmartin to Fianna Fáil. The request by the former Taoisigh Albert Reynolds and Bertie Ahern for donations from O'Callaghan was 'entirely inappropriate and was an abuse of power and government authority.'

Reserving some of its most trenchant criticism for Bertie Ahern, the tribunal rejected as 'untrue' the explanation he provided for the source of substantial funds going through his accounts in the early 1990s. It also, by extension, rejected the evidence of his friends and associates who claimed to have raised the so called 'dig-outs' in 1993 and 1994. It said that Ahern had failed to account for more than £165,000 that passed through his bank accounts in the early and mid-1990s. It also stated that a series of extraordinary and unprecedented attacks on the tribunal by ministers during 2007 and 2008 were designed to 'erode its independence and collapse its inquiry' into matters relating to Ahern.

Ahern described the tribunal's conclusions as 'unfair and inaccurate in regard to the evidence' and stated that he was 'incredulous' that the tribunal had rejected the evidence of his friends and others who, he said, had lent him money. 'In particular, I believe that the notion that I got large sums of sterling and dollars is objectionable, inaccurate and without an iota of foundation.' (See appendix 1, paragraph 41.)

Owen O'Callaghan also rejected the tribunal's findings and said he intended to challenge them in the High Court. In June 2012 lawyers on behalf of O'Callaghan began legal action against the findings. (See appendix 2.) On 16 May 2013 the High Court rejected a challenge by Owen O'Callaghan to the tribunal report and its finding that he was involved in making corrupt payments to councillors. O'Callaghan said he would appeal the decision to the Supreme Court.

——

In the wake of the report the leader of Fianna Fáil, Mícheál Martin, said he intended to call for the expulsion of Ahern from the party. Instead Ahern, Pádraig Flynn, G. V. Wright and the former senator Don Lydon resigned from Fianna Fáil before any expulsions took place. In late 2012 the party took control of Ahern's constituency offices in Drumcondra and associated finances. Councillor Anne Devitt of Fine Gael also 'stood aside', while Therese Ridge was expelled from the party.

For the future the Government agreed to examine the two hundred pages of recommendations in the damning report, including a proposal that the courts should be allowed to ban members of the Oireachtas who are convicted of accepting corrupt payments from holding public office, and to remove their pension rights. The report was referred to the Garda Commissioner, the Director of Public Prosecutions, the Revenue Commissioners and the Standards in Public Office Commission and was the subject of a three-day debate in the Dáil.

During the Dáil debate Deputy Caoimhghin Ó Caoláin (Sinn Féin) asked the Taoiseach, Enda Kenny, whether the state would issue an apology to Tom Gilmartin, given the findings of the report. There was no immediate response, though Kenny acknowledged that Gilmartin had been grievously wronged. The Government later introduced legislation aimed at preventing councillors from overturning the decisions of local authority management and planners, a practice that had contributed to the widespread corruption in the zoning process. However, so far it has failed to implement the recommendation of the Mahon Tribunal that political parties should make a far more detailed and extensive disclosure of their financial resources.

Media attention, which largely and inevitably focused on the report's findings against Bertie Ahern, waned after a few days, with a few exceptions, but most of the reportage confirmed the vindication of Gilmartin. The Independent News and Media group was forced to apologise and pay substantial damages to Gilmartin a few weeks after the report's publication, when three of its titles—the *Sunday Independent*, *Irish Independent* and *Herald*—misrepresented the tribunal's conclusions on the donation he gave to Pádraig Flynn for Fianna Fáil. Senior executives of Allied Irish Banks were also criticised in the report, and the bank stood accused of withholding information from its client, Tom Gilmartin, and in effect of colluding with the illicit payments to councillors, which were then reimbursed from Gilmartin's personal account. The bank's new chief executive, David Duffy, said he intended to ensure that the behaviour exposed by the embarrassing findings of the Mahon Report would not be repeated. 'I am confident that we won't be reading Mahon-style findings in the future culture of the bank,' he told the *Irish Times* in March 2012.

In response to some of the media commentary surrounding the publication of the report, Thomas Gilmartin (junior) went on RTE radio to welcome its conclusions, which accepted that his father gave his evidence 'in the honest belief that such evidence was true and accurate.' He also criticised the tactics of lawyers acting for Bertie Ahern, in particular their implication that his father might have suffered from mental problems. In an eloquent article in *The Irish Times* on 26 March 2012 he wrote that 'Ireland would never have found out about the corrupt activities of people like Frank Dunlop, nor the existence of a corruption ring at the heart of planning in Ireland . . . It is due to my father that the tribunal discovered that Bertie Ahern had huge amounts of money going through his accounts for which his explanations do not hold water . . . The report agrees that O'Callaghan did tell my father that he had paid Ahern, but it couldn't, because of Ahern's untruthful evidence, establish whether the payment took place—it could neither prove nor disprove it. My father was telling the truth all along.'

Referring to the demand for £5 million made on his father outside his meeting with Haughey and his ministers in Leinster House in February 1989, he said: 'Here is a man who was honestly motivated (and this is mocked by some commentators—but he could have stayed and made money in England where he was already successful) by a desire to try and provide jobs in Ireland being threatened inside the national parliament for refusing to pay up . . . The tribunal established that Flynn took . . . money despite the money being clearly intended for Fianna Fáil. The tribunal also established that Flynn's asking for and taking the money was corrupt but did not find that the giving was corrupt.'

He wrote that the rezoning of Quarryvale was utterly necessary, as the original town centre site at Neilstown was 'badly designed, badly located and poorly accessed. What exists at Quarryvale today, however, bears absolutely no relation to what my father had planned. The local people have been completely overlooked. The enduring victims of the corruption that infested Ireland during that period are the people who have to live in places where they have been sidelined and left to rot.'

When his father came to give evidence he was put through a 'sustained and systematic process of vilification and ridicule by politicians up to and including the Taoiseach and his cabinet, and also by prominent journalists and commentators.

'His evidence made possible the exposure of a litany of corruption that would never have been exposed otherwise. Ireland owes my father a debt of gratitude for doing what he has done. He is owed an apology by the State and by certain parts of the political and media establishment for what was done to him.'

It was Thomas who convinced his father to co-operate with the Tribunal from the outset in early 1998, at a time when many others were advising him not to get involved. Thomas knew that, at the very least, his father being able to air his story in a public forum could be a cathartic experience for a man who had kept quiet about the trauma he had experienced in trying to do business in Dublin. Even following his father's decision to withdraw co-operation with the tribunal following the decision, in late 1998, by the Revenue Appeals Commission not to pursue Charles Haughey for a £6 million tax demand, Thomas urged him to reconsider, which he finally did following Pádraig Flynn's 'Late Late Show' appearance. Thomas was by his father's side when he made his first public appearance at the Sherwin libel trial. He helped with the process of producing chronologies and statements, read the entire tribunal legal brief (amounting to tens of thousands of pages), put his father through his paces in practice sessions before his appearance, pre-empted lines of questioning by hostile counsel, and suggested lines of questioning to be pursued by their own legal team. Thomas was with his father every day of his time at Dublin Castle, and attended on behalf of his father when he was laid low by a quadruple heart by-pass. Without his son's work, Tom Gilmartin probably would not have appeared at the tribunal at all, and what has flowed from it would most probably never have been uncovered.

The role of his father in exposing corruption was also recalled in a special RTE 'Late Late Show' to mark the programme's and the station's fiftieth anniversary shortly after the tribunal's report was published. Gay Byrne said that one of the most dramatic moments of the long-running programme was Pádraig Flynn's appearance in January 1999, which effactually ended his political career and was the catalyst that brought some of Gilmartin's shocking claims to a mass audience for the first time. Some thirteen years later the country was shocked by the litany of corruption revealed in the report as a direct consequence of Gilmartin's story. Flynn's incautious and arrogant remarks that night were a major influence in convincing Gilmartin to co-operate with the tribunal of inquiry.

———

For Tom Gilmartin, the confirmation by the tribunal that it considered his evidence to have been honest came as no surprise, though it was of little consolation. 'What will be done about this corruption?' Gilmartin remarked to me in the early summer of 2012. 'What good is it to me? I got nothing but a lot of abuse and a load of lies told about me. My company and business are gone. But maybe this whole tribunal can ensure that no-one else will be the victim of such a conspiracy. If it does that it is worth the time and effort, but I wouldn't bet my house on it. As far as I can see, the tribunal report was buried a few days after it was published. The people who caused the rot are walking away scot-free. It's a great little country!'

A few weeks later, in August, there was a knock on the door of his Cork home. Two detectives from the Criminal Assets Bureau wanted to talk to him about his allegations of corruption involving politicians and others in the late 1980s. They wanted him to come to a Garda station in the city, with a solicitor, and make a statement, including information about sums he gave to Liam Lawlor all those years ago. Gilmartin declined the invitation and reminded the detectives that he had been granted immunity from prosecution by the DPP in 1998 in return for co-operating with the tribunal. He wished them well in their investigation and offered to give them whatever assistance he could to identify and deal with those involved in the corrupt activities he had exposed. He was not inclined to make a visit to a Garda station along with his solicitor, given the manner in which such an engagement could be misconstrued by some elements of the media if it was reported or photographed. The request for him to bring his solicitor also unfairly implied, in his view, some possible wrongdoing on his part.

The tribunal of inquiry, and Gilmartin's contribution to it, helped to explain the seeds of the economic and financial collapse and the reckless banking guarantee of 2008 that has left a massive anchor of debt on current and future generations of Irish people. It showed the extraordinary levels of graft and greed in which some of those with political and financial power are prepared to engage. The report may have come too late to help avert the disastrous collapse and loss of economic sovereignty but it remains a damning indictment of the behaviour of certain powerful political, business and banking interests during the 1980s and 90s. The investigation, though dealing only with a relatively short period, raises disturbing, and unresolved, questions concerning illicit political and business practices and the abuse of power by some of these powerful interests in subsequent years.

The tribunal found that Gilmartin's twelve central allegations proved to have substance, even if it could not get to the end of the money trail. Through his story, Tom Gilmartin has shone a bright light in a dark but deep corner of Irish political and commercial life.

POSTSCRIPT

In May 2013 the Government announced a plan to establish a new position of Planning Regulator, which was one of the recommendations of the tribunal report.

In July 2013 the corruption trial involving the businessman James Kennedy, Councillor Tony Fox (independent, formerly Fianna Fáil), the former councillor Colm McGrath and the former Fine Gael senator and councillor Liam Cosgrave (junior) collapsed after the key witness, Frank Dunlop, fell ill. Days earlier the case against the former Fianna Fáil senator and councillor Don Lydon was discontinued. The Director of Public Prosecutions had alleged that Kennedy paid Dunlop £25,000 in 1991 to bribe councillors in Dún Laoghaire-Rathdown to vote in favour of rezoning land at Carrickmines, county Dublin.

Following the collapse of the trial and the DPP's decision not to pursue the charges against the accused, the Mahon Tribunal published its findings in relation to the 'Carrickmines module' of its investigation. It concluded that Lydon, Fox, McGrath and Cosgrave had received corrupt payments from Dunlop, made on behalf of Kennedy. The report on the Carrickmines module had been withheld pending the outcome of the court proceedings.

In late July 2013 the tribunal approved the payment of their legal costs of €2.6 million to the builders Tom Brennan and Joseph McGowan, who were among those to make corrupt payments to Ray Burke and who were found to have hindered and obstructed its investigation. This followed a judgement by the Supreme Court in 2010 overturning the refusal by the tribunal chairman, Alan Mahon, to pay their legal costs to two directors of Joseph Murphy Structural Engineers, Joseph Murphy (junior) and Frank Reynolds, whom the tribunal found to have also hindered and obstructed the inquiry.

In March 2013 Des Richardson lost his High Court challenge to certain findings of the tribunal. He had claimed that the findings in relation to funds held by Roevin Ireland Ltd were 'wholly erroneous,' in that they claimed he could not explain the source of £39,000 held in the company's account. He said that tribunal lawyers had not asked him to explain the source of money in the account during his evidence. Ms Justice Elizabeth Dunne said that the tribunal appeared to have made a mistake in its findings, but that the error could be corrected by it. She said that an error of fact and an error of jurisdiction had been made that was 'not amenable to judicial review.' She also said that Richardson had not placed 'all his cards on the table' in relation to his application to the court, in particular his description in relation to soliciting funds from Pádraic O'Connor of NCB Stockbrokers and the manner in which the sum of £5,000 was obtained from the Roevin account to buy a bank draft that was provided to Bertie Ahern in 1993. O'Connor later told the tribunal privately that he had informed Richardson that he was not going along with the 'dig-out' story after it first emerged in September 2006 and could not understand why Ahern and his friends persisted with their claims about his alleged role as a friend and donor, knowing he would deny their assertions at the tribunal.

Also in March 2013, Des Richardson made a settlement with the Revenue Commissioners in respect of his company Willdover Ltd because of an under-declaration of VAT and of PAYE and PRSI. The company had been used by Richardson to invoice Fianna Fáil for his fees as party fund-raiser. The Willdover account was overdrawn on 22 December 1993 when a cheque from Fianna Fáil, signed by Bertie Ahern, was lodged to the account. On the same day Richardson wrote out a cheque on the account that was given to Ahern. He told the tribunal there was no connection between the two payments.

In August 2013 the editor of the *Sunday Independent*, Anne Harris, told the TV3 programme 'Print and Be Damned' that her predecessor and late husband Aengus Fanning had declined to publish the sensational details concerning Bertie Ahern's finances in April 2007 because he had made a deal with Ahern, who promised the newspaper exclusive stories relating to the forthcoming general election.

————

Another of the so-called 'dig-out' men, Jim Nugent, was in hot water when he became embroiled in a controversy surrounding 'top-up' payments to executives of the Central Remedial Clinic in Clontarf, Dublin, which assists people with physical disabilities. In November 2013 it emerged that the former chief executive of the CRC, Paul Kiely, had received no less than €136,000 per annum from the charity, including some from donations to an associated company, in addition to his publicly funded annual salary of €106,000, in breach of public-service pay guidelines. Kiely surfaced in the report of the Mahon Tribunal, which states that he wrote a letter as 'Director of Elections, Dublin Central Constituency', using the St Luke's address in Drumcondra, in which he refers to an 'inaugural Dublin Central Constituency Golf Classic' in St Ann's Golf Club, Clontarf, in October 1997. The tribunal was intrigued to find that a cash lodgement of £10,000 had been made to the mysterious B/T account two years previously, in July 1995, described to the tribunal as the proceeds of a 'golf fund-raising event in St Ann's.'

The tribunal report stated: 'Documentation was provided to the Tribunal wherein reference was made to an "inaugural Dublin Central Constituency Golf Classic" held in St Ann's Golf Club, Clontarf on 13 October 1997. Neither Mr Collins, nor any other witness, was in a position to explain why a golf classic fund-raising event was described as an "inaugural" golf classic in 1997 if, in fact, lodgements totalling £29,000 were attributable to such events two and five years previously.' The letter from Kiely to someone named Tony also promised to eliminate the 'constituency debt' as soon as possible. At the time, the tribunal pointed out, there was more than £35,000 in the B/T account.

Jim Nugent was chairman of the board of the CRC and a member of the board of the Friends and Supporters of the CRC, whose lottery proceeds part-funded the salary 'top-ups' of the executives. He took over as interim chief executive when Kiely's successor as CEO, Brian Conlan, resigned in early December before it emerged that he had also received 'top-ups' to his salary in breach of the pay guidelines. The appointment of Conlan, a serving board member, to the position in July 2013 was described as 'highly irregular' by the Health Service Executive, as it had not complied with normal procedures, including the interviewing of external candidates. Nugent and the other board members proceeded with the appointment despite the HSE's objections.

Bertie Ahern's former financial adviser Des Peelo was a former chairman and long-time member of the CRC board, as was the former Fianna Fáil TD, chief whip and Minister for Defence Vincent Brady.

In late 2013, Pádraig Flynn attracted critical media attention after it emerged that he had given a sermon at his local Catholic church in Castlebar, county Mayo, during which he spoke about the 'evils of money', among other themes.

In February 2014, investors purchased a 72.8 per cent stake in Liffey Valley Shopping Centre for €253m. This sale would appear to vindicate Gilmartin's assessment of the site's long-term investment potential.

———

Tom Gilmartin died on Friday 22 November, at the age of seventy-eight, several weeks after his admission to Cork University Hospital with a recurring chest infection compounded by a deteriorating heart condition. Doctors discovered the source of the virus causing the recurring lung infection, which at first responded positively to treatment. A plan to fly him to London for complex heart surgery was put on hold, however, as his condition weakened. Once again his kidneys failed, and as he was being prepared for surgery to open a blocked valve in his heart, he passed away.

In final conversations he once again expressed his concern at leaving behind his beloved Vera, his children and his sisters. He also complained that the stress and suffering he had endured over the years since he returned to do business in Ireland had irreparably damaged his previously sound health and constitution. However, he dealt with his serious medical condition with his usual good humour and expressed the hope and intention of being around for the launch of this book in the spring of 2014. Sadly, that was not to be.

His remains were removed from Cork and stopped in Grange, county Sligo, where the church was packed for a service attended by hundreds of people from the town and surrounding areas, including his native Lislary. He was buried in Vera's home place of Urris, on the Inishowen Peninsula in county Donegal, on Tuesday 26 November. During his funeral service his son Thomas spoke of his father's devotion to his wife and family and of his and their sadness that he had received no apology for the manner in which he was treated by those in positions of power in his own country. There were no political leaders at the funeral services, and no party issued a statement of regret at his passing.

In his eulogy in St Michael's Church in Urris, Thomas Gilmartin (junior) said: 'On behalf of my father's family—his wife, Vera;

his children, Liam, Anne, James, myself, and my wife, Emma; his granddaughter, Katie; and his sisters, Una and Chris—I would like to thank you all for coming here today, especially those who have travelled long distances. We are marking the passing of a truly remarkable man.

'It is difficult to know where to begin. There are so many stories, so many achievements, so many ways in which my father left his mark that I could keep you here until my *own* funeral if I were to try to include even *most* of it. Suffice it to say, he was a one-off. I said to my wife, in the hour after his passing, that there was now a Dad-shaped hole in the universe. Many of you knew him well, some from childhood, and will know exactly what I mean.

'Dad grew up in Lislary, county Sligo, the oldest boy born to James and Kathleen Gilmartin. As a boy he was able to handle horses, fish for his supper, work in the fields, and, like his father before him, was an expert ploughman. But apart from being physically strong and able from such a young age, he was extraordinarily intelligent and inquisitive about the world around him. It wasn't uncommon, even in recent years, to hear him recite entire poems, from Robert Service's "Songs of the Yukon", word for word, which he had taught himself as a youngster. Unfortunately, as was very common in the Ireland of the 1940s and 1950s, opportunities to make the most of his God-given talents were few and far between. Nonetheless, he managed to get a place at agricultural college, and did so well in his exams that he was told to get ready to come to Dublin to take up a job in the civil service. A short time later, he was told that his place had instead been given to someone who had not done anywhere near as well, someone who happened to have a well-placed relative. And so Dad was bound for Luton, in England, where many young men from his area had already gone to try to make a future for themselves.

'However, Dad always remained a proud Sligo man who never tired of telling stories about his adventures there as a young man. Forty-odd years in England did not leave even the slightest trace in his accent. When he spoke of Lislary and Grange it was with a mixture of love for the people and places he knew and sadness at the lack of opportunities given to him and many young men and women of his generation. Going back there last year, on what would be his final visit home, was a great privilege for my wife and myself. As we walked with him on the shoreline beside his birthplace, it was as if he were reliving his boyhood, and it was very moving to see the mixture of joy and sadness in him as he did.

'Luckily for his children, God had someone waiting for Dad in Luton, in the form of Vera Kerr. Mum and Dad worked hard to build a home for us, and even in the hardest times they were devoted to each other and to us. My mother was tireless in looking after both Dad and their children, which in turn allowed Dad to work hard and provide for us. And he achieved many great things. When Mum was set back by multiple sclerosis, Dad, to the very last week of his life, never ceased to worry about her well-being. We often laughed at the way in which the two of them would fuss over each other. Dad's love for Mum, like Mum's for Dad, was touching to behold. For Mum, and indeed for us, his children, the post-Dad era is going to be a strange and incomplete one.

'But it wasn't just our lives my father touched. Numerous people have told me, in recent days, about ways in which Dad made an indelible impression. Half an hour in his company was usually enough to ensure that he would not be forgotten. He also performed many acts of generosity and kindness and never said a word about them. Several examples have been given to us by well-wishers in recent days, revealing many things he never even told us, his family. It was the very nature of the man—full of love and compassion, particularly for those he felt had been given life's short straw.

'None of this is to say that he was a *complete* saint. Dad loved a bit of devilment too. He liked to tell a story of his youth, in Sligo, which involved a friend and himself at the wake of a neighbour. The neighbour was not a particularly nice person and had died in such a way that the body had to be tied down in order to lie straight in his coffin. Dad would burst into kinks of laughter recalling his friend sneaking in beside the coffin, cutting the straps, with the whole room thinking that the neighbour had come back to life as they sprang upright. It would take Dad about five minutes to recompose himself from the fit of laughing!

'He could also be a stubborn man! Dad, as many of you will know, liked his tea very strong. It was a running battle he had with waiters, nurses, and even with us, his family. I tried to convince him that adding any more tea to the pot would make the spoon stand upright—but *no*! There was always room for an extra tea-bag! Or four! In the last few weeks before his death he had come to dislike the taste of tea, and it was a sure sign that something had gone badly wrong.

'But Dad's stubbornness could be an asset too. When he came back to Ireland in the late 1980s, having been very successful in the UK, where he was very highly regarded, he did so because he felt that he could use the talents he had been gifted with in order to create jobs and prevent at least some people from having to take the same route away from their families and homeland that he had been forced to take. Unfortunately, my father was let down repeatedly by men for whom moral scruples, of the type my father lived by, were viewed as weakness. Later, giving evidence about his experience, he never wavered in his commitment to the truth, even when subjected to an extraordinary campaign of vilification. He would never perjure himself, even when it was disadvantageous for him to tell the truth, such was his honesty, so strong was his religious faith.

'Dad loved his country and was a proud Irishman. It truly grieved him, as the son of a man who fought for his country's independence, to see the sacrifices of his father's generation discarded by lesser men. It is a source of great sadness to us, his family, that Dad was never truly given the credit he deserved for what he did, or the apology he was owed for what was done to him. He deserved better.

'But that era was only a drop in the ocean compared to his life as a whole—the many achievements; the many lives he touched; the many people who loved him, both here and in England; and it is a source of great comfort to us as his family that so many hundreds of people have come to tell us about what Dad meant to them and about how sorely they will miss him. It is sometimes an exaggeration to say that we shall not see someone's like again, but in my father's case it is true. He was a one-off.

'We trust in God that he will find peace in Heaven and be re-joined with his beloved brother Jadel (James), his sisters Julann, Eileen, Maudie and Patsie, as well as his parents. We ask that you remember him, and us, in your prayers. Speaking for myself, I will miss him every day, and the rest of my life will be a much quieter and less colourful place without him to talk to. I was blessed to have him as my beloved father.'

APPENDIX 1

Extracts from the final report of the tribunal of inquiry

1. (Tribunal report, chap. 2, section 4.16) The Tribunal was satisfied that: Mr Lawlor arrived at the London offices of Arlington uninvited; purported to represent the Irish Government in relation to the proposed Bachelor's Walk development; used and promoted his position as a TD to persuade Arlington to pay him a monthly retainer (through Mr Gilmartin); and, unsuccessfully, sought a more substantial payment of a percentage take in the Bachelor's Walk development from both Arlington and Mr Gilmartin . . .

   (7.08) The Tribunal was satisfied that, on the basis of Mr Lawlor's representations, Arlington believed that Mr Lawlor was so close to the Government and the authorities in Dublin that a failure on their part to make significant payments to him might result in a lack of support by the Government and those authorities for the proposed development at Bachelor's Walk, rendering the aims of that project more difficult to achieve. The Tribunal believes that this is what prompted Arlington to expend almost IR£75,000 in payments to Mr Lawlor over an eleven month period. Having regard to the fact that he was an elected councillor and TD, Mr Lawlor's demands for payments and his acceptance of money in these circumstances was entirely inappropriate and corrupt.

2. (Tribunal report, chap. 2, section 10.13) The Tribunal was satisfied that Mr Gilmartin gave a true and accurate account of his meeting in late May 1988 with Mr Lawlor and Mr Redmond. The Tribunal accepted Mr Gilmartin's evidence that while Mr Redmond pretended to take a telephone call in his office, Mr Lawlor requested a payment of IR£100,000 for himself and a similar amount for Mr Redmond. It also accepted that Mr Lawlor either expressly or by implication made it clear to Mr Gilmartin that he would not realise his ambition to purchase and develop the lands at Quarryvale unless the substantial payments were made as demanded . . .

   (10.14) The Tribunal was satisfied that while Mr Redmond did not himself make any demand for payment from Mr Gilmartin on this or on any other occasion, he was aware of the demand being made of Mr Gilmartin by Mr Lawlor on his behalf and was, indirectly, party to that demand . . .

   (10.15) The said demand was corrupt.

3. (Tribunal report, chap. 2, section 16.06) The Tribunal was satisfied that Mr Lawlor did, as claimed by Mr Gilmartin, seek a 20 per cent stake of the Quarryvale project from him on two separate occasions. Such demands

were corrupt, having regard to Mr Lawlor's position as an elected public representative . . .

(16.07) Such requests by Mr Lawlor were consistent with his demand for a payment of IR£100,000 for himself and something for Mr Redmond in the course of the meeting in May or June 1988 with Mr Gilmartin and Mr Redmond, and with his demands of Mr Gilmartin and of Arlington Securities in relation to the Bachelor's Walk project.

4.   (Tribunal report, chap. 2, section 20.01) The Tribunal was satisfied that Mr Gilmartin did, as he claimed, meet the then Taoiseach and a number of Government ministers in Leinster House, and that this meeting took place in the early days of February 1989 . . .

(20.20) The Tribunal accepted Mr Gilmartin's evidence that in the course of his encounter with the unidentified man in Leinster House, he was provided with details of an Isle of Man bank account into which the £5 million was to be paid. The Tribunal accepted Mr Gilmartin's evidence that he had, for a period of time, retained the piece of paper on which the bank details had been written and which, Mr Gilmartin maintained, had been provided to him by the unidentified man. The Tribunal also accepted Mr Gilmartin's evidence that the piece of paper was subsequently destroyed by his son, in circumstances outlined by Mr Gilmartin, although the Tribunal regarded it as unfortunate that this information was not retained by him . . .

(20.21) The detail of Mr Gilmartin's recollection of the conversation between himself and the unidentified man was accepted by the Tribunal as being accurate. In particular, the Tribunal was satisfied that Mr Gilmartin was indeed threatened in the manner described by him in his evidence.

5.   (Tribunal report, chap. 2, section 14.05) The Tribunal was satisfied that, in the course of the meeting that took place between Mr Gilmartin and Cllr Hanrahan in Buswells Hotel, Cllr Hanrahan demanded IR£100,000 in return for his support for Quarryvale and that he sought IR£50,000 of this 'up front'. This demand was undoubtedly corrupt.

6.   (Tribunal report, chap. 2, section 23.13) The Tribunal was satisfied that a meeting scheduled for the morning of 22 February 1989, between Mr Redmond, county council officials, Mr Gilmartin and a number of his professional team was aborted and cancelled by Mr Redmond in the circumstances detailed by Mr Gilmartin in his evidence . . .

(23.14) The Tribunal was satisfied that, following a complaint to Mr Seán Haughey by Mr Gilmartin, the meeting with Mr Redmond and his officials was rescheduled and that Mr Haughey attended the meeting . . .

(23.15) The Tribunal accepted as true and accurate Mr Gilmartin's evidence that the exchange of words between Mr Haughey and Mr Redmond which culminated in Mr Redmond's stating 'ask your brother' and Mr Haughey responding 'I am not my so-and-so brother's keeper' did indeed take place . . .

(23.16) The Tribunal was satisfied that the actions of Mr Redmond, on 22 February 1989, were prompted by Mr Redmond's desire to thwart the progress of Mr Gilmartin's Quarryvale scheme.

7. (Tribunal report, chap. 2, section 31.05) The Tribunal was satisfied that Mr Gilmartin did receive a telephone call from an individual who introduced himself as 'Garda Burns', and that he was effectively warned away from the path that he had by then embarked on, namely dialogue with the Gardaí regarding allegations of corrupt practices and demands for money. It was common case that Mr Gilmartin's liaison with the Gardaí ended on 20 March 1989. The Tribunal was satisfied that the purpose of the telephone call (and, indeed its effect) was to, discourage, intimidate or warn Mr Gilmartin to desist from any further co-operation with the Garda inquiry. The Tribunal was also satisfied that, prior to the 'Garda Burns' telephone call, Mr Gilmartin had co-operated with the Garda inquiry and had provided them with information which he believed was true and accurate.

8. (Tribunal report, chap. 2, section 34.08) The Tribunal was satisfied that Messrs Dadley and Mould deliberately concealed from the Gardaí the true factual position regarding payments made to Mr Lawlor by Arlington. The Tribunal believed that Messrs Dadley and Mould's reluctance to apprise the Gardaí of the true position was probably because of a concern that any such admission of payments to Mr Lawlor would embroil them, and their company, in the Garda investigation, and that Arlington's payments to Mr Lawlor to assist them 'through the corridors of power', would become a matter of public controversy.

9. (Tribunal report, chap. 2, section 26.04) Of the three contemporaneous records of his contact with Mr Gilmartin in 1989 retained by Chief Superintendent Sreenan, only those of 9 March 1989 contained a reference to Mr Gilmartin's allegation that a demand for IR£5m had been made of him while he was engaged in business in Dublin. While the Garda final report ultimately furnished to the Department of Justice in May 1990 recited many of Mr Gilmartin's complaints, in various guises, the report contained no reference to Mr Gilmartin's allegation that a sum of IR£5m had been demanded of him.

10. (Tribunal report, chap. 2, section 47.10) The Tribunal was satisfied that Mr Flynn requested that Mr Gilmartin make a substantial donation, most probably at their meeting on 19 April 1989, and that the request was made on the understanding that steps would be taken to ease or remove obstacles and difficulties then being faced by Mr Gilmartin in relation to the Quarryvale project, which Mr Gilmartin perceived to be improper or unlawful.

11. (Tribunal report, chap. 2, section 48.01) The Tribunal was satisfied that . . . Mr Flynn wrongfully and, in the circumstances, corruptly sought a donation from Mr Gilmartin for the Fianna Fáil Party . . . Mr Flynn, having been paid IR£50,000 by Mr Gilmartin for the Fianna Fail party, proceeded wrongfully to use the money for his own personal benefit . . .

(48.10) The decision on the part of Mr Gilmartin to make a payment to Fianna Fáil through Mr Flynn was misconceived and entirely inappropriate. However, he did so in circumstances involving an element of duress or coercion, where he believed he had no choice but to act accordingly in order to avoid the obstructive and improper behaviour of elected public representatives and of a senior public servant, and (to use Mr Gilmartin's own words) to create '*a level playing field.*'

12. (Tribunal report, chap. 2, section 49.07) [*Re the Flynns' claim that they did not know that Mrs Flynn had opened three non-resident deposit accounts in AIB*] The Tribunal regarded the evidence tendered by Mr and Mrs Flynn in this regard to be astounding, incredible and untrue. The Tribunal was satisfied that at all relevant times both Mr and Mrs Flynn were aware that they had opened and maintained non-resident accounts in the period 1985–93, with a London address with which they had no apparent connection.

13. (Tribunal report, chap. 2, section 49.52) The Tribunal was satisfied, however, that the contrary was the case, and that the proceeds of lodgements to account no. 1000-022, including the IR£50,000 cheque given to Mr Flynn by Mr Gilmartin in late May/early June 1989, ultimately funded most or all of the purchase of the farm at Cloonanass in county Mayo. The Tribunal was also satisfied that only a small amount, if any, of that £50,000 was used by Mr Flynn for political purposes.

14. (Tribunal report, chap. 2, section 50.06) The Tribunal is satisfied that Mr Ahern's telephone conversation with Mr Gilmartin on 20 June 1989 took place and accepted Mr Gilmartin's recollection of that conversation. It was satisfied that Mr Ahern suggested, or requested, that Mr Gilmartin make a contribution to the Fianna Fáil Party.

(50.07) The Tribunal was further satisfied that in the course of his conversation with Mr Ahern on 20 June 1989, Mr Gilmartin informed Mr Ahern of his then very recent payment to Mr Flynn of IR£50,000 intended for the Fianna Fáil Party.

15. (Tribunal report, chap. 2, section 44.01) The Tribunal found Mr Gilmartin's account of a meeting with Cllr Burke during which Cllr Burke allegedly made reference to IR£500,000, to be confused and unreliable as to detail (including the likely date of the meeting). However, the Tribunal accepted that Mr Gilmartin had more than one meeting with Cllr Burke and that he had an encounter with him in 1990, at a time when he had paid over the balance of his full deposit for the Irishtown lands (the total deposit was IR£510,000).

(44.04) Notwithstanding the Tribunal's reference to the confused and unreliable nature of Mr Gilmartin's account of a discussion with Cllr Burke immediately prior to the trip to the airport, the Tribunal was satisfied that a discussion did take place in the course of which Mr Gilmartin understood that Cllr Burke was, in a roundabout fashion, seeking money for himself, or for Mr

Ahern. The Tribunal also believed that Mr Gilmartin's suspicion that he was being asked for money on Mr Ahern's behalf was fuelled by Cllr Burke's efforts to locate Mr Ahern in the course of his journey with Mr Gilmartin to Dublin Airport . . .

(44.05) The Tribunal had insufficient evidence to make a finding as to whether Cllr Burke, directly or indirectly, sought money from Mr Gilmartin, either for himself or for Mr Ahern. There was no evidence that Mr Ahern was aware of Cllr Burke's discussion with Mr Gilmartin or of Cllr Burke's attempts to locate him while en route to Dublin Airport with Mr Gilmartin.

16. (Tribunal report, chap. 2, section 50.25) Neither Mr Sherwin nor Mr Kavanagh asked Mr Flynn whether he had received any donation from Mr Gilmartin. The Tribunal found this failure to inquire of Mr Flynn remarkable, having regard to the fact that over a year previously, in June 1989, having being informed from a reliable source that Mr Ray Burke (then a Government Minister), had received a substantial donation intended for Fianna Fáil, Mr Kavanagh had telephoned Mr Burke to ascertain the truth of that information and had also raised the matter with the then Taoiseach, Mr Haughey.

17. (Tribunal report, chap. 2, section 6.10) The Tribunal was satisfied that from commercial/banking considerations, in particular, AIBs fear of an inability on the part of Mr Gilmartin/Barkhill to repay its debts to the bank, prompted them to pressure him to enter into an agreement with Mr O'Callaghan and ensure that it would be Mr O'Callaghan who would be the driving force in the Quarryvale project from February 1991 onwards.

18. (Tribunal report, chap. 2, section 32.70) . . . While the Tribunal could not determine with any degree of probability whether or not Mr Gilmartin was threatened in the manner described by him, it was nevertheless satisfied that Mr Gilmartin believed himself to have been threatened in the course of the meeting. Conceivably, this belief by Mr Gilmartin may have arisen as a consequence of the negative tone of the meeting, and because of references made to him about his previous business dealings in Northern Ireland.

19. (Tribunal report, chap. 2, section 9.03) The Tribunal was satisfied that the entity which Mr Dunlop promoted as the payment vehicle in this regard was Shefran. The Tribunal was satisfied that the agreement reached between Mr O'Callaghan and Mr Dunlop for the latter to be put in funds through Shefran was for the purpose of keeping the scale of the payments to be made to Mr Dunlop by Mr O'Callaghan secret from Mr Gilmartin. The Tribunal was satisfied that the scale of the Shefran payments made to Mr Dunlop allowed Mr Dunlop, at all relevant times, to have sufficient funds for the purposes of complying with requests or demands which he anticipated would be made of him by councillors . . .

(9.08) The Tribunal was satisfied that the IR£80,000 paid to Mr Dunlop over the course of three weeks in 1991 was never intended to be Mr Dunlop's fee as understood in the ordinary sense of the word. The Tribunal was satisfied that the primary purpose of Mr Dunlop being funded to the extent of IR£80,000 over a three week period in May/June 1991 was to provide Mr Dunlop with the facility by which disbursements could easily be made to councillors in the course of the Local Election campaign. Given the purpose for which Mr Dunlop was retained, namely to lobby councillors in support of the Quarryvale rezoning proposal, the provision of such funds to Mr Dunlop was made for a corrupt purpose . . .

(9.20) The Tribunal was satisfied that the primary purpose for the use of Shefran by Mr Dunlop in connection with Quarryvale was to facilitate the receipt of substantial funds from Mr O'Callaghan from which corrupt payments could be made to councillors in connection with Quarryvale and to conceal, from Mr Gilmartin, both the fact that such funds were being provided to Mr Dunlop and their scale.

20. (Tribunal report, chap. 2, section 19.07) The Tribunal was satisfied that Mr Fleming, when he sought information as to the purpose of the payments, was not provided with that information and was ultimately wrongly advised that the payments were connected with Mr Gilmartin, thus leading him to assign the payments in Barkhill's accounts as benefits which had been made to Mr Gilmartin . . .

(19.08) Ultimately, having regard to the manner in which the two 'expenses' payments were accounted for in Barkhill's books, it transpired in the absence of authority from Mr Gilmartin (and his wife) for doing so, he funded the payments made by Mr O'Callaghan to Mr Lawlor and Cllr McGrath.

21. (Tribunal report, chap. 2, section 3.57) The Tribunal was satisfied that, while the IR£70,000 paid to Mr Dunlop may have included an element of fees, its primary purpose and the greater percentage of it, was for payments to politicians associated with the Quarryvale project. Insofar as Mr O'Callaghan and Mr Dunlop intended that the IR£70,000 would fund Councillors who were likely to be candidates in the November 1992 General Election and the related Seanad Election, the Tribunal was satisfied that they were involved in an endeavour, the purpose of which was to compromise the required disinterested performance by Councillors of their duties in the making of a Development Plan, and as such the Tribunal was satisfied that the activities of Mr O'Callaghan and Mr Dunlop with regard to the IR£70,000 payment were corrupt . . .

(3.58) The Tribunal rejected Mr Dunlop's claim that he was unable to recollect the amounts of the payments and the identities of all those to whom he disbursed funds from the IR£55,000 withdrawn from his 042 bank account on 10 November 1992, and/or from the additional cash available to him at that time from other sources. The Tribunal was satisfied that Mr Dunlop withheld the identities of some of those whom he paid. The Tribunal believed it likely that those not identified by Mr Dunlop were public representatives.

22. (Tribunal report, chap. 2, section 17.11) The Tribunal was satisfied that at least some of the payments made by Mr Dunlop on the part of Mr O'Callaghan to or for the benefit of councillors through the mechanism of Frank Dunlop and Associates generated invoices were motivated by an attempt to influence those councillors in the performance of their public duties and were therefore corrupt. The Tribunal is also satisfied that Mr O'Callaghan was aware that some of the payments which he made to Mr Dunlop were being used for this corrupt purpose.

23. (Tribunal report, chap. 2, section 21.14) The Tribunal heard evidence of attempts by Mr Gilmartin to make contact with Cllrs McGrath and Gilbride on the evening of 17 December 1992. It was established, to the Tribunal's satisfaction, that his attempts were not successful largely because the telephones in the Fianna Fáil rooms in Dublin County Council were, on the evening in question, being manned by Mr Deane, in order to control contact by Mr Gilmartin with Cllrs McGrath and Gilbride.

24. (Tribunal report, chap. 2, section 26.34) . . . The coincidence in time between Mr Lynch seeking to speak to Mr O'Callaghan on 2 December 1992, which contact was followed by two further calls to Mr Dunlop's office by or on behalf of Mr Lynch on 15 and 16 December 1992, and the imminence of the Quarryvale vote, was remarkable. The Tribunal also noted Cllr O'Connell's late addition as a member of the UK FÁS delegation. As a matter of probability, Mr Lynch's telephone calls to Mr Dunlop on 15 and 16 December 1992 related to some extent to Cllr O'Connell's trip to the UK. However the Tribunal was not satisfied that Cllr O'Connell's absence from the County Council on 17 December 1992 had been 'orchestrated', as suggested by Mr Dunlop.

25. (Tribunal report, chap. 2, section 23.08) The Tribunal was quite satisfied that Mr O'Farrell was concerned about the articles and about Mr Gilmartin's possible response to them, particularly in the light of his knowledge, as of July 1993, of Mr Gilmartin's queries relating to and complaints about the large round figure payments totalling IR£150,000 which had been paid to Mr Dunlop via Shefran, and in light of the fact that in December 1992 Mr Gilmartin had threatened to go to the newspapers about his concerns. This information had impelled Mr O'Farrell to dispatch Mr Kay and Mr McGrath to meet Mr Gilmartin in London on 17 December 1992.

26. (Tribunal report, chap. 2, section 23.10) In a memorandum relating to a meeting between Mr O'Callaghan and Mr McGrath and Mr Chambers (General Manager of Corporate and Commercial) on 28 July 1993 there was no reference to any of the issues raised in *The Irish Times* articles or indeed to any matter referred to by Mr O'Farrell in his memorandum of 26 July 1993. The Tribunal found this absence of any mention or reference to the content of *The Irish Times* articles in such a memorandum, so soon following their

publication and Mr O'Farrell's memorandum relating to them, strange and it found extraordinary the suggestion as outlined in evidence that their content was not raised with Mr O'Callaghan, in the context of AIB's knowledge of the substantial round-figure payments to Mr Dunlop/Shefran and Mr Gilmartin's complaints in relation thereto . . .

(23.17) The Tribunal was satisfied that Mr O'Farrell raised the July 1993 *Irish Times* articles with Mr O'Callaghan in 1993 and the Tribunal did not identify any reason why he would not have done so, having regard to the fact that he documented his discussion of matters of a similar ilk with Mr O'Callaghan in 1995. The Tribunal rejected Mr O'Farrell's contention that *The Irish Times* articles were not raised with Mr O'Callaghan, having regard to, in particular, Mr O'Farrell and Mr O'Callaghan's then knowledge of Mr Gilmartin's complaints concerning Mr Dunlop and Shefran. It was simply not credible that this matter was not raised with Mr O'Callaghan by Mr O'Farrell, if for no other reason than for Mr O'Farrell to satisfy himself that the Quarryvale project would not become embroiled in public controversy.

27. (Tribunal report, chap. 2, section 3.108) The Tribunal rejected Mr Dunlop's claimed lack of recollection in relation to his requirement in September 1993 for IR£25,000 cash. Neither did it accept Mr Dunlop's claimed lack of recollection about the identity of the person or persons he met (for the purposes of disbursing money), in Powers Hotel on 17 September 1993. The Tribunal did not accept as credible, that Mr Dunlop could have forgotten the use to which he applied such a substantial cash sum, in circumstances where, shortly after receiving the cheque, he proceeded to encash it. The Tribunal was satisfied that Mr Dunlop chose not to disclose either the purpose for which a sum of IR£25,000 from Mr O'Callaghan which he effectively treated as cash, or the name(s) of the individual or individuals he probably paid money to on 17 September 1993 in Powers Hotel, a premises close to Leinster House.

(3.109) The Tribunal believed it probable that Mr Dunlop disbursed either the entire, or a significant portion of, the IR£25,000 cash to whomsoever he met in Powers Hotel on the 17th September 1993, and that, almost certainly, the beneficiaries were one or more politicians.

28. (Tribunal report, chap. 2, section 9.06) Having regard to the general thrust of what Mr Gilmartin conveyed to the Tribunal in 1998, and while particular details given by him about the Cork event were inaccurate (for example his reference to the fundraising dinner having taken place in Mr O'Callaghan's house, as opposed to Mr Welch's house) other details given by Mr Gilmartin to the Tribunal on 5 February 1998, and to his then solicitor Mr Smyth on 20 May 1998, were largely consistent with events involving Mr Reynolds which did in fact take place over the course of 11 and 12 March 1994, in particular, that he attended at an event in Cork, travelled to, and departed from Cork in a helicopter, and that on the following day he travelled to the United States in

connection with the St Patrick's Day festivities . . .

(9.07) Generally, therefore, in the context of events which have been established as a matter of fact by the Tribunal to have taken place on 11/12 March 1994, the Tribunal was satisfied that within a short time thereafter, Mr O'Callaghan apprised Mr Gilmartin of those events and in all probability mentioned that a collection had taken place at the dinner (as in fact it had). The Tribunal believed it quite possible that information which Mr O'Callaghan conveyed to Mr Gilmartin concerning a substantial donation to the Fianna Fáil Party was interpreted (albeit erroneously) by Mr Gilmartin as information that Mr Reynolds was the beneficiary of the fundraising event held on the 11 March 1994. It was certainly the case that the Fianna Fáil Party was a beneficiary of the fundraising event. The Tribunal was satisfied that Mr Reynolds was not the recipient of a £150,000 payment from Mr O'Callaghan on the 11 of March 1994, or on any other occasion.

29. (Tribunal report, chap. 2, section 1.251) . . . Having regard to the evidence heard by it, the Tribunal did not deem it appropriate in the circumstances to determine that this payment to the Fianna Fáil Party, and in particular the request made to Mr O'Callaghan by Mr Reynolds and Mr Ahern for a substantial payment, was corrupt. The Tribunal nevertheless considered that the concept whereby senior Ministers, together with a former Government Minister and EU Commissioner closely associated with that party, would actively engage in (what amounted to in reality) pressurising a businessman, then involved in lobbying the Government to support a commercial project, to pay a substantial sum of money to that political party, was entirely inappropriate and an abuse of political power and Government authority.

30. (Tribunal report, chap. 2, section 26.15) The Tribunal was satisfied that Mr Gilmartin repeatedly complained to AIB personnel about what he perceived to have been in effect the bank's failure to keep him abreast of all developments in the Quarryvale project, and particularly information relating to payments of money to third parties (and especially Mr Dunlop) by or on behalf of Barkhill.

31. (Tribunal report, chap. 2, section 30.08) . . . Although the Tribunal was unable to determine as a fact that an incident had occurred during a break at a meeting in AIB, as recounted by Mr Gilmartin, it was nevertheless satisfied, having regard, in particular, to Mr Maguire's evidence that Mr Gilmartin had genuinely believed that Mr O'Callaghan had eavesdropped on a conversation between himself and Mr Maguire and it was satisfied that Mr Gilmartin had commented thereon to Mr Maguire at the time and subsequently . . . The Tribunal did not believe it to have been the case, having regard to the foregoing, that Mr Gilmartin concocted the incident, although it was possible that he embellished aspects of it (and in particular his belief that Mr O'Callaghan fell from a cupboard).

32. (Tribunal report, chap. 2, section 20.16) Notwithstanding Mr Dunlop's denials

about any agreement for or discussion about Mr Dunlop being paid IR£1m from Mr O'Callaghan, the Tribunal was satisfied that by 1996 Mr Dunlop and Mr O'Callaghan were engaged in discussions about Mr Dunlop then receiving a substantial sum of money from Mr O'Callaghan.

33. (Tribunal report, chap. 15, section 2.05) On 4 October 1998 articles appeared in the *Sunday Business Post* newspaper written by one of its senior journalists, Mr Frank Connolly, under the heading 'Lawlor *'fees' now donations.'* The articles were accompanied by photographs of Mr Lawlor and Mr Dunlop. This was apparently the first occasion on which Mr Dunlop was publicly identified in relation to matters then being investigated by the Tribunal. The articles suggested that Mr Dunlop had been paid IR£500,000 in fees for his assistance in obtaining rezoning and planning permission for the Quarryvale lands. It also claimed that Mr Dunlop had confirmed that part of that sum had been used by him to make political donations, which it was said were fully documented. In sworn evidence to the Tribunal subsequently, Mr Dunlop accepted that he may have confirmed the figure of IR£500,000 to Mr Connolly. The article also stated that Mr Dunlop had confirmed that part of his duty as a lobbyist was to make political contributions to a range of politicians and political parties over a number of years.

(2.06) The Tribunal's first communication with Mr Dunlop was in the form of a letter addressed to him dated 6 October 1998 in which information was sought from him in relation to the articles which had been published in the *Sunday Business Post* on 4 October 1998 and other information relating to Quarryvale.

34. (Tribunal report, chap. 16, section 1.67) In the course of its public inquiries in the Quarryvale, Cherrywood, Balheary, Baldoyle/Pennine and Ballycullen/ Beechhill modules, the Tribunal established payments of approximately IR£400,000 as having been made to Mr Lawlor by individuals and/or entities associated with the lands which were the subject of inquiry by the Tribunal in those modules. More than four-fifths of this figure was found to have been paid within the period 1988 to 1993. The total found by the Tribunal to have been paid to Mr Lawlor, directly or indirectly, significantly exceeded the total payments which Mr Lawlor acknowledged receiving from those individuals/ entities, in statements or in the course of information provided by him to the Tribunal during its private inquiry and on the occasions when he gave sworn evidence to the Tribunal. The Tribunal was satisfied that Mr Lawlor, at all times in his dealings with the Tribunal, failed to disclose to it the total payments received by him from the individuals/entities associated with the aforesaid lands.

(1.68) In his dealings with the Tribunal, both in correspondence and in his sworn evidence, Mr Lawlor, to the extent that he acknowledged the receipt of money in relation to the Tribunal's inquiries in the aforementioned

Modules, invariably described these payments as consultancy fees or political contributions (mostly the latter).

(1.69) While the Tribunal did not always find it possible to determine the true purpose and reason for every payment to Mr Lawlor which was the subject of its inquiries, it was satisfied that the majority of the payments made to Mr Lawlor within the period 1988 to 1998 were payments which, having regard to Mr Lawlor's role as an elected councillor (until June 1991) and an elected TD (until 2002), were entirely inappropriate, improper and on occasion corrupt. The Tribunal was absolutely satisfied, that, with the possible exception of a few thousand pounds, none of the payments to Mr Lawlor could reasonably or accurately be described as political donations.

(1.71) In respect of the payments to Mr Lawlor investigated by the Tribunal, a clear and obvious link was established between many of those payments and the planning process (in particular the rezoning of land). The extent to which Mr Lawlor provided services in return for such payments was not always clear. Indeed the Tribunal was satisfied that on occasion money was paid to Mr Lawlor based solely on the perception on the part of a developer/landowner that it was necessary to keep Mr Lawlor 'on-side', for fear that not paying him would serve to negatively impact on a particular development or planning issue.

35. (Tribunal report, chap. 16, section 1.233) The Tribunal was satisfied that Mr Lawlor abused his role as an elected public representative (in his capacity both as an elected councillor until June 1991, and as an elected TD representing the Dáil Constituency of Dublin West) to a very significant degree, in that during the period of the late 1980s, and the 1990s, he provided services and advice to landowners/developers (including Mr Dunlop as their agent) in his capacity as an elected politician for personal gain. In effect, Mr Lawlor conducted a personal business in the course of which he corruptly sold his expertise, knowledge and influence as a councillor, and as a TD, for personal financial reward . . . The Tribunal was satisfied that decisions were made, on occasion, by developers/landowners (or Mr Dunlop as their agent) to pay Mr Lawlor for 'consultancy' services, in relation to the rezoning or development of their lands. This was not simply to have the benefit of his undoubted knowledge of the planning process and the influence he undoubtedly exerted over councillors, both as a councillor and as a TD, but was also to allay concern on the part of developers that a failure to engage with Mr Lawlor in this manner might result in a failure to have their property rezoned, or otherwise dealt with in the course of the planning process . . . Mr Lawlor's close involvement with landowners/developers (and particularly with Mr Dunlop as their agent) and his frequent demands for and receipt of substantial sums of money from them in the late 1980s and throughout the 1990s, coupled with his propensity to use false and fictitious business names and/or invoices to facilitate such payments,

rendered Mr Lawlor hopelessly compromised in the required disinterested performance of his public duties as an elected public representative.

36. (Tribunal report, chap. 2, section 32.70) The Tribunal was satisfied that in or about the spring of 1991, Mr Gilmartin was taken by Mr O'Callaghan to a meeting in a licensed premises in Clondalkin, and that the meeting was attended by Mr Gilmartin, Mr O'Callaghan, Mr McCann and Mr Jennings. It was common case that by April 1991, Mr O'Callaghan was informing third parties of meetings with, among others, representatives of Sinn Féin. Thus, as a matter of probability, the Tribunal was satisfied that Mr McCann's association with Sinn Féin was made known to Mr Gilmartin in some shape or form at the meeting . . . The Tribunal was satisfied that this was the only occasion when Mr Gilmartin attended a meeting involving a representative of Sinn Féin. This meeting was arranged by Mr Dunlop, probably at the instigation of Mr Lawlor. Mr Dunlop was not at the meeting attended by Mr Gilmartin . . . The Tribunal was satisfied that Mr Gilmartin's identification of Cllr Christy Burke as being the individual whom he met in the course of this encounter was erroneous, and it was satisfied that Cllr Burke never met Mr Gilmartin or Mr O'Callaghan. The Tribunal believed it likely that Mr Gilmartin's erroneous identification of Cllr Burke arose from the fact that Cllr Burke and Mr McCann bore a strong physical resemblance to each other, and it was satisfied that Mr Gilmartin's identification of Cllr Burke was not borne of any malicious intent on the part of Mr Gilmartin towards Cllr Burke . . . The Tribunal was satisfied that the meeting in a licensed premised attended by Mr Gilmartin, Mr O'Callaghan and Messrs McCann and Jennings, as a matter of probability, was conducted in a strained atmosphere. The Tribunal was satisfied, as a matter of probability that reference was made to Mr Gilmartin's previous business involvement in Northern Ireland. It was also satisfied that matters which almost certainly contributed to the strained atmosphere of the meeting included references made by Mr Gilmartin to corruption, and a reference by Mr Gilmartin to a payment of IR£50,000 to a senior politician (and which resulted in Mr O'Callaghan kicking him under the table).

37. (Tribunal report, chap. 2, section 2.19) The Tribunal was satisfied that Mr Dunphy gave his evidence honestly and in the belief that it was true and accurate . . . The Tribunal rejected any suggestion (to the extent that it was made) that Mr Dunphy embellished or otherwise altered his evidence to the Tribunal because of any sense of bitterness or anger on his part as to any past treatment of Mr Connolly or any issue relating to him, and which Mr Dunphy perceived as being unfair . . . The Tribunal was satisfied that Mr Dunphy, in his sworn evidence to the Tribunal, accurately recounted and described the words and terminology used by Mr O'Callaghan in discussions between the two men relating to Mr Ahern, Mr Reynolds and the issue of the granting of tax designation for the Golden Island development in Athlone . . . The Tribunal

was satisfied that Mr O'Callaghan made verbal statements to Mr Dunphy, to the effect:

- that Mr Ahern had been given an inducement or was 'taken care of' by Mr O'Callaghan in return for a promised favour.
- that Mr O'Callaghan gave inducements to politicians
- that Mr O'Callaghan found it necessary to engage in corrupt activity in order to successfully develop property in Dublin.

38. (Tribunal report, chap. 2, section 10.76) The Tribunal was satisfied that the B/T account was opened by Mr Tim Collins in 1989 for purposes other than the upkeep and maintenance of St Luke's, Drumcondra. The Tribunal rejected entirely the evidence of Mr Collins, Mr Burke and Mr Ahern as to the claimed purpose of this account.

(10.77) The B/T account was opened and operated in a markedly different fashion to that of other bank accounts associated with the Dublin Central constituency. Its opening and operation was to a very great extent kept secret, and active steps were taken by Mr Collins in 1989 and again in 1995 to ensure that correspondence and statements relating to the account were maintained within the IPBS branch or sent to Mr Collins' private address respectively, and not sent to the constituency office at St Luke's.

(10.78) The Tribunal was satisfied that the B/T account was not created or maintained as a 'building trust' account and that it was not established or operated as a fund for the upkeep and maintenance of St Luke's. Indeed the entire operation of the account from its inception in 1989 to January 2008 was the very antithesis of this claimed purpose.

(10.80) Equally, the Tribunal was satisfied that the B/T account was not an account used to fund political activity.

(10.81) The Tribunal was satisfied that at the time of the opening of the account in 1989, the letters 'B' and 'T' in the account's title 'B/T' stood for 'Bertie' (Mr Ahern) and 'Tim' (Mr Collins), in precisely the same manner as the letters 'D' and 'T' in a separate account within the same IPBS branch stood for 'Des' (Mr Richardson) and 'Tim' (Mr Collins).

(10.82) The Tribunal was satisfied, as a matter of probability, that the B/T account was operated (at least until 1997) for the personal benefit of Mr Ahern and Mr Collins.

39. (Tribunal report, chap. 2, section 1.188) The Tribunal was satisfied that, as of 10 November 1994, contrary to evidence given by Mr O'Callaghan and Mr Dunlop, (and, also, notwithstanding Mr Ahern's evidence) there remained on the part of Mr O'Callaghan and Mr O'Connor, and indeed of Mr Dunlop, every expectation that they would further progress their stadium proposals in subsequent contact with Mr Ahern.

40. (Tribunal report, chap. 2, section 13.01) Much of the explanation provided by Mr Ahern as to the source of the substantial funds identified and inquired into

[in] the course of the Tribunal's public hearings was deemed by the Tribunal to have been untrue.

(13.02) Because the Tribunal has been unable to identify the true sources of the funds in question it cannot therefore determine whether or not the payment to Mr Ahern of all or any of the funds in question were in fact made by or initiated or arranged, directly or indirectly, by Mr O'Callaghan, or, indeed by any other identifiable third party.

Conclusions of tribunal in relation to Bertie Ahern

41. (Tribunal report, chap. 17, section 1) The Tribunal rejected the evidence that in December 1993, there had been a collection organised by Mr Des Richardson and / or Mr Gerry Brennan from friends of Mr Ahern, or that IR£22,500 was provided to Mr Ahern, in the manner claimed, on 27 December 1993. Equally, the Tribunal was satisfied that Mr Ahern did not receive any such sum, either as a gift or as a loan, from the identified individuals.

(Chap. 17, section 7) Because the Tribunal was not provided with a truthful account as to the source of the said lodgement of IR£22,500 to Mr Ahern's bank account on 30 December 1993, it was unable to determine the original source of such funds.

(Chap. 2, section 2.20) The Tribunal was satisfied that Mr O'Callaghan informed Mr Gilmartin that he had paid sums totalling IR£80,000 to Mr Ahern. The provision of such information to Mr Gilmartin was not proof that such payments had indeed been made to Mr Ahern by Mr O'Callaghan.

Specifically in relation to the allegation that Mr O'Callaghan told Mr Gilmartin immediately following a Barkhill Board Meeting in AIB that he had paid IR£30,000 to Mr Ahern in return for an assurance that the Blanchardstown development would not receive tax designation status, the Tribunal accepted Mr Gilmartin's account as to the circumstances in which he was provided with such information.

The Tribunal was satisfied that Mr O'Callaghan was advised by Mr Ahern, the then Minister for Finance, at a meeting on 24 March 1994 that neither the Blanchardstown or Quarryvale developments would receive tax designation status. However, the Tribunal believed it to have been quite possible that Mr O'Callaghan had received a similar assurance on an unknown date considerably prior to the 24 March 1994, and that the reason for Mr O'Callaghan's again raising the issue with Mr Ahern on 24 March 1994 arose from a concern on his, Mr O'Callaghan's part, that Mr Ray MacSharry's then recent or imminent appointment to the board of Green Property PLC (the developers of Blanchardstown) might precipitate a reversal of Mr Ahern's earlier stated position that Blanchardstown would not receive tax designation.

(Chap. 2, section 1.134) The Tribunal was satisfied that the topics discussed at the meeting of 24 March 1994, were Mr O'Callaghan's concerns regarding the Blanchardstown tax designation issue and his plans for the 'All-Purpose National Stadium'. The Tribunal was satisfied that in all probability Mr O'Callaghan lobbied Mr Ahern for Government support and funding for the stadium project. It was inconceivable that such discussion would not have taken place, having regard to Mr Dunlop's letter of 1 December 1993 to Mr Ahern wherein a meeting was sought for Mr O'Callaghan with Mr Ahern regarding the stadium, and having regard to the fact that, as of 1 December 1993, Mr Ahern was in possession of documentation relating to the stadium project which had been enclosed by Mr Dunlop in correspondence with him. Moreover, it appeared to the Tribunal extremely unlikely that the issue of the stadium project and its funding would not have been discussed between Mr O'Callaghan and Mr Ahern, having regard to the fact that Mr Ahern had met Chilton and O'Connor on 11 March 1994.

(Chap. 2, section 1.136) The Tribunal was also satisfied, as a matter of probability, that in the course of Mr O'Callaghan's lobbying of Mr Ahern on 24 March 1994 with regard to the proposed 'All-Purpose National Stadium' Mr O'Callaghan sought to urge the merits of his stadium project over that of the then rival project being promoted by Ogden Developments. Mr O'Callaghan, in evidence, acknowledged having spoken to Mr Lawlor and Mr Dunlop about the Ogden proposal for a stadium development at the Phoenix Park racecourse and having relayed his concerns about that proposal to Mr Dunlop. In those circumstances it appeared inconceivable to the Tribunal that Mr O'Callaghan would not have urged upon Mr Ahern the merits of his proposal over that of a potential rival. That the possibility of a rival Stadium being developed was (and remained) a concern of Mr O'Callaghan's was documented in a note made by Mr Dunlop's solicitors Arthur Cox on 29 September 1994 wherein Mr Dunlop was recorded as having apprised his legal advisers of the rival Phoenix Park proposal, a proposal which, it was recorded, 'has frightened O'Callaghan'.

(Chap. 2, section 5.62) The Tribunal was satisfied that a significant portion (if not the entire) of the IR£30,000 cash which was lodged on 25 April 1994 came into the possession of Mr Ahern between 23 December 1993 and 25 April 1994.

(Chap. 2, section 5.39) On 8 August 1994, an account was opened at AIB, 37/38 Upper O'Connell Street, Dublin, in the names of Mr Ahern's then minor daughters Georgina and Cecilia Ahern, and the sum of IR£20,000 in cash was lodged to that account.

(Chap. 2, section 5.63) Similarly, the Tribunal was satisfied that a significant portion, (if not the entire) of the IR£20,000 cash which was lodged on 8 August 1994 came into the possession of Mr Ahern between 25 April and 8 August 1994.

(Chap. 2, section 5.64) The Tribunal was satisfied that Mr Ahern did not disclose to it the true source of the said lodgements in April and August 1994. The source of the IR£50,000 used by Mr Ahern to fund these lodgements therefore remains a mystery.

(Chap. 17, p. 2475, section 1) Mr Ahern maintained that this lodgement was comprised of approximately IR£16,500, collected for him by identified friends and then accepted by him as a repayable loan, together with Stg £8,000 approximately, presented to him following a dinner engagement in Manchester. The Tribunal rejected the evidence of Mr Ahern, and of others, to the effect that such collections had taken place and were the source of the funds lodged to Mr Ahern's account on 11 October 1994.

(Chap. 17, p. 2475, section 2) The Tribunal was satisfied that the said lodgement of IR£24,838.49 on 11 October 1994 had in fact been funded by Stg £25,000 cash.

(Chap. 17, p. 2475, section 3) Because of Mr Ahern's failure to account to the Tribunal for the source of the funds which comprised this lodgement, the Tribunal was unable to determine the source thereof.

(Chap. 17, p. 2476, section 1) Mr Ahern claimed that the source of this lodgement on 5 December 1994 was approximately Stg £30,000 cash provided to him by his friend Mr Michael Wall (as a fund for use in connection with 44 Beresford Avenue, Drumcondra), and which, in turn, he provided to Ms Larkin for lodgement to an account in her name. The Tribunal rejected the evidence of Mr Ahern and Mr Wall to the effect that Mr Wall paid approximately Stg £30,000 cash to Mr Ahern for the said, or any, purpose.

(Chap. 17, p. 2476, section 2) The Tribunal was satisfied that the source of the foreign currency which funded the lodgement of IR£28,772.90 on 5 December 1994 was not, as contended by Mr Ahern, approximately Stg £30,000 cash, but was in fact $45,000, cash.

(Chap. 17, p. 2476, section 3) Because of Mr Ahern's failure to account to the Tribunal as to the true source of the foreign currency which funded the said lodgement, the Tribunal was unable to determine the source of these funds.

(Chap. 17, p. 2478, section 1) The Tribunal was satisfied that Beresford was never beneficially owned by Mr Wall or intended to be beneficially owned by him. The property was beneficially owned by Mr Ahern between 1995 and 1997, and was legally and beneficially owned by Mr Ahern from 1997 onwards. The Tribunal rejected the evidence of Mr Ahern and Mr Wall which indicated otherwise.

(Chap. 17, p. 2476, section 1) This lodgement was comprised of two separate sums, namely IR£9,743.74 from an exchange of Stg £10,000 cash, and IR£2,000 cash. Mr Ahern maintained that the Stg £10,000 cash element of the lodgement represented part of a purchase of Stg £30,000 cash by him (or by others on his behalf), which in turn had been funded by some of the IR£50,000 cash withdrawn by Ms Larkin from the Larkin 015 account on 19 January 1995 (which had originally been lodged on 5 December 1994) following Mr Ahern's request that she return these monies to him. The Tribunal rejected Mr Ahern's evidence that he had purchased Stg £30,000 cash, and therefore rejected his evidence that the said lodgement of IR£11,743.74 on 15 June 1995 had been part funded by sterling purchased, as claimed, by Mr Ahern.

(Chap. 17, p. 2477, section 2) Because Mr Ahern failed to account to the Tribunal as to the true source of the said Stg £10,000 cash element in the lodgement on 15 June 1995, the Tribunal was unable to determine its actual source.

(Chap. 17, p. 2477, ssection 1) [*Re lodgement of £19,142.92 to account of Ahern on 1 December 1995*] This lodgement was funded entirely by Stg £20,000 in cash. The Tribunal rejected Mr Ahern's evidence that the Stg £20,000 was purchased by him (as part of the Stg£30,000 purchase referred to above). It followed therefore that the IR£19,142.92 lodgement was unrelated to the IR£50,000 which had been withdrawn in cash by Ms. Larkin from the Larkin 015 account on 19 January 1995.

(Chap. 17, p. 2477, section 2) Because Mr Ahern failed to truthfully account to the Tribunal as to the source of the sterling used to fund the IR£19,142.92 lodgement on 1 December 1995, the Tribunal was unable to pronounce as to its source.

Note on discovery orders

Perhaps the most powerful inquiry tool available to a tribunal established pursuant to the Tribunals of Inquiry (Evidence) Act (1921, as amended) in its quest to establish facts is its power to order the discovery of documents. The Tribunal made more than nine thousand discovery orders in the course of its work, many of them directed to financial institutions, as part of a process to identify the movement of funds into, and out of, the bank accounts of individuals and companies.

APPENDIX 2

Statement by Owen O'Callaghan
Irish Times Friday, 23 March, 2012
© Irish Times, 2012

The following is an edited version of a statement issued by Owen O'Callaghan in response to the Tribunal's findings.

'I want to make it quite clear that I utterly reject the findings of the Mahon tribunal and that I intend to seek their judicial review in the High Court. The tribunal arrived at its conclusions based on procedures which by any reasonable criteria have been biased, unfair and unjust.

'There are so many deficiencies in the way the tribunal went about its work that it is difficult to know where to start. But failing in any way to subject the evidence of its star witness, Tom Gilmartin, to even cursory examination is probably the most striking.

'The tribunal through its quite extraordinary protection and mentoring of Mr Gilmartin has produced what is clearly an inevitable result having regard to all that has been spent on the process. On any reading Mr Gilmartin's evidence was inconsistent, contradictory and unreliable.

'In a judgement of the superior courts of this country his evidence was decried as being unreliable. Yet it appears from the report that his evidence remains the principal foundation for all of the adverse findings against me. It is simply breathtaking that the tribunal appears to have accepted every allegation made by Mr. Gilmartin as the basis for their report

'In the course of litigation taken by me against the tribunal, one of the Supreme Court judges, Mr Justice Hardiman, said that the tribunal had displayed such bias against me, in favour of Mr Gilmartin, that the tribunal should not be permitted to continue the investigation any further and should be stopped by the courts from any further investigation into me or my companies.

'Mr Justice Hardiman's criticisms of the tribunal are remarkable and trenchant. They reflect his deep unease at the manner in which the tribunal was conducting its business and should give pause for thought to any fair-minded person reading its findings.

'... There was considerable support right across the political spectrum for the then Quarryvale project. Like many other businesses and individuals at that time, I supported the election campaigns of politicians who long before my involvement in the project had declared their strong support for the project.

'I find it incomprehensible that the tribunal should conclude, as it has, that this support amounted to corruption and that this compromised the "required disinterested performances by councillors of their duties."

'The findings of the Mahon tribunal against me, having regard to the evidence given at the tribunal, are simply not sustainable.'

Notes

[a]   Ahern and O'Callaghan consistently denied that any such payment was made or received when the allegation first surfaced several years later.

[b]   AIB memo of meeting, 23/11/1990. (Tribunal report, chap. 2, section 3.17.)

[c]   AIB memo, 4/12/1990. (Tribunal report, chap. 2, section 3.21.)

[d]   Dunlop had become a central cog in a 'system operating on Dublin County Council whereby a nexus of councillors—Fianna Fáil, Fine Gael and certain Independents—proffered their support in terms of signing motions, for consideration during the course of the Development Plan, and in terms of support in the Chamber, in return for cash.' (Tribunal report, quoting Dunlop, chap. 15, section 11.02). While the 'system' had existed for several years, and Dunlop became involved only as a medium between developers and councillors on Liam Lawlor's invitation some time in early 1990, he 'substantially perfected, expanded and exploited it to a hitherto unachieved level.' (Tribunal report, chap. 15, section 11.07.) In the process he was acquiring vast sums from his clients, a small portion of which he used to buy the votes of councillors for rezoning proposals or material contraventions of the development plan and ensuring that 'the financial rewards for the relevant landowners/developers were enormous by any standards.' (Tribunal report, chap. 15, section 10.01.)

[e]   Details of this exchange are in the transcript of the tribunal hearings and cross-examination of Owen O'Callaghan on 30 September 2008 in relation to the article in the *Sunday Business Post* on 13 December 1992.

[f]   In 2004 the Supreme Court upheld a High Court decision in favour of RTE, following a lengthy libel action.

[g]   During this period I contacted a man who had handled offshore accounts in Bank of Ireland in the Isle of Man in the late 1980s and early 90s in an effort to track down the identity of those behind the account number given to Tom Gilmartin in Leinster House. He had since been transferred to the bank's Jersey branch, before he moved to the Cayman Islands. I eventually found him at a finance house in the United States through an internet search that brought up his name and a photograph of him attending a golf outing with his colleagues. When I contacted him by phone he said he would not comment on his work with Bank of Ireland in the Isle of Man. His last words were 'How the fuck do I get my name off the internet?' The identity of this person was passed on to the tribunal.

h   Liam Lawlor was born in 1944 and became involved in the refrigeration
business on leaving Synge Street Christian Brothers' School, Dublin, in the
early 1960s. He was a member of Fianna Fáil until his resignation from the
party in June 2000. He was a member of Dublin County Council, representing
the Lucan Ward, from 1979 to 1991. He lost his seat in the 1991 local elections.
Lawlor was a TD representing the constituency of Dublin West between 1977
and 2002, with the exception of the periods from June 1981 to February 1982
and November 1982 to February 1987, when he was out of office. The loss of
his seat in the 1982 general election was attributed to his role in zoning and
planning controversies. At various times during his political career he held the
positions of chairperson of the board of the Eastern Regional Development
Organisation and chairperson of the Joint Committee on Commercial
State-Sponsored Bodies, from which he was forced to resign in 1989 after it
emerged that he was a non-executive director of the Goodman firm Food
Industries, which was seeking to buy the state company Irish Sugar. As
chairperson of this committee Lawlor had access to confidential information
on the internal affairs of the Sugar Company. He was a member of the Select
Committee on Members' Interests of Dáil Éireann (commonly known as the
Ethics Committee) and vice-chairperson of the Finance and Public Services
Committee. Between 1982 and 1987 he was a paid full-time national organiser
for Fianna Fáil.

INDEX